HISTORY OF WORLD ARCHITECTURE

Pier Luigi Nervi, General Editor

ORIENTAL ARCHITECTURE
Mario Bussagli

Contributions by
Paola Mortari Vergara,
Arcangela Santoro,
Chiara Silvi Antonini,
Adolfo Tamburello

Translated by John Shepley

Harry N. Abrams, Inc., Publishers, New York

Produced under the supervision of Carlo Pirovano,
editorial director of Electa Editrice

Design: Diego Birelli, art director of Electa Editrice

Photographs: Federico Borromeo

Drawings: Studio of Enzo Di Grazia

Library of Congress Cataloguing in Publication Data

Bussagli, Mario.
    Oriental architecture.
    (History of world architecture)
    Translation of Architettura orientale.
    1. Architecture, Oriental. I. Mortari Vergara Caffarelli, Paola. II. Title.
NA1460.B8713 722 74–4024
ISBN 0–8109–1016–0

Library of Congress Catalogue Card Number: 74–4024
Copyright 1973 in Italy by Electa Editrice, Milan
All rights reserved. No part of the contents of this book may be
reproduced without the written permission of the publishers
Harry N. Abrams, Incorporated, New York
Printed and bound in Japan.

PREFACE

Architectural criticism has nearly always been concerned with the visible aspect of individual buildings, taking this to be the decisive factor in the formulation of value judgments and in the classification of those "styles" which appear in textbooks, and which have thus become common knowledge. But once it is recognized that every building is, by definition, a work subject to the limitations imposed by the materials and building techniques at hand, and that every building must prove its stability, as well as its capacity to endure and serve the needs it was built for, it becomes clear that the aesthetic aspect alone is inadequate when we come to appraise a creative activity, difficult enough to judge in the past, rapidly becoming more complex in our own day, and destined to become more so in the foreseeable future.

Nevertheless, what has struck me most, on studying the architecture of the past and present, is the fact that the works which are generally regarded by the critics and the general public as examples of pure beauty are also the fruit of exemplary building techniques, once one has taken into account the quality of the materials and the technical knowledge available. And it is natural to suspect that such a coincidence is not entirely casual.

Building in the past was wholly a matter of following static intuitions, which were, in turn, the result of meditation, experience, and above all of an understanding of the capacity of certain structures and materials to resist external forces. Meditation upon structural patterns and the characteristics of various materials, together with the appraisal of one's own experiences and those of others, is an act of love toward the process of construction for its own sake, both on the part of the architect and his collaborators and assistants. Indeed, we may wonder whether this is not the hidden bond which unites the appearance and substance of the finest buildings of the past, distant though that past may be, into a single "thing of beauty."

One might even think that the quality of the materials available not only determined architectural patterns but also the decorative detail with which the first simple construction was gradually enriched.

One might find a justification for the difference in refinement and elegance between Greek architecture, with its basic use of marble—a highly resistant material, upon which the most delicate carvings can be carried out—and the majestic concrete structures of Roman architecture, built out of a mixture of lime and pozzolana, and supported by massive walls, to compensate for their intrinsic weaknesses.

Would it be too rash to connect these objective architectural characteristics with the different artistic sensibilities of the two peoples?

One must recognize, therefore, the importance of completing the description of the examples illustrated with an interpretation of their constructional and aesthetic characteristics, so that the connection between the twin aspects of building emerges as a natural, logical consequence.

This consequence, if understood and accepted in good faith by certain avant-garde circles, could put an end to the disastrous haste with which our architecture is rushing toward an empty, costly, and at times impractical formalism. It might also recall architects and men of culture to a more serene appraisal of the objective elements of building and to the respect that is due to a morality of architecture. For this is just as important for the future of our cities as is morality, understood as a rule of life, for an orderly civil existence.

PIER LUIGI NERVI

TABLE OF CONTENTS

FOREWORD

The publication of a volume devoted solely to the architecture of middle and eastern Asia clearly reflects the new interest in the artistic culture of those great Asian civilizations that—by a possibly controversial definition—may also be called "Far Eastern." *Oriental Architecture* brings together and synthesizes in one volume the architectural developments of seven large regions—all of them marked by complex historical vicissitudes, by equally complicated social phenomena, and by an extraordinary richness of thought. The customary rule is to compile a separate volume for each cultural area, or at least to devote one volume to each of the major cultures of these regions. There are, however, in addition to certain contingent and absolute requirements that preclude these alternatives, theoretical and scientific reasons, which are set forth more fully in the Introduction, that justify a unified treatment of the architectural works here examined. Above all, there exist undeniable ties and relationships that link together these highly diverse artistic cultures.

The attentive reader will soon discern the nature of the more obvious of these relationships—which do not reside merely in matters of type or technique, or in the predominant use of particular materials, since these are often of a religious and spiritual character—as well as the existence of minor but widely radiating currents of taste, and of influences and pressures. The latter, while sometimes involving countries very remote from one another, have nevertheless served to produce a dense network of lesser ties that evidence what we might call the "differentiated unity" of Asia.

The contributors to this volume (all teachers at the University of Rome) are Italian scholars with varying backgrounds—linguistics, history, art history—whose interest in the study of the figurative arts in Asia has been inspired by their specialties. They all bring to their respective discussions the enrichment of the particular studies in which they have participated. The result is a kind of *concordia discors* that in part corresponds to the objective requirements of the individual fields of the contributors, who will sometimes emphasize rhythms of development, at other times historical conditions, spatial values, or technical data, according to their sensibilities, their preferences, and even their basic training. Moreover, it was no easy task to confront the problems of Asian architecture and to remove them from the accompanying art historical context of the other figurative arts; throughout Asia, architecture is considered a minor art and is not always easily separated from sculpture and, to a lesser degree, from painting.

There have even been serious difficulties in the choice of illustrations. Except for Federico Borromeo's photographs, taken especially for this volume with a skill that is not merely technical but also that of an enthusiastic lover of Asian (especially Indian) art, it was no easy matter to collect suitable, new, and previously unpublished material. On the other hand, in some regions—such as Central Asia—there has been scant survival of significant monuments; what little remains can in no way be compared with the wealth of other areas. The well-known political conditions in such countries as Vietnam have hindered specific photographic projects, and consequently there is a considerable disproportion between the visual documentation for some regions and other richer and more accessible ones.

Despite these handicaps, this volume represents a necessary preparatory move toward wider and deeper investigations that, among other things, will inevitably have to confront the problem of figurative space in the Asian world. On the formulation of this problem—by no means easy because it collides with the entire history of art of the adjoining European continent, and with the scientific and philosophical conceptions elaborated by individual civilizations—depends the possibility of a single basic critical standard, one common to such highly different worlds and capable of bringing research on the artistic phenomena of Europe and Asia to the same level. It is now time for the history of art to become a single history—even though cultivated by specialists in diverse regions of the world—with similar (if not necessarily identical) problems, views, and methods, differentiated only by the diversity of documentary evidence and by the methods employed in approaching aesthetic values.

Final judgment on this volume is naturally up to its readers, whether they be specialists or not, and the book's fate is primarily entrusted to them. For us, as authors, it is already a satisfaction to be able to offer and reveal to a wider public the architectural treasures of civilizations that have developed parallel to our own, and which represent not its antithesis but its completion and its reciprocal parameter of measure.

Mario Bussagli

INTRODUCTION

The characteristic forms of Asian architecture are still one of the most striking and familiar aspects of the artificial "Oriental" world that our increased knowledge and facility in mass communication cannot successfully eliminate. The taste for the fantastic and exotic, however slight today, may be said to be ingrained in the human spirit, and for historical reasons is particularly felt by Western man. The Great Wall of China, any of the pagodas of the Far East, the stupas of India and the Indianized world, the great temples of China, Japan, and Southeast Asia—all evoke an indefinable sense of wonder, a mysterious and diverse presence that shapes itself in a primarily emotional way, even though its effect upon us has been given lucid literary expression by a number of our best writers. But an evaluation of this kind, which we might call sentimental-exotic, remains a superficial one, and is in any case the fruit of a European-centered view, or at least extraneous to the very world that produced the monuments of which we speak. In reality, these and an infinite number of other architectural works reflect the social, economic, and historical structure of an immense and varied world, subject to transformations that are no less felt for being slow and conflicting. The sum of the Asian experiments, the series of critical problems faced, and the variety of technical results obtained thereby are not inferior to those that have ripened over the centuries in the West, even though there is a general tendency to contrast Asian architecture with what is vaguely and generically defined as Western.

In no Asian civilization has architecture ever been considered one of the major arts. The heaviness of the materials employed, and the quantity of technical data necessary for planning and construction, have led to the conclusion that it is hardly spontaneous, not easily appreciated, and therefore the product of the craftsman rather than a work of art. Thus, the technical texts of India—to begin with, the *Mānasāra*, which though late is one of the most complete—enumerate with great precision the various aspects of the technical training necessary for the architect. These include geology, geometry, magic, religion, artistic techniques, and even psychology (the latter to assist in dealing with workers). Indeed, the whole implies a specialized body of learning that is certainly uncommon and quite different from that of Western classical or Renaissance architects, not to mention any modern or contemporary ones.

In the Far Eastern world, where wood is deliberately employed and architectural forms are placed within the sphere of nature—one thinks of gardens and of the Sino-Japanese ability to exploit the natural surroundings of a building—the architectural work takes its place on a lower scale in a hierarchy of artistic values wherein painting, calligraphy, poetry, and music stand at the top. In recent decades, Far Eastern concepts and techniques have been translated, with considerable

freedom, into new and strikingly contemporary architectural terms, even calling for materials absolutely different from the ancient and traditional wooden structures. Through a combination of varying circumstances, the traditions of Japan and the renewed creative capacities of her great contemporary architects have produced vast echoes in Europe and America. A great part of this sincere interest is due to the efforts of Japanese architects to reconcile the significance and continuity of their tradition with the inevitable change and updating of their culture, which is driven by an urge to create new symbols and new common values acceptable to a spiritually, economically, and socially reinvigorated world.

That these efforts are perfectly justified and valid is an undeniable fact; consequently, the entire span of Asian architecture cannot be judged merely as an historical and archaeological phenomenon, nor should we study its works as a simple heritage of the past. With the fluctuations and continual variations in the scales of values adopted by all human civilizations, it can still be a source of suggestions and of possible inspiration (likewise for experiments unknown to the Western world), and it may well be capable of future developments. In any case—setting aside historically documented amalgamations of East and West—there can be no doubt whatsoever that the Asian experience remains a parameter of comparison for the architecture of other continents. To recognize it as such will enrich our historical and aesthetic vision, and among other things will help us to confront the question of the allegedly irreconcilable opposition between Asia and Europe in the architectural sphere.

But is it really legitimate to speak of an Asian architecture? The various artistic civilizations of Asia display enormous differences among themselves, and the response of Asian man is likewise different in varying climatic and environmental situations. As a result, the vast series of socio-cultural phenomena and their related reflections in architecture as manifested during centuries and millennia would seem to deny the methodological correctness of a unified treatment. To judge by appearances, an approach of this sort can be justified only by a tenuous and debatable geographical bond.

In reality, all of Asia is overlaid by an imposing complex of cultural phenomena that tends to unify its broad areas on partially homogeneous grounds, which in turn are strengthened and extended by mutual influences, contacts, and exchanges. Moreover, the economic and organizational structure of the Asian world, however fractured, obeys a series of common choices and preferences; its architectural works, expressing as they may highly different aspirations and intentions, remain above all unmistakably Asian. The prejudicial question on which the validity of this essay—and, in part, of those that follow—

depends can be answered in the affirmative, since even if one takes note of the aesthetic, functional, or technical differences that separate these works, tastes, and tendencies, it is not difficult to perceive their common foundation and the extensive interplay of mutual influences.

Naturally, in a book such as this, it is necessary to rely on available sociological data, and to consider also the philological and psychological approaches. The true protagonist of our research is, however, the artistic phenomenon in itself, evaluated and considered both on the sociological (especially symbolic and religious) plane and in its historical and political context, despite the obvious limitations imposed by the almost complete anonymity of the artists involved (particularly in the architectural field) and by the relatively sparse nature of the philological evidence.

The northern stretches of the Asian continent, corresponding to the area of tundras and forests and to part of the central strip of deserts and steppes, were almost completely unacquainted with architecture until very recent times. Only underground tombs of various types (such as chambers or pits), indicated on the surface by rings of stones, tumuli, or in some other manner, demonstrate the existence of a desire to build, obviously prompted by the impulse of sacred and funerary values. Much rarer in occurrence and more recent in date are certain subterranean dwellings that respond to climatic requirements—protection from the cold, for example—and to functional values that can be understood only in terms of a particular religious culture. The marks of shamanism so overload such structures with symbolic values that, once they are divorced from the culture that produced them, the solutions adopted for accessibility, livability, and the very life in common of the hierarchical group served by them are rendered absurd. They are typical examples of a symbolic and magical functionalism so exaggerated as to be an extreme case even for Asia.

Chinese literary sources mention the small fortified "cities" in wood and stone built by certain nomadic groups as they became progressively sedentary under the influence of Chinese culture. No examples have survived, just as almost nothing, except for fragments, remains of the fourteenth-century Catholic churches in Mongolia (in the Gothic style but with ample concessions to Chinese techniques and materials) built by Giovanni di Montecorvino. These scant remains comprise almost the entire architectural heritage of the nomadic peoples and hunters of the north. We must remember, however, that the felt tent of the nomads, a true masterpiece of practicality and rationality, itself reproduced the shamanistic symbolism of underground dwellings, which thus appears as an indispensable requirement.

Apparently, an enormous portion of the Asian continent was for a long time devoid of important architectural forms. Until quite recent times, there were no actual urban agglomerates; we can say that the urbanization of this immense area is connected with the history of the last two centuries and has developed primarily along Russian lines, with considerable intensification in the last few decades.

It is thus the great sedentary, agricultural civilizations of the south—including all the territories of China and Korea, as well as the Japanese archipelago—that have expressed themselves in valid and coherent architectural forms capable of broad development. These forms, when placed according to type and purpose in urban contexts and in very diverse groupings, can be better understood by an examination of the essential outlines of the Asian city.

The Asian City

Throughout Asia the city has had a very different meaning from that it possesses in the West (first, Classical Mediterranean, later European). It is still less important than the village as a human habitat, which is in fact the fundamental agglomerate in all sedentary Asian societies. Apart from the existence of modern megalopolises such as Tokyo, for example, the distribution of the population into hamlets, the tendency toward isolation, the conservatism characteristic of the village, and the continual rapport of man with nature—whose gigantic forces are manifested in Asia with a violence unknown in the West—have not been devoid of consequences in the field of architecture. In Indian villages, for example, the principal construction remained for centuries the Vedic altar, a structure rigidly connected with symbolic requirements, even down to the number of bricks employed, and with ritual function. Concepts of durability, aesthetic value, and rationality in the modern sense have not been taken into consideration, however. This psychological attitude has its repercussions on other aspects of religious architecture. Certain works, intended to serve as votive offerings, are built without any interest either in durability or Vitruvian *firmitas*, and thus assume a meaning that is inconceivable to the West. A Buddhist stupa, solid in construction and lacking interior space, may have been erected for the sole purpose of "acquiring merit"—in other words, to better the fate of the patron and builder in his future lives. If the stupa were to crumble or be demolished immediately after being perfectly completed, this would have no importance, since the act of faith that presided over its construction had already been carried out.

For tens of centuries, all of Asia lacked the necessary prerequisites whereby the bourgeois class (artisans and merchants) might have acquired an economic strength that would resolutely reflect the life and functions of the cities. The hostility of the central powers toward the mercantile and craft guilds is amply shown both by Indian texts on political theory—these embrace the idea that the *śrenī* (guilds), because of their wealth, constitute the principal danger to the sovereign[1]—and by the Confucian contempt for trade.

As a result, there existed no juridical foundation permitting the formation of civic autonomy and the recognition of the urban community within the outlines of an independent civilization, distinct from the surrounding ones—as occurred, for example, in Italy. In China, the building of a new city was one of a number of works carried out by the state, and the planned urban centers served as an instrument of central power. Their purpose, in fact, was to ensure the transportation, storage, and distribution of principal goods, not to mention their military and internal security functions. Nor could it have been otherwise, since all Chinese imperial governments considered the entire territory under their rule as a unified whole.[2]

What was therefore planned for the Chinese populace was a general system by which they would be distributed throughout cities and lesser centers according to the needs foreseen and imposed by an absolute power—one that, despite being abstract and remote, in theory excluded free activities and had no interest in favoring the city over the village. It was not accidental that inside the cities themselves each quarter was isolated and autonomous in its relations with the local authority. The connection between house and street was bound up in precise rules that, in the more ancient periods of the empire (roughly speaking, from the second century B.C. to the ninth century A.D.), granted free and direct access to the street only to the highest functionaries. The necessity for police control and the desire to shatter any sense of civic unity account for the imposition of a particular physical aspect on the Chinese city that would be unacceptable in other civilizations. Distinguished by the presence of city walls and constructed on a grid plan (confirmed in a later period by Marco Polo's description of Cambaluc, present-day Peking), the urban nucleus was essentially an instrument of oppression. Only under the Sung, at the end of the tenth century, did this significance begin to diminish, even though the central government still remained abstract and remote, circumscribed as it was in its decisions and administrative activity by the sphere of the court. The Mongol invasion was to reduce the importance of the city once more, as a result of the nomadic origins of the new rulers and their characteristically imperial vision with its overtones of universalism.

Something similar happened in India too, where the political division of the immense subcontinent exposed its inhabitants to continual fluctuations in the ruling power because of the expansion and collapse of various state structures. Curiously enough, throughout the centuries and despite complex historical vicissitudes, the only agency to remain firm and operative was the land office, on which the tax yield depended—especially in such an agricultural society *par excellence* as that of India.

There can thus be no doubt that one of the basic characteristics of Asian unity is precisely this complex socio-economic structure that reduces the importance of the city to a minimum, while absolutely excluding the formation of any autonomous powers of an urban kind. Even when the collision with the Islamic world led to the emergence of great Muslim cities, and when coastal centers appeared that were to be Europeanized by commercial expansion, the Asian city was never to achieve autonomy. In short, in no instance did it succeed in expressing any bourgeois strength from its own core. Islam itself, which granted a wider cultural, religious, and administrative importance to the urban nucleus and moved it closer to European examples, was unable to impart a juridical appearance or an operative autonomy to civic centers. The colonialist drive created mercantile and military bases, especially on the coasts, but had neither the aim nor the possibility of reproducing European-style urban structures in Asia for the benefit of the Asians. For the colonial rulers, the city was likewise an instrument of power, though naturally, from their contact with various economic systems, the natives of the surrounding areas were able to derive some advantage.

Thus there arises once again, in relation to the value and function of the Asian city, the much-discussed problem of the "Asian mode of production," which, among other things, is said to constitute one of the undivided and unifying components of Asian society. Actually, this expression, coined by Karl Marx, becomes more precise when defined as a "despotic village economy,"[3] since it is characterized by a combination of the production activity of village communities and the economic intervention of a state authority that exploits and at the same time directs them. There is no doubt, however, that at the root of all sedentary Asian societies there has been maintained, for extremely long periods and in different forms, an interest in public works that the state (or sovereign) provides for and executes. These works are controlled and administered in the same manner as commerce, many mining and refining industries, transportation, and various other activities, with the state (or sovereign) theoretically limiting its own power only in relation to the capacity of its subjects for endurance and survival. This centralization, this despotic authoritarianism, was preserved even when the political acts of the sovereign were based on a humanitarian ideology and formulated according to concepts of universal brotherhood, respect for life, and "nonviolence." Such was the case of Asoka (c. 269–232 B.C.), the third and greatest sovereign of the Maurya dynasty, the first Indian empire. Asoka, who derived the foundations for his own political vision from Buddhist ethics, undertook great public works—streets, hospitals, reservoirs, cisterns, commemorative and symbolic pillars. His was an Asian state, and though paternalistic and only mildly oppressive, was still incapable of breaking the truly tyrannical patterns of his ancestors.

In addition to this pronounced tendency toward centralization, private property and initiative were hindered by all legislative and fiscal means. Thus there existed a basic antagonism between the masses of subjects and the bureaucratic apparatus of the state, making it very obvious why private property did not confer any real political power. It is for this reason that Asian societies, except when they come into violent contact with other, totally different social structures—and in particular with colonialist capitalism—appear almost incapable of rapid development. This does not mean that they are immobile or identical among themselves. Inversely, it is hardly correct to say, as does Chesneaux, that "the theory of Asian society is a myth, rather than a useful scientific hypothesis," it being understood that this theory applies primarily to the more productive agricultural areas. The Central Asian area, in the centuries from the beginning of the Christian era to its total conquest by the Turks (ninth to tenth centuries A.D.) does not enter into Chesneaux's description because the economic basis of the entire region was essentially mercantile. The western area, where greater agricultural development was possible through artificial irrigation, produced state structures of the semifeudal type or, more precisely, alliances of small semiautonomous potentates under a theoretical authority. The other districts, corresponding to the present Sinkiang region in China, saw the emergence of caravan city-states (each with a different cultural structure) founded on oases. Here human habitation, limited by the hostility of the desert and other obstacles, could not be dispersed in a network of agricultural villages. Very close in its outlook to the medieval European world, Central Asia was the only area to make the city the synthesis of a refined civilization and to develop a kind of bourgeois class. A tangible factor was the decentralization of the monastic complexes, which tended to detach them from the restless life of the urban nucleus, thus confirming the importance of religious thought. Nevertheless, in the entire range of Asian civilizations, this remains an extraordinary and fundamental exception. Despite its militarized and strongly bureaucratic state organizations, this region was the only one capable of developing a very profitable socio-economic structure and of ensuring that its commercial and cultural activity extended over an enormous territory.

Unfortunately, for various reasons, we cannot trace with precision the genesis of this urban structure, which in the West took shape predominantly in the form of large castles and in the East in actual cities. In the latter area, archaeologists have primarily unearthed monastic agglomerates and religious constructions hewn out of rock, which better survived the vicissitudes of the centuries. With the advance of Islam into the area, even though the mercantile economy that had created the splendor of Central Asian civilization was not wholly destroyed, new urban centers of the Muslim type emerged. They would have a physical character of their own, generally not much different from that of Iranian cities or other regions of the Muslim world. Only Samarkand—the sole great love of Tamerlane—was to have the strange destiny of becoming the capital of an ephemeral empire created simply for its embellishment. We might add, in evaluating the "Asian mode of production" theory in relation to architecture, that another exception is found in the theocracy of Tibet, where the economic structure of the plateau took the form of a mixture of livestock breeding and laborious agriculture within the very framework of a state that, after a phase of kingship, was clearly based on religion and entrusted to monastic hierarchies. Here the Asian mode of production does not take the classical Marxist form (actually derived from the India and China of the nineteenth century); nor does it adhere to the more precise definition stated by Chesneaux, which we have followed while yet proposing certain general characteristics.

We still find the state in Tibet promoting large works (though by means of religious communities), but the development of private property and even the yield from the scarce amount of arable land are hindered by magic and superstition, elements that were backed up by the spiritual authorities. Deep plowing, for example, was prohibited so as not to offend the klu, the spirits of the earth—corresponding to the naga, or deified serpents of India—who might in turn revenge themselves on the entire country.

This fragment of medieval civilization, with its mystical and magical setting that has lasted until recent years, has also produced highly valid architectural forms that are without doubt Asian. They are specifically Tibetan as well, and have been erected in relation to a number of diverse elements that take their place within the framework of the lamaistic social order, a strongly hierarchical one albeit along lines that differ considerably from other Asian civilizations.

We can conclude therefore that a critical examination of the Asian mode of production shows that, however vast, it does not appear to be limited in space, since something similar can be found in other areas, and that it most certainly varies in time. Nevertheless, this much-discussed economic phenomenon offers two constant characteristics whose unifying importance cannot be denied—the state's interest in public works, and the relative lack of private property and initiative. For these reasons also, the architecture of Asia appears predominantly religious. Great monumental works could be realized primarily in terms of particular cultural structures, in a world where political theories and the practice of government conferred on the holders of power a single possibility for a dialogue with subject groups; this possibility was limited to the sphere of their common acceptance of metaphysical values, whether magical or religious. In other words, religious faith and religiosity were the only common ground for rulers and subjects. This implies the existence of patterns of thought that tend, independent of the reality of economic drives, to accentuate religious speculation to degrees unknown in the West—this on the basis of a total lack of opposition between the sacred and the profane (since the sacred in itself pervades even the slightest act of daily life) and on the conviction that there exists no definite orthodoxy, every form of religious thought being capable of approaching the truth and leading to salvation.

Whether this last circumstance means the reabsorption of the individual into the energy of the universe, or his survival in one or another of the paradises or "pure" lands imagined by the mystics, has no importance. Rather, what counts is that the reality of religion has, for the Asian world, a consistency and importance greatly superior to what we might find outside that continent. Possibilities for meditation were offered by the dispersion of its inhabitants in the immense network of villages. That unique factor, or the separation of religious souls in monastic agglomerates far from the structures of cities, may—in the immobility of a life devoid of shocks—have facilitated spiritual attitudes that in other worlds would be inconceivable. Furthermore, in this case the underdevelopment of cities would be indirectly responsible for a particular Asian mode of thought—one that certainly varies and is often contradictory if we compare the predominant lines of thinking in this or that civilization, but that is nevertheless diffused from one end of the continent to the other and that is essentially devoted to metaphysical speculation.

It is certain that the underdevelopment of Asian cities acts to exclude such concepts as those of *polis, civitas,* or *commune*. What is lacking is the sense of the fraternal group, exposed to external pressures equally dangerous to all and committed to responding collectively to challenges which, if not met and overcome, would threaten the life of all. With the exception of the Central Asian city-state, this is the characteristic common to the great mass of Asian populations; thus, the Japanese *shimin* is a simple translation for the English word and concept of the "citizen," while *chōnin* ("city dweller") is certainly not the French *citoyen* of Republican fame, and even less an expression interchangeable with the Latin *civis* or Greek *polites*. On the other hand, much as some scholars may try to deny it, the religious component in Asian thought remains the determining one to this day, accentuated as it is by the values derived from paranormal experience, and by a remote and intense stratification of the analysis carried out in the depths of the unconscious since earliest times. In conclusion, there is no doubt that historical materialism is one key by which to grasp forms and phenomena of a history as complex and tumultuous as that of Asia. It is, however, not the only one, much less one that can throw light for us on architectural phenomena of broad significance in which a predominant part is played by the collective unconscious—what the Indians call *prakrti*, or "nature."

The Characteristics of Asian Architecture

We are dealing here with a unique economy that excludes any speculation in the building industry, reduces private initiative, and favors the formation of specialized or semispecialized autonomous groups in building construction. The architecture of Asia assumes a special significance when one considers that the curves of economic profit and semiprofit react on it only partially. External intervention such as the state initiates—which may reflect the faith or pride of a sovereign, the religious devotion of high personages, or the interest of the nobles or high bureaucracy, depending on time and place—or the kind produced by religious communities do not allow for situations similar to those that came to fruition in the Classical, medieval, and Renaissance West. It is obvious that, in a world sincerely and profoundly pervaded by deep religiosity, the desire for art is concentrated on religious works of major importance. Nevertheless, aesthetic considerations also play a part in constructions of purely practical utility, and to a greater extent in expensive dwellings. In medieval Japan, one actually notes an interchange between villas and sacred buildings, as shown, for example, by the monastery containing the *Hōōdō* (phoenix hall): originally a villa belonging to the Fujiwara, it was transformed into a sacred building by the regent Yorimichi of the same family.

Traditionally set into their natural surroundings or embellished with artificial references to nature itself—ponds, miniature gardens, "dry" rock gardens using gravel to symbolize water—the villas and large isolated dwellings of the Far East, especially those in Japan, are enlivened by a highly refined taste. It is here in these buildings that one finds the clearest anticipation of modern architecture. For, as we have already noted, conceptions, models, and construction elements from the Japanese tradition have been taken up and translated into other materials by great modern architects—from Ludwig Mies van der Rohe, Walter Gropius, and Frank Lloyd Wright to the present Japanese masters (not excluding, in some phases, Kenzo Tange himself).

The importance of the religious component invests Asian architecture with a complicated system of symbolic allusions. Its historical development might be traced almost completely on the iconological level and by the iconological method, even though this would reveal only a single (albeit important) aspect of a broader and more complex reality. One must, however, keep in mind that the religious component is not homogeneous. In its enormous vitality, it follows divergent lines and even offers substantial variations within the same current or sect, depending on time and place. The phenomenon, encouraged by the systematic lack of a rigid orthodoxy, is especially evident in the wide expansion of ecumenical religions that have collided with areas dominated by very different civilizations; this happened to Indian Buddhism and Hinduism, Persian Manichaeanism, and other lesser known religious currents. In this light, the presumed immobility of Asia can hardly be said to exist because of the polemical vigor of its innovators and commentators, its teeming sects, and the wealth of its mystical experience—a heritage transmitted to groups very much vaster and more prepared than their Western counterparts to receive it.

But this religious interest, however predominant and in a certain sense the summation of its various cultures, does not bar Asia from other interests and areas of speculation. In the so-called humanistic sciences, a number of ideas and theories systematized by the West in modern times were strikingly anticipated in Asia. In psychoanalysis, linguistics, political theory, in the search for paranormal possibilities, even in many fields of technology, Asia has arrived at astonishing results that the West has been slow in realizing, and in some spheres, we have only begun to acknowledge that our own culture is capable of such awareness.

In the fields of economics, politics, and social organization—taking into account the circumstances we described earlier—one can discern behavior or lines of systematic organization that do not always have a secure ideological basis, that respond from time to time to changing practical needs as well. With no revolutionary impulse, but rather by a slow evolutionary process, these patterns have a profound influence on the most intimate fabric of human society. The effort to single out and define the phenomena to which they give rise is always a difficult one; only rarely does it succeed in providing exhaustive data for modern methodological research. But it has been possible to glimpse ancient economic and ecological crises due to overproduction, problems of minting, monetary circulation,[4] inflation, devaluation, stockjobbing, the planned hoarding of gold or silver coins in contrast to the bimetallic intercontinental circulation of coins that prevailed until the first century A.D. Thus, there is an immense sector of activity, thought, and organization that barely emerges from the available documents. We can attribute this to the nature of the documents themselves (based as they are on patterns of thought, and with intentions foreign to everything that might interest modern specialists in these fields), the chronological uncertainty of the huge mass of available texts, and their division into a myriad of tongues and not easily legible scripts.

Thus it remains an arduous task, even with the help of all auxiliary documentation, whether archaeological or not, to establish precise relationships between the figurative arts (particularly architecture) and whatever sociological, economic, and political data can be recovered by the widest and most patient research.

The inadequacy of religion alone as a key to interpretation is thus obvious, and it is for this reason that one can justify the fact that an Indian—whether Hindu, Jain, or even Muslim—is and always remains above all an Indian, just as a Japanese—atheist, Christian, Shintoist, or Buddhist—is and remains always a Japanese. Bonds exist that develop from a wider cultural fabric transcending religion and manifesting itself in infinitely diverse ways: from structures of logic to ways of expression and communication, to examples of coherent and tangible collective thought, easily defined as the mode of Asian thought but in reality various and elusive, even though offering, from one civilization to another, common essential lines that are remarkably clear. Obviously, the mode of thought also varies in time both in the religious sector and in other fields, without abrupt turns or revolutions, but still with considerable vitality, except during the phase of benumbed immobility immediately following the decisive impact of the colonialist West. Architecture reflects these variations to some extent, since even in Asia it is the principal interpreter of a complex reality in which, however, fixed and more or less undivided points stand out.

The relation between man and nature, resolved in various forms to the disadvantage of man, who is seen as a fragile creature incapable of opposing the violence of natural forces, almost always takes the form of an artificial symbolism that alludes to the extinction of the human being within the very essence of the universe. A geocentric vision, theories concerning a multiplicity of magical centers (which also have an effect on the form and location of sacred monuments), an indifference toward the individual and the resulting supremacy of the universal and absolute over the individual ego, the greater importance attached to the concept of space as compared to that of time—all these are common Asian elements that have had considerable repercussions in the sphere of the figurative arts, including architecture. Clear-cut and linear in the Far East, hyperplastic in India and in Indianized areas (where it is always connected with sculpture), Asian architecture elaborates an infinity of types different from those of the West, and which at times correspond to exclusively Asian needs. We might mention "umbrella and sunshade" architecture, to use Le Corbusier's expression for his planning at Chandigarh, extending it beyond India to a vast Far Eastern area.

We can also speak of life as it is lived at ground-level, since in many countries (particularly Japan) human existence in the house is conditioned by the Eastern manner of sitting, and does not observe the Western system for household living. Thus, the floor is not only a surface to be walked on, but a welcoming support, neat and polished, while the furnishings are kept low. Elsewhere—in Muslim Asia, for example—we find cushions and rugs as a distant memory of life in tents. We may also recall the *ratha*, the Indian temple in the form of a chariot that merges the choreography of large processional carts with the values of architecture. The relatively illogical principle of its design freezes in stone the slow motion of the carts themselves, filling them with devotional significance and with sexual symbolism as a lesson in life (the classic example is the Temple of the Sun at Konarak, which represents the chariot of the sun god Surya). But the relation between the characteristic social structures of Asia and its architectural types emerges from other examples.

The huge fortresses referred to as "villages with inhabited walls" correspond to the nomadic shepherds' need for security while they were in the process of becoming settled. Their dwellings and storerooms were built into the enormous thickness of the walls (some eighty feet), while the inner rectangle remained free to shelter herds and flocks. Functional in their way, these structures had a combined significance—as an enclosure for animals, as a village, and as a fortified dwelling place for the group. From a socio-economic crisis that involved restricted populations and from the conflict between two hostile worlds (the nomadic and the settled), there emerged shortly before the middle of the first millennium B.C. a complex, organic, architectural structure that cannot be matched elsewhere. Similarly, the Potala at Lhasa and the "castle" at Leh, both in Tibet, are constructions of multiple significance. The nine stories refer to cosmological fantasies, and aside from their symbolism, they represent a combination of palace, fortress, and holy place (they contained, among other things, numerous temples and chapels). Fruits of a society that one might call theocratic—if Buddhism can be said to admit the concept of God as conceived in the West—the two Tibetan complexes combine the sum of religious, political, military, magical, and ecclesiastical values. We refer, of course, to the organizational and hierarchical values of a religious elite.

The architectural phenomenology of Asia thus cannot be compared, under certain aspects, with that of any other civilization. In the hierarchy of the arts, before full contact with the West occurred, architecture was considered by all Asian civilizations to be at an inferior level, since it could be executed immediately and individually. Its use of heavy construction materials, even when the material was wood, required the solution of static and therefore technical problems, as well as the employment of a great number of skilled workers. Even if architecture interpreted the needs of a fixed society and satisfied the taste of that group, it was not held to be capable of the same immediate expression as painting and sculpture. This attitude led to a frequent recourse to symbolism that could easily be understood and appreciated by broad levels of the population.

As a consequence of this approach, the architectural work came to be evaluated and understood primarily in terms of its symbolism. Among all the sources of symbolic inspiration, India is undoubtedly the greatest, not only because she elaborates different forms of sym-

bolism, but also because her religious thought has set up wide-ranging currents that impinge on various local impulses, which thus meet and adapt to one another. Other sources of symbolic inspiration can be singled out—besides those from archaic cultures—in the Iranian and Central Asian area and in the Far East. The predominant motif among them all is the representation of the totality of space and thus of the cosmos.

Such a representation may be unified, as in certain Buddhist stupas, or divided, as in the Temple of Heaven in Peking, where the three-tiered sacrificial area (with nine steps leading up to it to represent the nine levels of Heaven) is completed by a pavilion to the divinity, along with other symbols from Chinese cosmography. The square plan of the other constructions standing before the temple and of certain architectural elements, taken together or as details, allude to the shape of the earth (in Chinese cosmology, the earth is square and the sky round).

The motifs of the world axis and the center of the universe frequently recur in Asian architecture, modulated in various forms according to the period and to particular religious trends. The symbolic Indian source (which is, in its turn, made up of distinct parts but unified by a profound reworking of external influences) remains dominant in every case.

While always primarily inspired by India, Asian architecture in general displays two different modes of construction. With relation to the Asian problem, it is customary to use the word "constructed" for any work in stone, wood, brick, or other material that is built to resolve static and technical problems similar to those revealed in works created by other civilizations. We can by this means distinguish it from architecture that is "cut" into the rock, in which all static problems are resolved by the cohesion of the rock itself. The term "open-air architecture" is not exact, since works cut into the rock exist that are in every way analogous to those that are "constructed"—that is to say, provided with outer and inner space. Nevertheless, rock-cut architecture is found primarily in caves, and in such cases is devoid of outside space. Furthermore, the façades (with or without verandas) have the single purpose of marking and framing in a pleasing manner the openings (for entrance and illumination) necessary for the utilization of these constructions, whose inner space tends to connect the sacred with the essence of the earth.

All cut architecture, however, is a form of pseudo-architecture. While lacking static problems, it uses pillars, ribs, posts, moldings, and spires—the presence of which allude to similar elements in constructed architecture, though they lack any functional purpose beyond the symbolic one. Agreeable to Asian taste and techniques, this type of architecture was extended even to the interior of China. The collaboration between architect, sculptor, and painter is all too evident, to the extent that in the caves of Central Asia, where the petrographic structure of the rock (flaking, crumbling, sliding) prevents careful work, the assistance of the painter or sculptor modeling the divine images in stucco or in plaster on rocky outcrops becomes indispensable and predominant. As for the paintings that adorn the interiors of the cave temples, whether in India or Central Asia, they reveal above all the unconscious desire to dispel the heaviness of the massive, gloomy, encumbering material, which is made even more so by scant illumination. This wish to open windows onto an edifying world that has something of the fabulous can be seen as constant. It was destined to end by exhausting itself in the "tapestry" wall paintings of Tunhwang (at the Central Asian border where the properly Chinese area begins), which, together with the ceiling decorations, have the clear purpose of concealing the walls and the surface of the rock.

If there exist architectural works devoid of external space, there are also typical constructions that lack interior space, and which are therefore similar to giant sculptures. In particular, the Buddhist or Jainist stupa often has no internal space, even though its characteristic symbolism suggests different forms. It may stand for a representation of the whole universe (seen, so to speak, from the outside); it is then formed by a supporting body and a hemispherical or bell-shaped cupola that simply alludes to the celestial hemisphere hanging over the earth, which in Buddhist and Indian cosmology is discoidal; or it may allude to the cosmic mountain, the axis of the universe, sometimes being completed by other symbolic elements that refer to the upward surge of the heavens.

In this second case, the derivation from the Mesopotamian ziggurat is obvious, especially in the stupa with superimposed terraces that imitate a similar meaning in a different form. Sometimes stupas of this type reach gigantic dimensions, like the Borobudur in Java, which is an entire hill transformed into a Buddhist symbol. In India, the form of the stupa tends to be modified by a vertical thrust that depends on taste, and perhaps on the social environment of the particular area. Thus, the so-called stupa of Kanishka—of which only the foundation remains—bore witness to the pride and devotion of the sovereign. Its wooden superstructure reached a height of almost 640 feet, according to later accounts by Chinese pilgrims. It was the magical center of an immense empire in which paranormal powers undoubtedly played a significant part, and was thought to be the highest tower in all of India.

This verticality had conspicuous echoes primarily in China, where the pagoda with its tower was nothing but the transformation of the vertical stupa into an architectural structure provided with organic interior space, thus resuming the same symbols and modifying only their proportions and importance.

Wooden architecture, which prevailed in the Far East, became remarkably widespread in other areas. Apart from the western regions of Central Asia, where whole palaces—Pjanzikent in Sogdiana, for example—were built of wood and survive only as charred remains from the fires that destroyed them, the entire early phase of Indian architecture reveals its unmistakable derivation from wooden prototypes. Not only do stone structures display joints derived from wooden ones, but sculptured ornamental motifs take the place of fastening quoins or of (clearly enlarged) metal nails. Usually we find floral rosette motifs, or, less often, narrative bas-reliefs enclosed in circles, which are interesting for their solutions of compositional and perspectival problems in fully exploiting a circular space. It has been thought that the use of wooden architecture in India and Iran was derived from the Indo-European building tradition. The transition to stone would have taken place at different times in the two countries and for somewhat different, if similar, reasons. In India it occurred late, in part under Iranian influence (the isolated pillars of Asoka), and in part as the manifestation of a liking for cut architecture. Constructed architecture emerged on the basis of the experience accumulated in the use of perishable materials. Its decoration is sometimes created by techniques characteristic of the working of materials other than stone—for example, the collaboration offered by the guild of ivory workers in erecting one of the stupas at Sanchi—and with the purpose of fixing sacred and edifying values in lasting structures. In Iran, on the other hand, stone architecture had a ceremonial and choreographic significance, gave ample development to interior space by exploiting the use of wooden horizontal beams, and exalted the power and regal functions of the ruler.

Stone, worked and employed in accordance with all the experience acquired throughout the ancient Near East (including the territory of the Greeks in Asia Minor), tended to give solidity and permanence to the center of an ecumenical empire that was the religious and magical point of reference as well as a political and administrative seat. Around the large stone constructions, conceived for ceremonial purposes, the dwelling sections remained chiefly in wood. Here the old Indo-European tradition took its place, without disappearing entirely, beside the experiments re-elaborated by a different world, to whose physical aspect contributions had been made by Indo-European groups arriving in the area conquered by the empire in previous periods. It is obvious that the tradition of wooden architecture persisted tenaciously for a number of different reasons, and that the economic factor was not the most important. In the Indian world, on the other hand, the superimposition of Indo-Europeans on Indus civilization produced a social change and a halt in activity that, in the field of technique, brought about a decided regression in the use of brickwork.

But if the Indo-European tradition is linked to wooden constructions, the wooden architecture of Asia is obviously not entirely Indo-European. The ecological structure of the continent suggests the use of wood as the primary construction material. In certain civilizations, such as those of Central Asia, China, and Japan, it preserves its pre-eminence; in India and Iran, it recedes in the face of brick and stone, despite intermediate phases, as shown by mixed structures (wooden planking in the stupa of Kanishka) and by such examples of coexistence as the capital cities of Iran.

Conclusion

The Asian world, in the broad outlines of its social structure, manifests itself as a complex of highly evolved civilizations in which political power is unlimited and tends to become oppressive, self-preserving, and thus traditionalist, independent of the aspirations and sentiments of the ruler or rulers holding power. With the exception of those areas where the nomadic cultures and mercantile civilizations of Central Asia developed, the Asian economy is an agricultural one; the city plays a secondary role, while private wealth, mercantile or otherwise, does not confer political power. The subjected masses, whatever their class, have no political choice and cannot overthrow the system under which they live, being at best capable only of changing their rulers.

This lack of choice on the political level is, however, accompanied by considerable freedom on the religious one. This does not exclude traditionalist, habitual, or superstitious ties; what counts in the final analysis is simply one's own convictions and conscience. The paths that lead to the truth are infinite and equally valid. From this arises the prestige and universal value of the religious art work—in particular of the architectural work, which is the sum of esoteric and exoteric wisdom and the precise testimony of a proclaimed truth.

Asian thought, open to every kind of research and speculation, never denies mystical, paranormal, or meditative experiences. Even China—which transforms the essential lines of its own political system into something religiously intangible, reducing the defense of the system to a conflict between *fas et nefas* and neglecting to develop a law, an *ius*, formulated to uphold individual freedom—welcomes such great mystical and meditative trends as, for example, Taoism and Ch'an Buddhism, which expand human consciousness to dimensions beyond the normal ones. There exist thus certain fundamental attitudes of Asian man that—being shared—allow us to consider the whole continent as a unit, a coherent ensemble, made dynamic by economic, political, and cultural phenomena.

In these areas, it is easy to trace the speed of transmission and the extent of expansion of religious ideas, as well as the influences and superimpositions (more or less justified) that manifest themselves with extreme frequency in the sphere of religious thought, but the contacts and borrowings in the other fields are proportionately rarer and less active. Though the Asian architect is never a philosopher or scientist, his creations almost always mirror some religious and philosophical speculation; its essence is grasped by the artist's creative inspiration and aesthetic sense, becoming fixed in forms and examples that in their turn may influence the further development of religious thought. The latter is also a vision of the world, though it usually ignores certain particular aspects and problems of individual and social life, which are considered illusory and thus negligible. In the religious sphere, the individual is virtually free, for persecution is rare, but the development of religious thought unfolds in competition among the various trends. Each of them, therefore, is obliged to undertake activity that we might define as suggestive edification (occult persuasion based on symbolism), and which prompts it to attempt a total detachment of the metaphysical and religious world from the reality of daily social life. Asia also stands in this conflict between two equally pressing realities—the mystical one of divine experience and the sensory one of everyday life. This does not detract, as we have said, from the fact that no opposition whatever exists between the sacred and profane; the religious reality transcends and pervades the existential one, to form a unity with components that only the most recent criticism has begun to analyze with any precision.

These are the undivided foundations that justify the assumption of this book, which is the treatment in a single volume of the architectural works produced by very different civilizations, capable of expressing themselves in styles and forms quite remote from each other, but always united against a common background that we can only define as Asian. As for the sequence and variation of such styles and forms, it will be the task of the individual authors to present their phenomenology and development. I hope merely to have sketched, if only in broad outlines, the unifying characteristics of Asian civilization as they relate to architecture.

Mario Bussagli

1. *Mohenjo-Daro (Pakistan), plan of the city (from Volwahsen, 1969).*
2. *Mohenjo-Daro, view of the Great Bath.*
3. *Mohenjo-Daro, remains of constructions and drainage canal.*

At the beginning, in the third millennium B.C., the most important aspect of Indian architecture was centered on urban planning. It is apparent that the problems that arose were faced and resolved by avant-garde solutions unique for so remote a period. In a context of rigidly planned, standardized structures and works, two great metropolises, Mohenjo-Daro and the city known to us as Harappa, reveal the prevalent city-planning interests of their unknown architects. What counts is the city itself—in its entirety, in its perfect correspondence to an incredibly modern rationalism, in its simple presence. Monuments in the true sense, whether sacred or profane, are lacking, and the search for variations in taste and conception of individual architectural works is slight. Planned, functional, with its dwelling units made uniform according to the social class of the inhabitants, constructed of baked bricks but with an ample use of wood for superelevations, Mohenjo-Daro—India's most ancient city—takes its place in a vast phenomenon of urbanization extending in isolated spots over an enormous territory (Plate 1).

At the same time, large cities were emerging in Turkmenistan (Namazza-tepe and other centers on the Tedzent River), and in Afghanistan (Mundigak and Shahr-i-Sokhta on the Hilmand River), but the economies sustaining them were very different from and less complex than the system that produced urbanization in the Indus basin. The activity of these proto-civilizations was remarkable, so much so that the influence of the Afghan cities of the Hilmand reached the eastern shores of the Arabian peninsula. It cannot be compared, however, to that of Indus civilization. The difference in level is shown by the lesser rationality of the urban structure (which was sometimes grandiose), by more restricted economic specialization, and by the absence of writing. However, the Turkmeno-Afghan phenomenon—whose physical aspect we now know with some precision as a result of very recent discoveries—also sheds light on the genesis of the proto-Indian civilization of the Indus.

After a preparatory phase (improperly called pre-urban) characteristic of the archaic center of Kot Diji and other lesser ones, the Indus basin saw the almost sudden emergence—in the first half of the third millennium—of a splendid civilization, whose territory was the vastest among ancient civilizations. City planning reached extraordinary levels of activity and rationality. The metropolises were laid out on a grid plan (the sign of precise and rigorously maintained planning) and there is every indication of a division into neighborhoods in accordance with the productive specialization of the inhabitants, along with a highly modern interpretation of the distance between home and place of work. The project bespeaks a hierarchical social structure, which seems to be confirmed by the presence of fortified citadels with huge

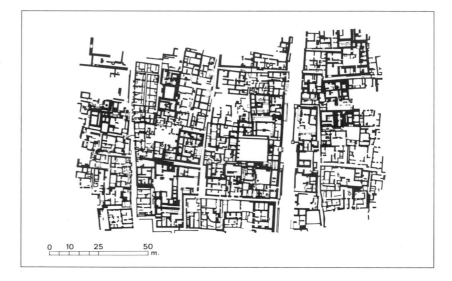

4. *Lothal, drainage canal.*
5. *Rajgir (Rajagriha), walls of the ancient city.*

6. *Patna (Pataliputra), column from the palace of Asoka.*
7. *Lauriya Nandangarh, commemorative column of Asoka with inscription and seated lion.*
8. *Fortress of Allahabad, commemorative column of Asoka (originally from Kausambi).*

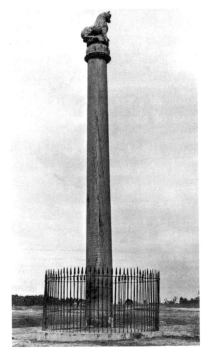

9. *New Delhi, Kotila-i-Firuz Sah, column of Asoka (stamba).*

walls, erected on an artificial elevated base. The citadel, in fact, may have been the seat of a strongly oppressive oligarchical power, besides being a secure refuge during invasions (which were unlikely and are in any case undocumented) and during the frequent floods. Strict rationalism is shown by the installation of public utilities—caravan resting places at the large street crossings, grain silos with openings at the top, public baths that may have had a sacred character (Plate 2), drainage canals and sewage systems (Plate 3). It is possible that the physical orientation of the city was in accordance with the prevailing winds, so as to ensure occasional cleaning of the streets by natural means.

The civilization of the Indus Valley declined because of a profound ecological change produced by its own expansion and activity. The colossal demand for baked bricks and construction lumber brought about extensive deforestation in the entire basin. This in turn led to more frequent and destructive floods, a threat that increased with subsequent changes in the incline of the river bed, altered as well by slow coastal earth tremors. The energy and activity of the bearers of this civilization, predominantly proto-Dravidians, are evident in their capacity to reconstruct immediately those cities destroyed by the river. Mohenjo-Daro, for example, was rebuilt at least seven times. Nevertheless, these ancient builders were caught in a vicious circle of which they were unaware, and by their very capacity to respond promptly to the violence of nature, ended by increasing this violence themselves. With their energies exhausted, the civilization they had created declined and ultimately disappeared (the Aryan invasion about the middle of the second millennium B.C. was also a contributing factor).

The economic structure—based on intensive agriculture, on the cultivation of flax and cotton, on exports and trade (by land and sea) over a wide area—permitted the accumulation of great wealth. Nevertheless, there are no traces of temples, nor of the pomp that usually accompanies royal courts. The complex religiosity of the peoples of the Indus excluded the use of large sacred images, and must very likely have caused them to turn more to psychically evocative forms and to orgiastic rites than to concrete representations.

The concept of the city, with the exception of its public bath and the so-called palace of Mohenjo-Daro (which—approximately 240 by 82 feet—was one of its large, functional, but not rich buildings), was formulated according to a collectivist utilitarianism and a planned functionalism. In all likelihood, these two factors subordinated any aesthetic considerations to the prevailing requirements of the urban system. All the houses, some of which had more than one story, had central courtyards on which the doors and windows opened. Entrance doors were placed on the lesser side streets. As a result, the principal

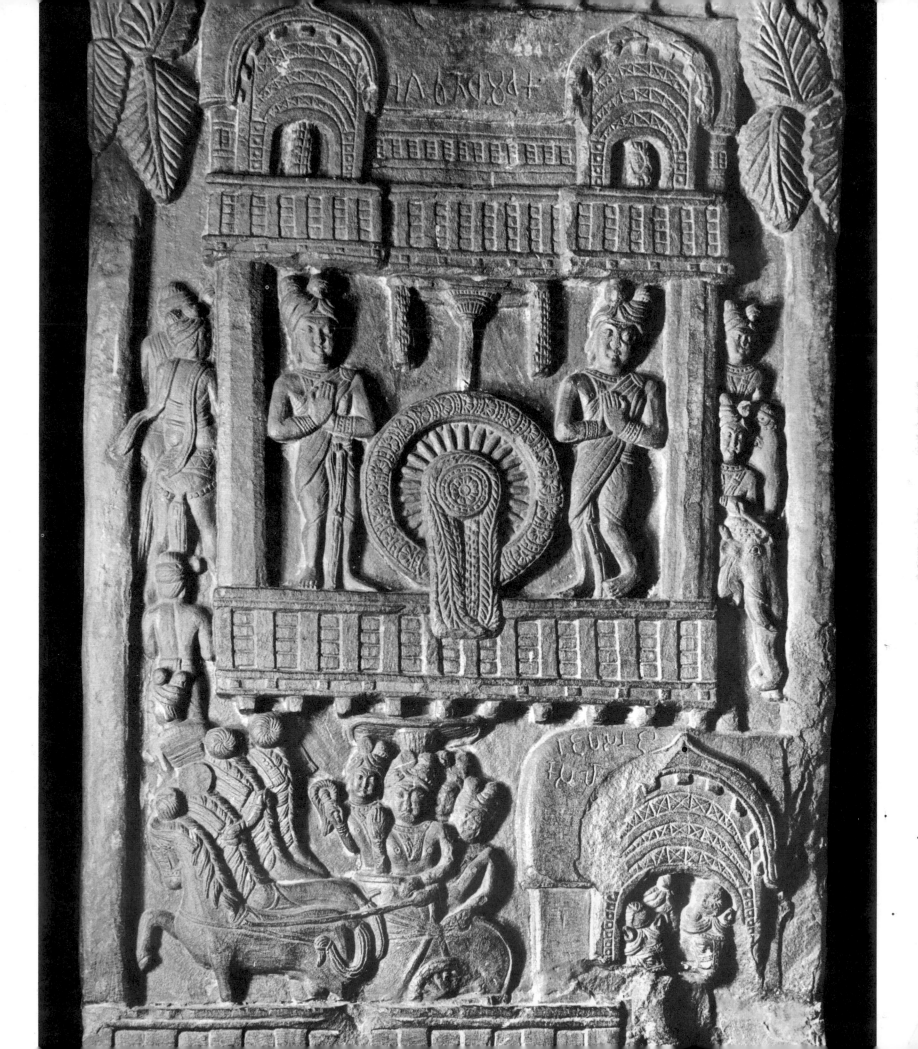

streets, which were not wide, were lined by walls that were uninterrupted except by cross streets; there were no recesses or openings of any other kind. Thus the architectural work was the city itself, not the temple, which did not exist or was replaced by the public baths. Neither was it the palace, which was of such remarkable size but nevertheless does not exhibit the magnificence of this vanished world.

Of the proto-Indian phase, also characterizing the now-buried dry docks of the port of Lothal (Plate 4), not much survives. The collision with Indo-European civilization, which violently superimposed itself on that of the Indus, probably gave rise to intermediate and restricted forms of culture, but only at the level of the village or small town. Such forms, however, are dubious and had no results, since the Indo-European architectural tradition was founded on construction in wood. The walls of Rajagriha (modern Rajgir), an ancient semilegendary capital, are the only architectural vestiges (Plate 5) that remain of a long period extending until the invasion of Alexander the Great into northern India and the founding of the first national Indian Empire, the Maurya dynasty. Creative effort at that time was directed only to poetry and religious thought, which explains why the period in question is generically called Vedic. The large collections of sacred hymns called the *Vedas*, together with a respectable body of texts of another kind, formed the basis of this Brahmanic culture.

Construction was in wood and, given the characteristic climate of the subcontinent, wood could not last for long, not even in such areas more favorable to its preservation as those of the mountainous arc in the north. The preservation of wooden architecture in some regions—in Kashmir, Nepal, and Bhutan—does, however, arouse one's interest in the techniques and forms employed. Elsewhere, the difficulty of providing for a sufficient quantity of suitable lumber, the further threat to its preservation caused by various animal species (especially insects), and the wish to create durable works worthy of religious prestige—all reduced wooden architecture drastically. Naturally, we have no way of determining how the total disappearance of possible, and even imposing, wooden constructions may have altered the evidence now available to us. Suffice it to recall, in this connection, that the wooden superstructure of the so-called stupa of Kanishka at Shah-ji-ki-Dheri (near Peshawar) carried it to a height of 638 feet, more than doubling the height of the masonry structure; only the rectangular foundations remain today. If the stupa had not been celebrated for various reasons, and if Chinese texts had not spoken of it as the "highest tower" in all of India, we surely could not have imagined the importance of its integration of materials.

The prevalent use of wood has caused a considerable gap in the history of architecture, extending over a period of time that greatly

16. *Sanchi, complex of temples: plan of the site; plan and elevation of the Great Stupa (from Volwahsen, 1969).*

17. *Sanchi, reconstruction of the holy site; in the foreground, the Great Stupa (from Volwahsen, 1969).*

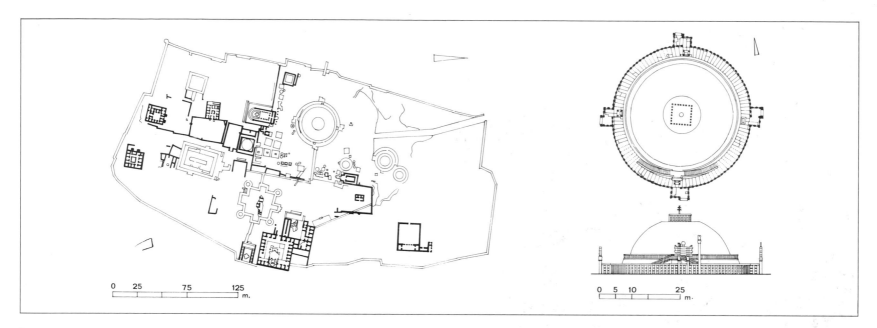

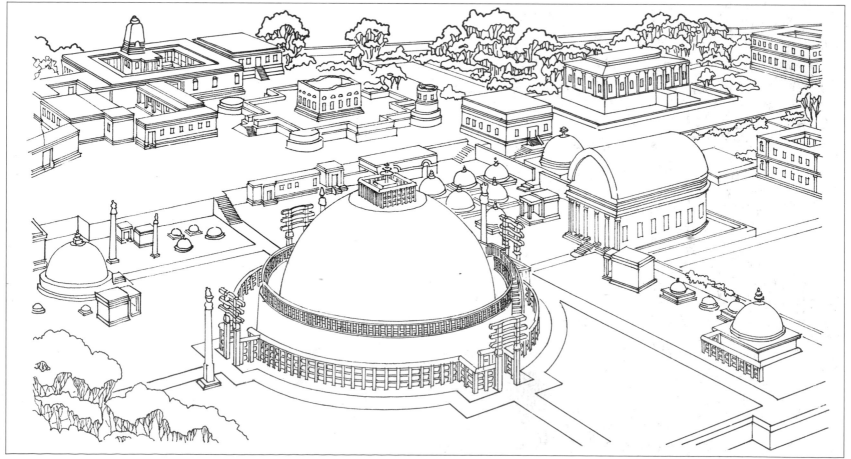

exceeds half a millennium. The only available evidence we have that is worthy of attention begins to come to light in the Maurya period, when the subcontinent was practically unified from the political standpoint and was strongly pervaded by Buddhist thought, which Asoka—the last of the great Maurya rulers—tended to transform into a political ideology. Open to wide contacts with different worlds as a result of Alexander's expedition and the influx of refugees loyal to the defeated Persian Empire, in contact and conflict with the Greek world created by Alexander's successors, India reached a truly significant turning point. In the area of construction materials, we find the first documented use of stone by means of a technique that was derived in part from foreign influences, and in part by imitating techniques used for other materials or discovering them anew. As for brick, whether raw or baked, there existed important ancient traditions that had been only partially lost.

First of all, in the Maurya phase, we find the appearance of stambas, isolated pillars topped by a capital supporting symbolic animal or inanimate figures (Plates 7, 10); their function is primarily magical and religious. They are, in fact, symbols of the "center," in that they indicate the point of convergence—and hence of irradiation—of paranormal forces that, spreading outward, uphold a particular religious persuasion. It is more likely that they were erected by Asoka and not, as some scholars believe, by his father and predecessor, Bindusara (Plates 8, 9). They were, in practice, Persian construction elements used in a different way. By losing their static function as supports, they became true symbols yet preserved their entire original appearance, including the characteristic bell-shaped capital (called Persepolitan), which culminates, however, in the final esoteric sign (Plate 15). From this capital, the use of which became very widespread even in plastic decoration and edifying narrative sculpture, the round amalaka (or cushion-shaped) capital characteristic of later Indian architecture was eventually derived. The form would also be used as the outer termination of the cupolas of temples, likewise designated as amalaka.

Rock-Cut Architecture

The first dated evidence of rock-cut architecture goes back to the Maurya period. In the Indian world, it is necessary to distinguish, over a long period of time, between truly constructed architecture (improperly called open-air architecture, as mentioned in the Introduction) and the kind that is cut into the rock, frequently inside caves in homogeneous rocky embankments where there is a sheer cliff (Plate 11). This type of construction is typical of India. Rock-cut architecture emerged as a result of the rapport that Indians almost instinctively feel to exist between the sacred sphere and the bowels of the earth. It later spread

over a considerable part of Asia, following the extension of Buddhism outside India (the sacred home of Buddhism), though with certain variations in technique and interpretation. We may consider it a traditional religious element, linked to the diffusion of Indian taste and to a particular persistence of its symbolic values, which at times undergo the effects of adaptation to cultural environments highly different from their original one.

Rock-cut architecture is always of a particular kind, one in which all static problems are automatically resolved by the cohesion of the rock itself. Since constructions in caves are endowed exclusively with interior space and only a bare suggestion of a façade that may or may not have a veranda, it is easy to observe in them elements that—though devoid of any static importance—tend to preserve the appearance of the interiors of constructed works. Their presence reveals the concern of the builders to respect a taste (and a symbolism) that by that time had become traditional. If static problems do not exist in works of this kind, there obviously exist others, deriving from the technique for excavating the rock[1] (based on the use of chisels and iron wedges of various sizes and on the creation of parallel excavation galleries) to the effects of light and shadow produced by the scant penetration of light from the outside. On the other hand, the technique of cut architecture was extended with the passage of time to virtually monolithic constructions endowed with both interior and exterior space. It is a sort of sculptured architecture, suggested in part by the hyperplastic character of Indian architectural taste, and evidenced by such famous works as the celebrated temple of Kailasanath at Ellora erected by the Rashtrakuta dynasty between the middle of the seventh and the middle of the eighth century A.D. (Plates 86–89) or the stupendous chapel near Kalugumalai, dedicated to Siva by the Pandya rulers of southern India.

Outside Indian territory proper—in the Khulm Valley in Afghanistan—we find a rather ancient example of cut architecture, one that dates back to the fourth or fifth century A.D. This is the stupa (Plate 49) and adjoining monastery of Haibak, known to the ancients as Samangan or Simingan. The monastery, cut inside a cave, is characterized by an unusual plan whose function is exceptional and symbolic, with small half-columns topped by Ionic half-capitals. These represent the translation into rock of particular static solutions that pertain to Sassanian Iran, adopted to support the cupolas overhanging square rooms. But the most interesting monument of the Haibak complex is the stupa. This is the term for a certain kind of construction with a full cupola and rich in symbolic values, used both by Buddhists and Jains. Here at Haibak the cupola, or rather pseudo-cupola, representing the celestial vault as observed from the outside, is monolithic and full as usual. Unlike constructed cupolas, however, it could not accommodate

23. *Sanchi, Stupa No. 3.*
24. *Magadha, city gate of Kusinagara; reconstruction from a relief on the southern gate of the Great Stupa at Sanchi (from Volwahsen, 1969).*
25. *Sanchi, Stupa No. 2.*
26. *Bhaja, rock sanctuary, exterior.* ▷

27. *Bhaja, Chaitya No. 12, section (from Volwahsen, 1969).*
28. *Bhaja, Chaitya No. 12, interior, nave; in the background, the stupa.* ▷

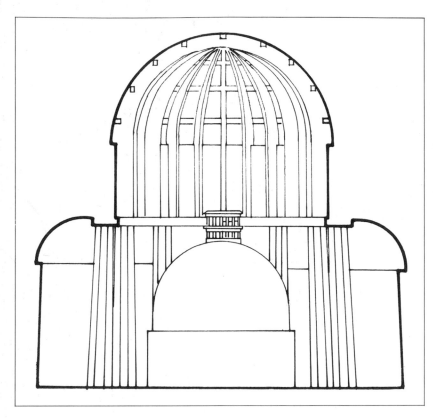

29. Bedsa, entrance to the chaitya.
30. Bedsa, interior of the chaitya, detail of capitals. ▷

◁ 31. Bedsa, interior of the chaitya.
   32. Bedsa, interior of the chaitya, sculptured reproduction of the exterior of a
       house.

in its interior what is called the foundation deposit, the necessary and consecrating element of every Buddhist stupa, always connected with the "body" and word of Buddha.

The Haibak construction, which required strenuous economic and technical efforts, as well as an enormous amount of labor, was not perfectly orthodox. Moreover, if it is true that the trench that was dug to isolate the form of the cupola was supposed to be filled with water,[2] the stupa would have represented the terrestrial disk surrounded by the ocean. In this case, even symbolically, the stupa at Haibak would not have been entirely traditional, since its significance, rather than being cosmological, would seem to have been connected with the earth and ocean. The *harmikā* (the balcony over the cupola, which here has a cell) represented the point of intersection between the human and the divine, thus making concrete a concept widely developed in Mesopotamian ziggurats. Surrounded by a ring of water and partially visible in the reflection, the stupa at Haibak must have represented a true *unicum*. Symbolism aside, the exceptional character of the work is important to us in that it shows that both methods of rock-cutting had reached beyond the territory of India between the fourth and fifth centuries. It reveals, too, that there existed a desire to create unusual effects—the symbolic and ornamental association with water is almost a kind of liquid architecture—and an interest in the creation of forms deliberately devoid of interior space. There is no need, therefore, to wait for later periods in order to place cave architecture side by side with the rock-cut constructions that have both interior and exterior space.

As for works extracted from caves, the first that we know goes back, as mentioned earlier, to the Maurya period. It is dated by the inscription recording its origin in the twelfth year of Asoka's reign—that is, 256 B.C., according to the most generally accepted chronology. Known as the cave of Sudama, it is situated in the Barabar Hills and is a proto-Hindu temple structure remarkable for its singularity. Rectangular in plan, with an entrance on one of its long sides, it displays a false vault, curved so as to assume the form of a half-cylinder laid on the sectional plane, parallel to the perpendicular face of the cliff into which it is constructed. It ends, however, in a circular apse connected to the principal area by a narrow opening. Seen from inside the principal area, the apse is convex rather than concave. In the view from the interior of the nave, it imitates in stone a circular hut (or rather semi-hut) with a projecting ogival roof. This choice of form for the apse, almost separated from the body of the temple, is probably connected with the significance that round huts covered with leafy branches assume in the coronation ritual (*rājasūya*). The hut, in this and other cases, is likened to the matrix of the earth. Related to the god, placed inside the rock, and realized in stone to defy the ravages of time, the

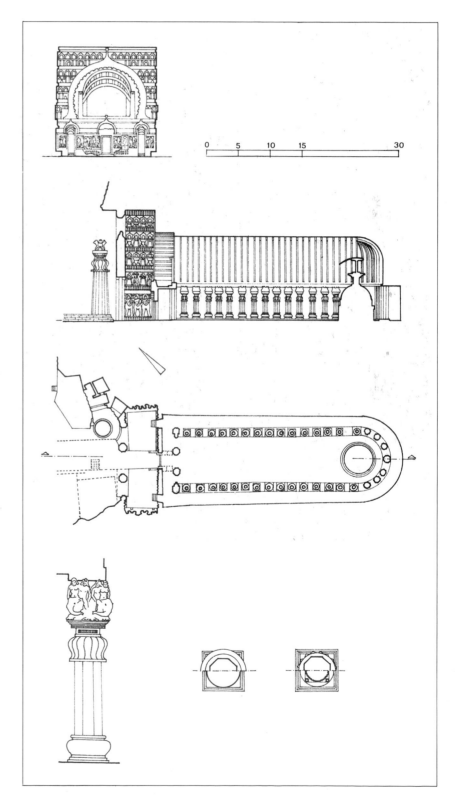

◁ 36. *Karli, interior of the chaitya, nave with the stupa.*
   37. *Nasik, sangharāma, exterior of Chaitya No. 18.*
   38. *Nasik, sangharāma, interior of Chaitya No. 18.*

47

39. *Udayagiri, caves of Rani Kanaur, exterior.*
40. *Taxila, temple of Jandial.*
41. *Taxila, Temple of the Double-Headed Eagle on the site of Sirkap.*
42. *Taxila, distyle in antis temple on the site of Sirkap.*

43. *Taxila, city walls of Sirkap.*
44. *Taxila, small stupa on the site of Sirkap.*

46. *Taxila, Dharmarajika stupa.*
47. *Taxila, temple of Kunal.*
48. *Taxila, remains of a monastery near the temple of Kunal.*

false hut of the cave of Sudama alluded to the rule of the god over the entire universe, perhaps with reference to the possibility of evoking the divinity itself on the part of meditating priests.

Architecture in Wood and Stone

The most important aspect of the false hut in the cave of Sudama is its demonstration of the profound influence exercised by wooden constructions over those in stone. Here symbolic reasons prompted the imitation in stone of a circular wooden hut. Elsewhere, the interdependence of wooden and stone constructions is confirmed by a quantity of secondary data. Thus, the balustrades that define the sacred area around Buddhist stupas—though made of stone—display joints that are absolutely identical with wooden joints, and simulate in their heaviness the balustrades constructed with large logs (Plates 13, 14). With all the irrationality of adopted solutions (requiring much labor and the resolution of considerable technical difficulty), they confirm that the use of stone imitates—for reasons of taste as well—that of analogous constructions in wood. Ornamental rosettes, with or without figures, but in which the motif of the lotus corolla always recurs (Plate 12), are placed at the points of intersection of the upright posts and the crosspieces—precisely at the points where cones and wedges functioning as nails were inserted into wooden constructions. Elsewhere, as for example in the chaityas (or sanctuaries) of Bhaja and Karli, wood was actually employed to complete the interior structures of rock-cut constructions. In fact, in the two cases mentioned, the ribs of the vault are of wood; they are thus ornamental elements that allude to methods employed for wooden buildings unknown to us. They indicate, however, the existence of a definite and deep-seated taste that could not be ignored without extreme effort.

The use of such lasting materials as stone and brick is primarily connected with sacred constructions. Moreover, in Buddhist and Hindu India, even if a constant and substantial commitment to lasting works of art did not exist, there was an inevitable tendency toward building in a durable fashion.

Durability and Economics

In non-Indian civilizations, it would seem absurd to detach the architectural work from the concept of durability. Usually, the collapse of a scarcely finished construction, even in regions bordering on India, was due to technical deficiencies and was considered a true calamity. Roman prisoners and the emperor Valens himself (head of the Eastern Roman Empire from 364 to 378 A.D.) were assigned by their Persian captors to the arduous construction of a bridge, Bandi-Kaisar ("Caesar's bridge"), which is still in use. The explicit recognition of

49. *Haibak (Afghanistan), monolithic stupa, detail of upper part with terrace cell* (harmikā).
50. *Stupa from Taxila (Taxila, Museum).*
51. *Kabul (outskirts), stupa of Guldara.*

54. *Sanchi, Temple No. 17.*
55. *Nalanda, votive stupas in Area 12.*
56. *Nalanda, temple in Area 3.* ▷

Roman technical superiority, even in the midst of a desire to humiliate the conquered foe, was obvious. This superiority translated itself into terms of durability still more than into terms of building science.

In India, especially for the Buddhist population, there existed instead a notably different standard of judgment. If a work was built in order to acquire merit, which was to a greater or lesser extent a constant aspiration, what mattered most was the intention and the sacrifice in money and labor involved in carrying it out. The work, seen as a votive offering, was a gift, a donation of invested wealth and labor. Therefore, even if it collapsed upon completion, it nevertheless had already fulfilled its function. From the economic and technical standpoint, this concept had curious results. Construction frequently brought about only a limited circulation of wealth from the patron to the builders (who were also motivated in part by a desire to acquire merit), since the work created was an end in itself and in theory was not built to last. From the technical point of view, this mental concept ensured that the builders preferred inexpensive, makeshift techniques, quickly applied, and paid only cursory attention to problems of stability. The widespread use of stucco in the northwest can be connected almost always with this desire to build hastily without an excessive concern for a structure's durability.

Naturally, when there was a question of glorifying a site of extreme religious importance, or when the patron attributed a particular value to the work he commissioned, the incentive toward lasting construction, maintenance, restoration, or indeed reconstruction became the rule. Furthermore, durability contributed to the fame of a particular temple or sanctuary. Tradition, reasserting itself, imparted a particular vitality to the architectural complex, resulting in a constant influx of pilgrims and casual visitors—a virtual reflex activity whose importance (economic as well) cannot be denied. In other words, a derivative economic traffic (in votive offerings, souvenirs, temporary facilities for food and lodging, etc.) flourished around the holy centers, involving not only the clergy, but also—and primarily—the groups and individuals attached to this marginal economy. Thus it happened that there emerged around every stupa or temple of some importance temporary dwellings designed to be inhabited by those who lived off the fame of the temple, as well as other constructions suitable for sheltering this traffic. Moreover, the very structure of the huge medieval temples—frequently formed by a group of different constructions contained within a single consecrated rectangular enclosure—was connected with such services as the temple itself required, and with the presence of this marginal but by no means negligible economy that had installed itself outside the enclosure.

For other reasons, not the least being the limited need for interior

space in Hindu temples, the solution of problems of stability was based on an exploitation of gravity that featured building enormous walls, with the entire structure diminishing upward like a pyramid. Form and decoration were often obtained by subsequent cutting and carving. Still, even though a remarkable number of Indian works have survived the ravages of time, the characteristic relativism of Indian thought with respect to the importance given to architectural works (and not only to these, but to all of sensory reality) constitutes a degree of appreciation that is undeniable. However, this appreciation must be viewed beside the characteristic coexistence of constructed and cut architecture, along with the relative implications of works "cut in the negative sense"— that is to say, in caves (with interior space only)—and those "cut in the positive sense" (with exterior space, either with or without interior space). These observations, implying as they do a highly special flexibility in the evaluation of the architectural media, are sufficient to underscore the originality and autonomy of the architectural phenomenon in India.[3]

Aesthetic Value

In the traditional hierarchy of artistic activity, India bestows the highest value on poetry, the theater, dance, painting, and music. Architecture, along with sculpture and the minor arts, was considered almost a craft, even though it required of the architect exceptionally vast knowledge touching on the most diverse fields, including empirical knowledge of a geological sort and other related subjects that can be called geomantic. Indian aesthetic thought excludes architecture from the major arts—while yet demonstrating in a thousand ways an awareness of the undeniable rapport that links it to society and to the tastes of the immense world of which it is an expression—because of the vast technical component that the act of building involves. Even apart from the highly binding prescriptions of the texts, architectural structures were built very slowly, by masses of men engaged in hard labor over long periods of time and using technical means that further increased the distance between the intention of the artist and the final realization of the work. In short, the architectural work did not correspond finally to the aesthetic canons suggested by philosophical speculations.

There is no doubt that Indian religious architecture, predominant in its importance and abundance, reflects Indian civilization better than any other of its means of artistic expression. That civilization, as we know, leaves the widest possible margin for religious speculation. Apart from the sacred significance attributed to construction materials (whether wood, stone, or brick),[4] Indian architecture obeys a unique— that is to say, a religious and symbolic—"functionalism." The very act

of building—which began by determining the rapport between the universe and the chosen terrain, with geomantic appraisals and the exorcising of *bhūtas* (demons and spirits) from the site as well as gods other than those to whom the temple was dedicated—had the value of a magical rite. There was a full awareness of the "sacrifice" of which the earth was victim, withdrawn as it was from cultivation and destined to support the weight of the wall structure. It was thought necessary to placate the earth through the rite of *vastuśamana* in order to establish a favorable relationship between the creative force of the earth itself and the human work that was to rise on it. There existed thus a kind of rapport between architecture and nature, formulated on the basis of invisible forces rather than on those of aesthetic harmony. Now, the magical basis of such rituals, the multiplication and interweaving of symbolic elements, the very fact that the construction of a religious structure could be likened to a liturgical act—all seem to have excluded in the most absolute fashion any urgent search for *rāsa*, a term that refers to the very substance of the aesthetic experience (although it has numerous meanings, the chief one being "flavor"). But if traditional classifications relegated architecture to a secondary plane, the works created were not rendered less valid thereby, as is proved by the universal appreciation accorded them today. Nevertheless, even in the Indian world and despite their negative premises, works of architecture enjoyed a popularity that precluded any complicated reading of the symbolic and religious values they incorporated.

We find traces of this in literary works: temples, independent of their symbolism, are compared in their bulk to huge mountains,[5] but still more significant is the suggestion offered by the *Cūlavamsa*, a Pali-Singhalese work, which in describing the ruins of Polonnaruwa (Plates 184–192) compares them to old men who bend more and more toward the ground with the passage of time. The same text speaks of constructions that, "rising in stone or brick, create a pleasure for the eyes." This clearly corresponds to a particular impression aroused by the work of art outside of its religious and symbolic implications. The critical attitude reflected by the Pali-Singhalese text, like that shown in other works that strive to express the grandeur of certain temples through unexpected or daring metaphors, leads back to one of the most valid and widespread currents of thought.

The aesthetic speculation of Dandin, Sanskrit author and poet of the sixth century, points out in fact that the *rāsa* to which we refer is nothing but a state of mind, a sentiment intensified by a combination of different elements but essentially a normal one (which as a result can be perceived and expressed in the literary forms of which we have spoken), even when it is prompted by forms that turn out to be partially accidental, as in the case of the Polonnaruwa ruins. It is obvious that

66. *Aihole, temple of Durga, exterior of apse.*
67. *Aihole, temple of Durga, detail of sculptured decoration of a pillar.*
68. *Aihole, temple of Durga, exterior.* ▷

the exterior decoration—constantly hyperplastic due to the insep-arable relation between architecture and sculpture—has an influence on the impressionistic value aroused by the enormous size of religious architectural structures. Because of such a phenomenon, the symbolic component of the work and the myriad images adorning its exterior intervene almost unconsciously; they blend into a single significance that is generally connected with the mountain, with its upward thrust, and with a vision that reunites the concretions of the earth—that is to say, mountains—with a spiritual effort at elevation. The direction of the effort is toward achieving a reality that precludes all that is relative or contingent.

From the Western viewpoint—and limited to sacred Hindu buildings—the effect of the massive temples could be said to have been close to the Baroque in some respects, especially in the movement of surfaces and the resulting play of light and shadow. It was admittedly a swollen, heavy, and exotic Baroque, but rich in effects and rendered abstruse by the diversity of its artistic language and expressive means. Indeed, the decoration and the treatment itself of the images obeyed a foreign and vexing taste when measured against Western choices and experience. Nevertheless, it was precisely because of this similarity, superficial and poorly understood though it was, that even the Indian experience helped (indirectly) in the paradoxical definition of the Baroque as a "category of the human spirit," at a particular moment when critical thought was directed at this artistic trend.

In reality, the architecture of India can be evaluated only on the basis of the culture that produced it, it being understood that it offers universal values, suggestions, and sentiments no different from those recorded in Indian literature. The degree and intensity of these im-pressive appraisals are obviously modified as a result of the modes of thought and fixed hierarchies of values corresponding to the diversity of those cultures that from time to time have confronted the discovery or the knowledge of Indian architecture. In any case, there is a clear aesthetic difference between Buddhists and Hindus, which can be related to the essence of their respective quests for truth. The search of the Buddhist is directed toward an ideal of peace and serenity; in Hin-duism, there is a prevailing dynamism (and a movement of architectural volumes) that attempts to express a divine majesty shining through the very life of the universe. The first philosophy, however linked to cosmic symbolism, is based on a human measure. The second has as its parameter the rhythm of life of the universe; it transcends the individual and his destiny, as well as his range of mental sentiments, to express an overwhelming awe of the sacred.

This is not to deny that the great sacred works of Buddhism and Hinduism are the fruit of a highly particular social situation that concentrates the tremendous efforts of generations therein, to the

73. *Mamallapuram, Dharmaraja* rath *(monolithic chariot-temple), elevation, section, aerial view, and ground plan (from Volwahsen, 1969).*   74. *Mamallapuram, Descent of the Ganges, rock sculpture.* ▷

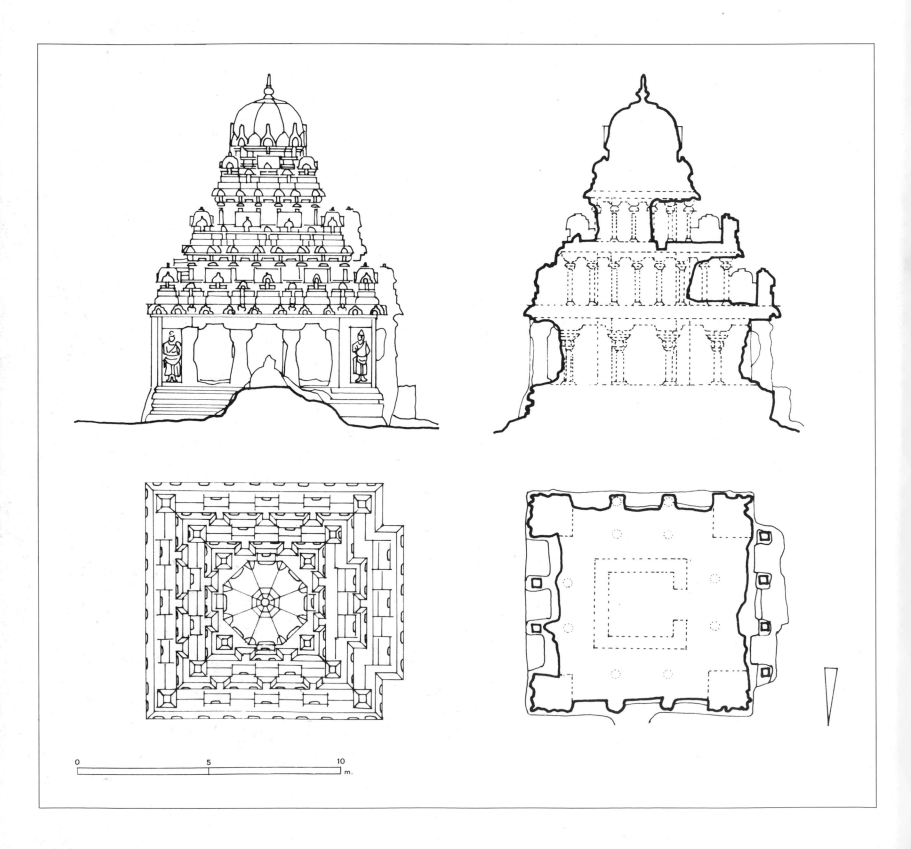

detriment of other undertakings which the religious spirit (in its way relativistic because lacking in real barriers of orthodoxy) of Indian culture has made to appear less urgent. The drive toward the Absolute, an essential concept of Indian religious speculation, made the reality of social conflict fade. The result has been a lack of interest—not only theoretical—in history and the wish to react to the pressure it exercises upon individuals through a sense of community[6] (Buddhism) and through a hopeless, extremely resigned isolation (Hinduism). Only the certainty of endless reincarnation attenuates the instinctive terror of death, rendering less miserable the life of beings crushed by insuperable, intertwined, oppressive hierarchies. The only full, free, fundamental, and respected choice was that of religious belief. Ideas of this kind were reflected in the field of the figurative arts, and thus also in architecture, producing—along with other profound components—forms and effects that in other civilizations could not even have been imagined. Created by great if anonymous artists, these forms were in essence *prakṛti*—that is to say, nature—not only because they were in harmony with the natural surroundings, but also and above all because they were deeply rooted in civilization, in man, in the Indian world in its entirety. For *prakṛti* is, after all, the collective unconscious of the Indian people.

The Dominant Theme

To judge by the quite numerous and systematic treatises, the fundamental motif of Indian architectural constructions is the representation of the center. It is a theme equally valid for architecture and for city planning. Every temple or palace was an *axis mundi*, a sacred center in which the celestial, the terrestrial, and even the infernal worlds met (Plates 16, 17). By extension, this symbolic motif also recurred in the plan of cities, it being understood that in all of India, down to our own day, the essential unit of human agglomeration is the village. Thus, the motif of the center found its place in the theoretical plans of cities, whether these were square in shape (the square being the symbol of the ordered world, the perfection of form and of order); rectangular, with the principal streets inscribing a rhombus; or even more abstract (circular, semicircular, or triangular).

The idea for the round plan may be of foreign origin—perhaps Assyrian, by means of the Parthians—but in every case these geometric figures had their own value and symbolic meaning. The constant significance underlying these various symbols is that of converting the magical forces of the soil—pre-existing or assembled and condensed by preliminary foundation rituals—into a basis of support for human cohabitation and into a form of breath or of life, in unison with the rhythm of the cosmic breath. The search is for a human dimension for cities, in order that men may feel therein the rhythm of the universe,

which is likewise achieved through the geometric treatment of the indefinite (but not infinite) space of the urban complex. On the other hand, the concept becomes changed and exaggerated when it is a question of sacred constructions. Here the geometric tendency, since it alludes to a greater intensity of the sacred, is even more evident. The plan of a stupa in various periods will be frankly circular (Plate 59), including its surrounding enclosure; or it may display a circle inscribed in a square (Plate 51), or even series of squares. The plan of the Hindu temple will on the contrary be primarily an enclosed rectangle (Plate 57), though sometimes the sides of the enclosure are segments of reversed ellipses; the disposition of the buildings, which can vary considerably, will sometimes be symbolic and sometimes quincuncial, with one building at each corner and one at the center (Plate 56), thus exploiting the diagonals of the rectangle as axes for the placement of structures in space. In every case, there is an obvious attempt to provide isolated visibility for the principal building, which nevertheless forms part of the total order of symbolic (and thus artificial) space constituted by the whole. In a certain sense, this arrangement endowed the hemispheres of stupas and the huge masses of medieval temples with a prominence that alluded symbolically to the mountain *par excellence*—the cosmic pillar, the axis of the world, made concrete by its man-made replica.

There is clearly, with respect to sacred monuments, a shade of meaning different from what we find in the Western world. In fact, there exists between the sacred and profane a characteristic dichotomy in location that does not exactly correspond to what occurs in the West, especially insofar as theoretical implications are concerned. Sacred constructions are frequently decentralized with respect to urban agglomerates, when not actually isolated. They may be temple cities (Madura), combined temple and monastery complexes (Ajanta), or—as previously stated—isolated temples that attract to their precincts groups of persons having economic connections with the life of the temple. In all such cases, we are in the presence of "centers" in themselves, whose magnificence forms no part of an urban context, but emerges from the desire for a deliberate and specific encounter with the sacred. As such, these centers were purposely created to be alien to the city, but in a form different from that of the Christian monastery or abbey. The city, in its turn, was seen as a consecrated and functional center, designed to connect the sacred with the daily life of a mass of human beings who availed themselves, as a specific and ready reference point for their spiritual needs, of the religious construction that in theory was always placed at the center (but that in practice might be located differently, even though gravitating directly toward the center). The dichotomy between sacred and profane is here reduced to a

different degree of intensity. This same human mass—which is never capable of conferring real autonomy on its own city—knew, in return, that it lived in an urban environment where every detail acted to convert the invisible magical and religious forces into influences that were protective, creative, and responsive to the order and divine law that reigned within its walls.

Thus, we find in the texts that the basic structure—generally a rectangular grid—is overlaid by a street pattern that increases the symbolic values of the urban center. Such insertions also provide solutions that satisfy the demands of traffic relating to the location and function of the city itself. A fortified city might be in the form of a *padma* (lotus blossom), preserving the inner network but enclosing it within a quadrilobate ring of circular, octagonal, or hexagonal bastions whose lobes correspond to the corners of the basic square. Other theoretical plans may call for a greater width of the streets, which were oriented in a particular direction; or situate the buildings— always with the basic network in mind—in such a way as to form a symbolic figure (the swastika, for example). Nevertheless, beyond these theoretical considerations, the social reality of the Indian world has conditioned the growth of its cities, producing spontaneous variations in the basic grid pattern and the symbolic geometrical figures. The grid, rigid and undivided, bound up with a town plan, appears at its clearest only in the metropolises and cities of the Indus Valley culture. Although it is impossible to reconstruct the successive stages, it is known that from these derive the erudite and speculative plans already to be found in the Vedic phase, but which were to be fully developed in technical writings only much later.

It is certain nevertheless that the division of the space under construction into a network of squares and—subordinately—into triangles emerges from requirements of a religious and symbolic kind. However, the geometric treatment of the available space is very different from what we find in modern architecture, and leads to what we might call a multiple visibility for the work. This is because the work itself, as a result of its symbolic significance and its representation in concrete form of a vertical axis (the magical *axis mundi*), must offer equally valid and total views from all sides, thus being subject to a scheme that is more sculptural than architectural. Even the word "façade" takes on a shade of meaning quite different here from its use in the European world and in some other parts of Asia. The façade is determined by points of access to the interior, whose existence it underlines, but it does not prevail over the lateral or apse views. Its symbolism as the center carries the Indian architectural mass as much as possible toward plastic values.

The Development of Architecture in India

It should be pointed out that—aside from the Vedic altar to be found in every village, and which, in its simplicity, is as charged with symbolism as any of the great architectural works—the architecture of India has obviously experienced oscillations in religious thought. It thus keeps pace with the rise of Buddhism, and is later modified by the affirmation of certain trends in Hinduism and the consolidation of Jainism. Nevertheless, it was Buddhism alone that imparted to India a pre-eminent position in the international sphere. It was the expansion of Buddhism—a clearly Indian religion, though heterodox with respect to its Vedic-Brahmanic-Hindu background—that in fact produced Asian humanism. The spread of properly Hindu thought was more limited and less rich in suggestions capable of development.

Beginning with the Maurya period, or more precisely with the reign of Asoka, the architectural constructions that have come down to us are for the most part Buddhist. However, in addition to stambas (isolated pillars), we also find chaityas (sanctuaries) and viharas (monasteries). Besides the chaitya of Sudama that we have already mentioned, there is that of the Lomas Rishi cave, which also displays an entrance with the characteristic *kūdu* (horseshoe arch) that surmounts and frames the entrance and that was to become one of the most widespread motifs in Indian architecture (Plate 11). Used also for upper windows in other typical constructions, it carries over into its execution in stone (as in the caves at Kanheri and Karli, and the early Ajanta caves) the characteristic traits of the wooden *kūdu*, a proof of its derivation from a wooden architecture that has disappeared. As for civil constructions, there remain the foundations of Asoka's palace at Pataliputra (now Patna; Plate 6), whose splendor was described by the Greek Megasthenes, Seleucid ambassador to the Maurya court. The royal palace on the ancient site of Sirkap at Taxila most likely belongs to the same period; only its ground plan survives, though other remains (Plates 40–44, 46–48, 50) testify to the former richness of the site. It is very probable that the palace at Pataliputra, destroyed by fire between the fifth and seventh centuries A.D., was partly laid out according to the plans for Achaemenid palaces, taking its inspiration from a similar concept of royalty.

Later centuries offer a much wider panorama. The stupa, as we have often had occasion to mention, is a construction lacking interior space. As a characteristic sacred building, it assumes very different forms in its Indian development, as well as in its diffusion over all of Buddhist Asia. It has a multiple symbolic significance: as a magical center (the axis of the world); as a representation of the universe, seen from outside; as a tomb, cenotaph, or reliquary; as a reminder of edifying or miraculous events. It can also be built as a votive offering or as a sign of the faith erected on new, vast territory. It replaces the importance of the altar and can be considered an architectural image of the Buddha, whose essence permeates the entire universe. Finally, it can vary greatly in size and form, from miniature replicas a few inches high (but with the same importance) to mountain stupas such as the Borobudur of Java, which is an entire large hill transformed into a symbol (Plate 201).

In the period under consideration, we find a number of famous stupas, ranging from that at Bharhut (whose decoration is an example of a school of sculpture in which independent characteristics are mingled with a desire to avoid the anthropomorphic representation of the Buddha by substituting symbols) to the stupa of Buddh Gaya (a reminder of the Buddha's Enlightenment) and the celebrated group at Sanchi in Madhya Pradesh (Plates 18, 21, 22). Stupas at this time are surrounded by a *vedikā* (fence) with open *toranas* (gates) at the cardinal points consisting of vertical posts with horizontal beams (Plates 23–25). The stupa itself, cylindrical at the base, rises into a body with a false hemispherical dome called an *anda* (egg) surmounted by a kind of small belvedere, the *harmikā*, at whose center an axis—with a series of parasols often diminishing in diameter—represents both the axis of the universe and Buddha.

The period of construction of the stupas at Sanchi is rather controversial. The most probable date is the second or first century B.C., which is almost certainly the date for the so-called Great Stupa, the focal point of the entire sacred complex situated a few miles outside the city (Plates 19, 20). The presence of one of Asoka's pillars confirms the holy tradition of the site from somewhat earlier periods and may supply some foundation for the emperor's presumed visit to pay homage to a small Buddhist community that had settled in the surrounding hills. But, aside from the considerable sacred significance of the complex, what is important is its intermingling of architectural and figurative evidence that can be deduced from the decorations. Here the stupa is truly the image, or rather the epiphany, of the Buddha, of his Law that rules the universe (serving in fact in aniconic representations to express the Buddha's presence), and is moreover a psycho-cosmogram. The form, suggested by the apparent aspect of the vault of the sky, implies in its turn the total presence and intangibility (ascribed to the foundation relics) of the Buddha, who in this way is seen not as a human teacher but as the essence of the universe.

The type of stupa with a hemispherical dome is also found in the Andhra school. For example, we have traces of the foundations of the huge stupa at Amaravati, where the diameter of the sacred area is several hundred yards, as well as the remains of other works of the same kind, though smaller in size, found at Nagarjunakonda, Gum-

82. *Kalugumalai, monolithic Vettuvan Koil temple.*
83. *Pattadakal, temple of Mallikarjuna.*
84. *Pattadakal, temple of Mallikarjuna.*

madidirru, Prolu, and Guntupala. The domes, more globular, were grafted onto drum bases much higher than the examples at Sanchi. This data is supplied by reliefs with sculptural representations of local stupas; from these we can also see that the stupa of the Andhra school considerably modifies the appearance of the entrance to the sacred area. The *vedikā* (the openings in the outer fence) were flanked with images of facing lions placed at the tops of the posts, while the outer edge of the raised circular walk surrounding the drum halfway up displayed projecting balconies that faced the gates. On these balconies, side by side and joined at their capitals, five pillars of equal height were erected. Their symbolic significance is unknown, but it is assumed that their practical use was to support oriflammes or banners that had a ritual meaning. The presence of verticalized bands, almost surfaces— alternately carved and empty and thus contributing to effects of light and perspective—modifies the globular mass of the stupa and diminishes its isolation while enclosing the dome, conceived so as to exceed a hemisphere in curvature, in a kind of crown. There is thus a change in style that derives from the cultural conditions of the Andhras and from a state of mind that foreshadows future developments in Indian art, which were to be more balanced and knowledgeable.

In the northwest Indian regions—that is, the area of expansion of the so-called Greco-Buddhist art of Gandhara—the stupa acquires a strong vertical thrust. This thrust is frequently obtained by wooden super-structures that must have included series of terminal parasols, trans-forming the stupa into a conical trunk that sometimes rose to consider-able height. We know of this verticality through models, sometimes very elaborate, or through the small stupas to be found in areas outside the Indian subcontinent (in Afghanistan or Central Asia), which though late are sufficient to indicate the direction taken by the Gandhara stupa. An upward thrust, a mysticism not unlike what we find in the Gothic, characterize these productions of the north, from which derive, by various intermediate stages, the Tibetan chorten, where even the dome is distorted to take on the shape of an inverted pot (the term "pot" serves as a technical one). Lamotte has given us an accurate listing of Indian tower stupas, almost always some 200 feet in height, to be found primarily in the Gandhara region.[7]

The importance of the Gandhara school is not really limited to stupas, though some of these, as in the Takht-i-Bahi complex, find their place in rather scenographic overall solutions that surely show traces of the Classical and Hellenistic component fundamental to this school. Proceeding from the fortifications of Bactra (today known as Balkh), with their Parthian-style decorations and high embrasures, to such Hellenistically inspired cities as Ai Khanum ("Lady Moon" in Uzbek)—which is situated at a bend of the Amu Darya River and preserves the agora, principal street, citadel, and even a *heroon*—or the

86. *Ellora, Kailasanath, elevation, transverse section, and plans; at the right, elevation of a monolithic column in the courtyard of the temple (from Volwahsen, 1969).*

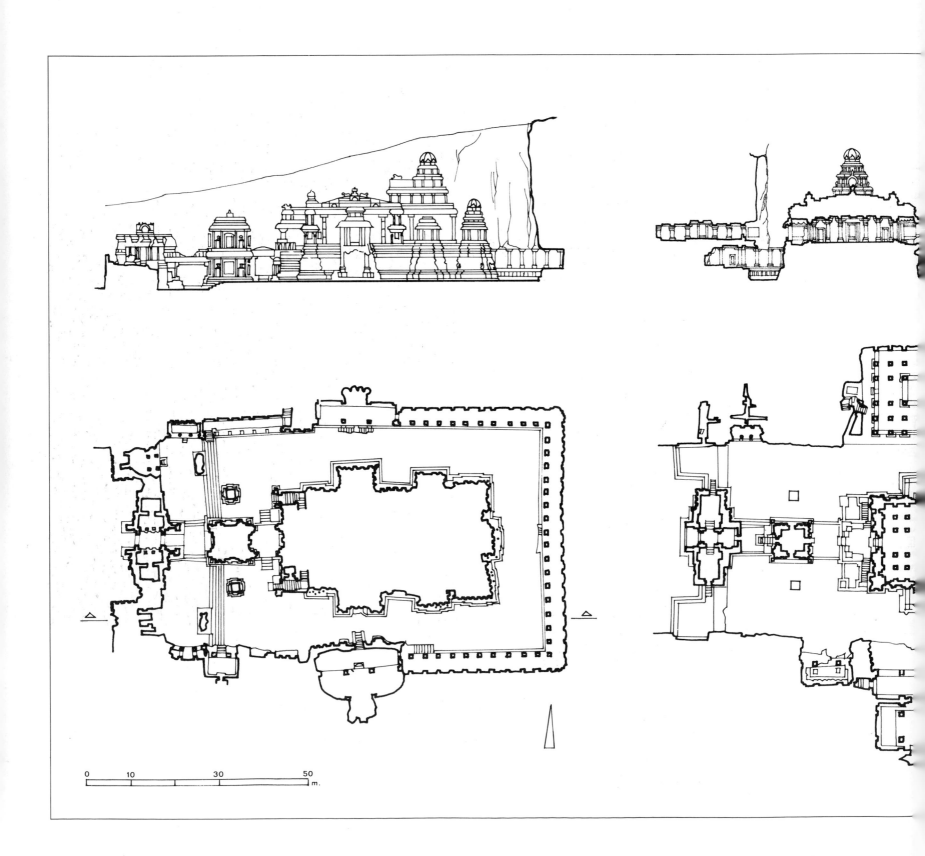

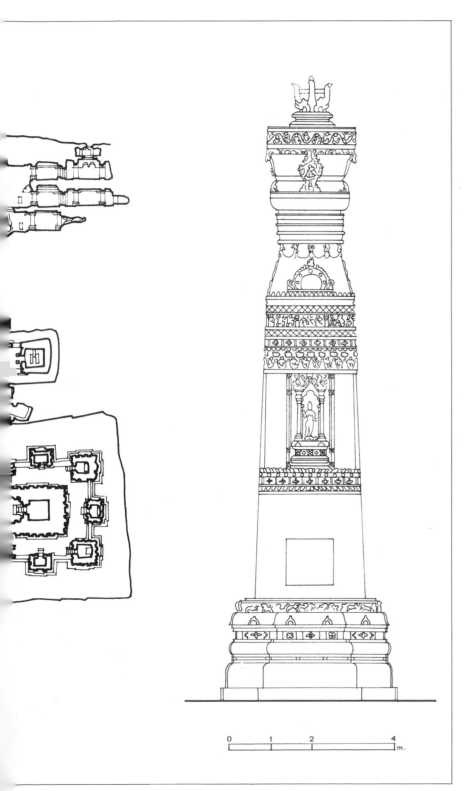

0 1 2   4
m.

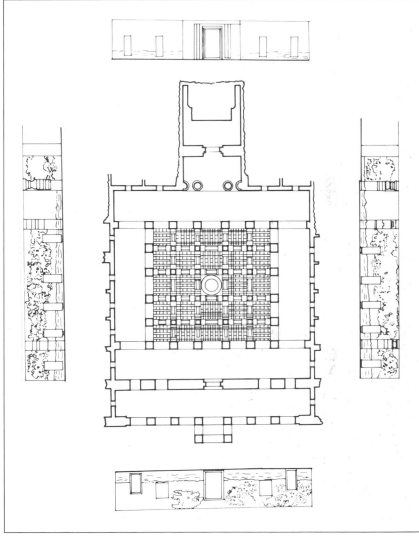

93. *Ajanta, Cave No. 2, plan.*
94. *Ajanta, Cave No. 6, plans of the lower and upper levels.*

95. *Ajanta, Cave No. 9, plan of the chaitya.*
96. *Ajanta, Cave No. 10, plan of the chaitya.*
97. *Ajanta, Cave No. 19, interior of the chaitya, stupa with a representation of Buddha in high relief.* ▷

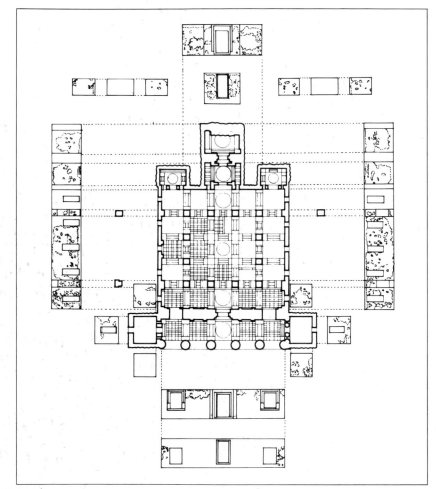

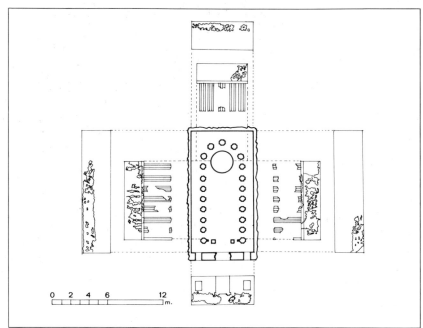

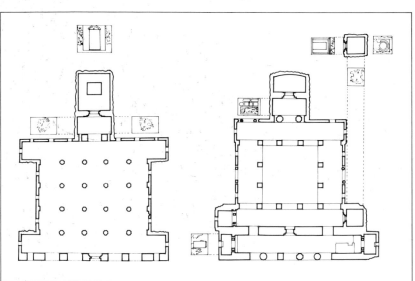

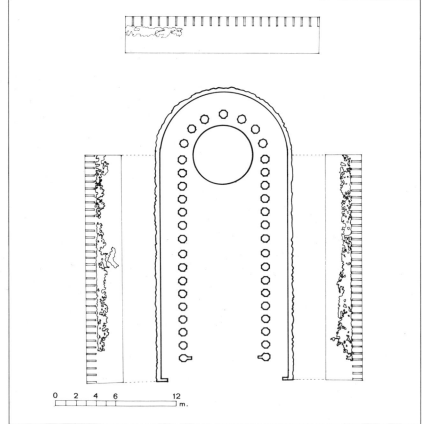

complex of Kapisa-Begram, one arrives back on properly Indian soil at Taxila. Here we recall Charsadda and Puskalavati, the Greek Peukelaotis and in some respects the sister city Taxila. In practice, virtually all urbanization in the Gandhara region is Greek in character, based on Hellenistic models that are modified only to the extent that local taste suggests different solutions, as for example in the skyline of the chapels that top off the stupa of Takht-i-Bahi. This is not to deny that Gandhara architecture, though employing round support towers, octagonal motifs even in domes, and other elements of foreign derivation, is essentially an autonomous architecture, primarily "constructed," in which Indian, Classical, Iranian, and perhaps Central Asian elements come together. The temple of Jandial at Taxila (Plate 40), for example, is a distyle *in antis* modified to suit the needs of a fire cult. But the Classical component—smothered in such gigantic works as Surkh Kotal (Plate 45), which nevertheless preserves Greek elements—sometimes comes to the surface again in the plan of sacred complexes (Mohra Moradu, Jaulian, and Loriyan Tangai). Here space is divided into an aligned order that places the principal monument at the center, leaves one wing available for cells and chapels, and reserves the other for the erection of the votive stupas. The vertical thrust, already mentioned, is not only an anti-Classical element, but a search for particular effects, deriving from a conception of space entirely foreign to India and nevertheless clearly Gandharan.

In the development of the stupa, the square or rectangular base on which the cylindrical body of the dome-topped drum is grafted becomes a verticalizing element by means of the steep staircases that ascend to the base of the central body of the stupa itself and that are placed at the four sides. Even when the plan of the base is more involved, becoming cruciform or star-shaped, the conception of the space remains an upward one, in a controlled succession of superimposed and diminishing horizontal planes. There remains the overall conception—multilateral (and indeed capable of being enjoyed from every point), static at the base, but animated in the conical trunk of the upper structure. In practice, it can be made objective through the superimposition of the different forms that strengthen the vertically oriented precision of the imaginary line from which the stupa's constituent forms derive.

As for such later stupas as those at Sarnath and Nalanda, one notes an increase in mass and a feeling of heaviness in the constructions. At Sarnath (Plate 59) the superimposed cylindrical masses, with collar fittings and greatly flattened terminal ogives, show a structural tension that seems to radiate over the surrounding space. At Nalanda (Plate 55) the staircases for access, projecting from the square base so as to form a cruciform plan with a central square, produce effects of geometric and

101. Osia, temple of Harihara 1.
102. Osia, temple of Harihara 2. ▷

103. *Osia, temple of Surya 2.*
104. *Osia, temple of Surya 2, detail of the* mandapa.

105. *Osia, view of the reservoir and underground palace.*
106. *Osia, veranda of the underground palace.*
107. *Osia, partial view of the reservoir.* ▷

108. *Osia, temple of Pipala Devi.*
109. *Gyaraspur, Char-Kambha (temple with four columns).*
110. *Gyaraspur, Ath-Kambha (temple with eight columns).* ▷

111. *Gyaraspur, Indola portal.*
112. *Gyaraspur, temple of Mahadevi.*

◁ 113. *Gyaraspur, temple of Mahadevi.*

114. *Schematic representation of a* nāgara *temple (from Volwahsen, 1969).*

115. *Evolution of the plan of a temple from the square form to a polygonal form based on the presumed chronological division of the circle. Example: plan of the holy cell of the temple of Brahmesvara at Bhuvanesvar (from Volwahsen, 1969).*

(in a certain sense) of abstract movement that in any case are very far removed from the Indian taste for curvilinear values and soft, rounded forms. As its use spread over Asia, the stupa achieved enormous dimensions, as at Borobudur in central Java during the ninth century (Plates 201–203); became a commemorative monument, as happened in Central Asia; or lost its character as an architecture without interior space by having a chapel with an image of Buddha installed in the cupola (or rather in the *anda*).

Cave Architecture

The ancient examples from the Maurya period were followed by a considerable range of works hollowed out of the rock, especially of the sanctuaries known as chaityas (though the Sanskrit word is connected with funeral rites of cremation and the ashes of the dead). The chaitya appears to be related to the stupa only by the fact that it contains one in its interior. The plan of the chaitya, of particular interest for its balance and harmony, displays in its final development a particular form, with a semicircular apse and false lateral naves that are too narrow for effective use. At the same time the chaitya becomes elongated (Plates 29–32). At Bhaja the ratio of width to length, unusually marked by the large central cupola surmounting the stupa, is 1:2.5 (Plates 27, 28); at Ajanta, taking into consideration all the chaityas on the site, it can be reckoned at 1:2.7; at Karli it is clearly 1:3. With the passage of time, chaityas thus become larger and more magnificent, approaching, even if remotely, the Western basilica; this means that there was an increasingly broad participation in religious ritual, with a profound change in the social composition of those attending. Moreover, the fact that not only monks but the laity as well participated in rites, exegesis, and the study of doctrine is shown by the large meeting halls for both groups that are already indicated at Bhaja (Plate 26).

Experts all agree in their estimation of the Karli complex (Plate 36) as one of the finest artistic achievements of cave architecture—a credible observation, but one that shows how easy it is to perceive the care and application that went into the construction of these works. Similar works, built in the open, influenced those extracted from caves, and this explains why at Karli we find the repetition of an interesting solution for the façade with three entrances (Plate 35), and especially a greater interest in the external space, something already to be seen at Ajanta (Cave No. 19—Plate 97—belonging to the Gupta period).

Sangharāmas (certain monasteries) cut into the rock deserve mention along with chaityas. Their cells had (and have) a quadrilateral plan, frequently square. They opened onto an inner court—square or rectangular—while a colonnaded veranda ran in front of the cells

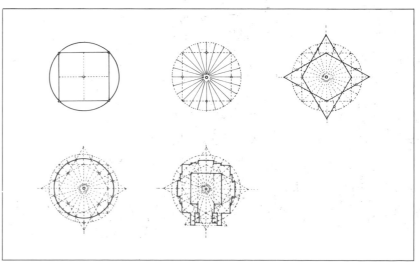

themselves (Plate 34), shielding them from the sun and allowing persons to pass from one to another under cover; this was also useful during the monsoon season. The *sangharāma* often had two stories, or indeed three. Derived from constructed examples, rock-cut monasteries (requiring a truly enormous expenditure of labor) were almost always more regular. We might mention those of Kondane (Plate 33), Pitalkhora, Nasik (Plates 37, 38), and Karli, as well as Ajanta (Plates 90–99) and the Jain monasteries of Orissa (Khandagiri; Udayagiri, Plate 39). In general, the ceiling of the meeting hall is not sustained by pillars, but in later periods (from the beginning of the full Gupta phase on—that is, from the fifth to the eighth century) the hall becomes hypostyle, while the full development of excavation techniques is shown, so far as *sangharāmas* are concerned, in the two large monasteries of Ellora (eleventh and twelfth centuries). This is an observation, however, that applies primarily to cut decoration, concentrated on pillars and friezes.

Beginning with the Gupta period, while stonecutting techniques improve, there is a growth in the importance and spread of constructed works, which is likewise related to the rebirth and consolidation of Hinduism. The temple of Kailasanath at Ellora (Plates 86–89), built by Emperor Krishna I of the Rashtrakuta dynasty, is also the fruit of this technical progress. Construction lasted from 756 to 773—that is, during the reign of Krishna I—and the complex, which was slightly larger than the Parthenon in plan and one and a half times as high, was completed down to the last detail in less time than it would have taken to build it in masonry. The construction—or rather, the cutting—proceeded from top to bottom, thus avoiding the need for scaffolding, and the work took shape on the basis of a very detailed plan that was carried out with exceptional care.

A different example, also with regard to the techniques employed (wet wooden quoins), is offered by the seventeen temples of Mamallapuram (Plates 73–80), of which the one known as the Seven Pagodas preserves archaic Dravidian features. They were cut out of hard granite and are slightly earlier than those works on the island of Elephanta in the harbor of Bombay, which partly echo the style of Ellora and contain the three-headed figure of Siva known as Mahesamurti. These are the last great rock-cut works. From this point on, open-air constructions predominate.

Temples

It is not easy to discern the genesis of the typical and so-called medieval temples of India. There may be an indication of it in a small circular chapel at Bairat near Jaipur that goes back to the third century B.C. It originally contained a stupa, but—except for the foundations—little remains today of this wooden and brick construction. As

118. *Bhuvanesvar, temple of Muktesvara.*
119. *Bhuvanesvar, temple of Rajarani.*

120. *Bhuvanesvar, temple of Brahmesvara, plan, elevation, and section (from Volwahsen, 1969).*

121. *Bhuvanesvar, temple of Brahmesvara, axonometric drawing (from Volwahsen, 1969).*

122. *Bhuvanesvar, temple of Lingaraja, schematic elevations of the two principal buildings (from Debala Mitra, 1961).*

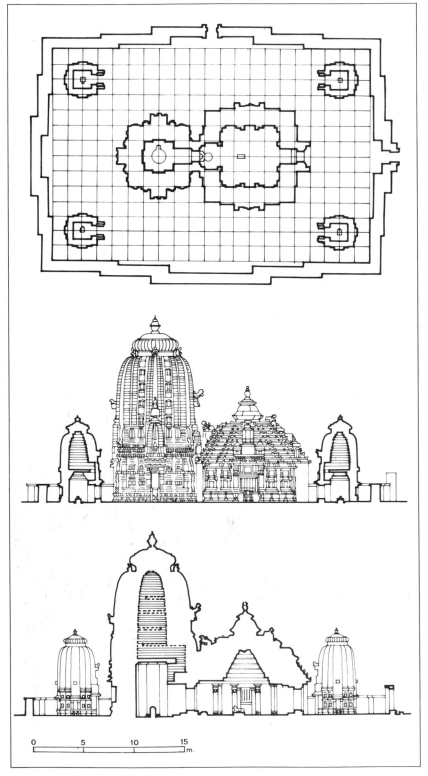

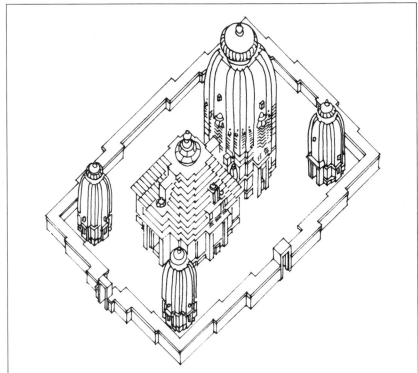

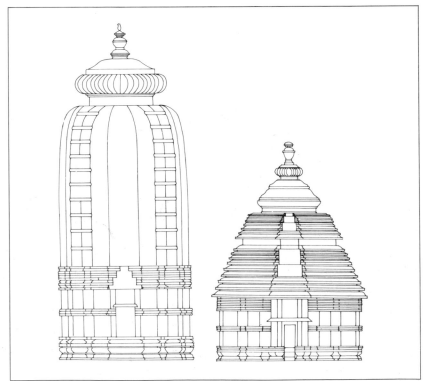

124. *Modhera, temple of Surya.*
125. *Modhera, temple of Surya; in the foreground, the brick terrace.*
126. *Modhera, temple of Surya; in the foreground, the brick terrace.*

127. *Khajuraho, temple of Kandariya Mahadeo, elevations and plan (from Volwahsen, 1969).*

128. *Khajuraho, temple of Laksmana and temple of Siva.*

129. *Khajuraho, temple of Kandariya Mahadeo.* ▷
130. *Khajuraho, temple of Kandariya Mahadeo, detail of the decoration.* ▷

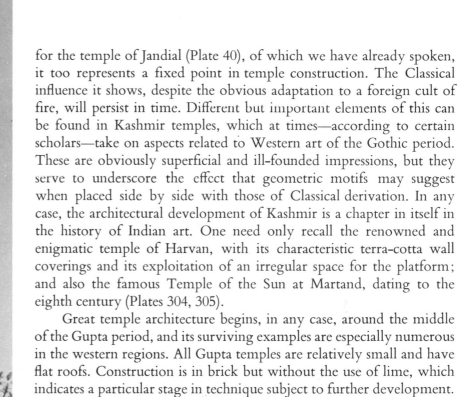

for the temple of Jandial (Plate 40), of which we have already spoken, it too represents a fixed point in temple construction. The Classical influence it shows, despite the obvious adaptation to a foreign cult of fire, will persist in time. Different but important elements of this can be found in Kashmir temples, which at times—according to certain scholars—take on aspects related to Western art of the Gothic period. These are obviously superficial and ill-founded impressions, but they serve to underscore the effect that geometric motifs may suggest when placed side by side with those of Classical derivation. In any case, the architectural development of Kashmir is a chapter in itself in the history of Indian art. One need only recall the renowned and enigmatic temple of Harvan, with its characteristic terra-cotta wall coverings and its exploitation of an irregular space for the platform; and also the famous Temple of the Sun at Martand, dating to the eighth century (Plates 304, 305).

Great temple architecture begins, in any case, around the middle of the Gupta period, and its surviving examples are especially numerous in the western regions. All Gupta temples are relatively small and have flat roofs. Construction is in brick but without the use of lime, which indicates a particular stage in technique subject to further development. It is significant that one of the best examples, the sixth-century temple at Deogarh near Jhansi (Plates 52, 53), employs iron pegs to hold the masonry together, an expedient that permitted the erection of a small tower over the sacred chapel. The heart of the temple—as is always true of any Indian temple—was formed by a small cell; closed except for the entrance, it was called the *garbha griha*, since it was here that the principal and holiest image was kept. By means of a vestibule called the *antarba*, the cell communicated with the *mandapa*, where the faithful carried out their devotions. Originally, the *mandapa* was a separate building. This room was in its turn preceded, as one entered from the outside, by an *ardhamandapa* portico. This succession and linking of different rooms, prescribed by the texts, is preserved throughout the centuries, along with the custom of leaving the main cell free of decoration; only the proportions and minor details vary. If we keep in mind, however, the extent of Indian territory, the variety of cultures it contains, and the very long period of architectural activity, we must concede that there is a certain uniformity in temple architecture.

One of the oldest temples for the phase we are considering is undoubtedly the one known as No. 17 at Sanchi (Plate 54). It has been definitely dated to the fifth century A.D. and is square in plan, with a columned portico that recalls a Greek temple, though this does not imply an actual derivation from or dependence on Greek models. Temple No. 18, which follows it in numerical sequence, has been largely destroyed; all that remain of it are tall columns surmounted by a lintel, giving a curious combined effect of classicism and modernity (Plate 71). It may have been topped by a low curvilinear tower, but

132. Gwalior, temple of Sas-Bahu.
133. Gwalior, temple of Sas-Bahu.
134. Gwalior, small temple of Sas-Bahu. ▷

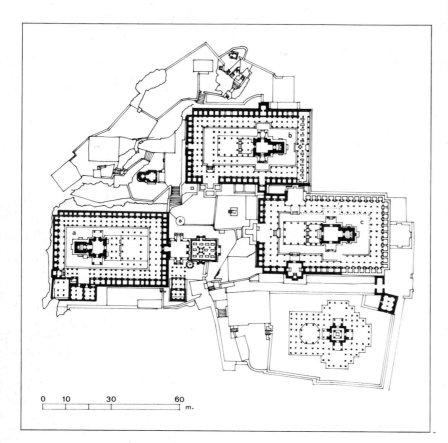

135. *Rajputana, Mount Abu, complex of Jain sanctuaries: a) plan of the temple of Vimala; b) plan of the temple of Tejapal; c) plan of the temple of Adinatha (from Volwahsen, 1969).*

136. *Rajputana, Mount Abu, temple of Dilwara, interior of the* mandapa. ▷

◁ 137. *Rajputana, Mount Abu, temple of Dilwara, interior of the dome.*

138. *Puri, temple of Jagannatha.*
139. *Gangaikondacholapuram, temple of Brihadisvara.*
140. *Belur, temple of Cennakesava.*

there is little basis for this hypothesis, which anyway does not resolve the problem of variations and types of temple structures presented by many incomplete temples. It is certain that the simplest solution, the flat roof, did not satisfy Indian taste, even though others offered serious technical difficulties. The preference, for symbolic reasons, was a projecting roof with jutting rows of stones placed on successive levels, on which smaller buildings seem to rise, their presence modulating the space into continuous denticulations. The surface tension is broken and the building acquires mass and body in an exceptional and pleasing way.

The development of the Indian temple from the sixth to the eighth century can be easily reconstructed—though not without uncertainties—from the important architectural complex constituted by the cities of Badami (Plates 61–64), Aihole (Plates 65–69), and Pattadakal (Plates 83–85), the political and religious capitals of the Chalukya rulers. In Aihole, the temple of Durga, the great goddess of war, is probably the earliest known example of the sikhara temple with a curvilinear roof, of which we will speak later, along with that of Laksmana at Sirpur. Unfortunately, the latter is completely in ruins and difficult to reconstruct in its original form. The other sikharas at Aihole are dated slightly later, and the problem of the development of Indian temples begins to be complicated by chronological uncertainties. We are unable to properly place works in other regions of India, with the exception of those in the Tamil area ruled by the Pallavas, political rivals of the Rashtrakutas and at the same time their emulators in the field of architectural construction.

There is, however, no need here to concern ourselves with political conflicts between little-known dynasties in medieval India, even though such conflicts were important and profound. Yet it is an interesting fact that Vikramaditya II, who won Kanchipuram from the Pallavas and made large donations to the Brahmins, the poor, and the temples of the city, carried away with him to Kanara a number of great Tamil artists and architects, to whom he gave special honors. Among these men we find mention of Chattara, Revadi, and Ovajja; we know too that Gunda, who was responsible for the construction of the temple of Virupaksha, was originally from the south. Such information shows a tendency to mitigate the anonymity of artists and testifies to the fame that some of them enjoyed. It may also help to explain the spread of technical and stylistic solutions from one region to another, over great distances, and the reception accorded to the style (or at least the taste) of the Pallavas, even outside their own territory and independent of political vicissitudes.

Indian architectural treatises distinguish two principal types of temples: the *nāgara* and the *dravida*. Both words have an ethnic refer-

141. Tanjore, temple of Brihadisvara, entrance portal.
142. Tanjore, temple of Brihadisvara, ground plan and section of the cell (from Volwahsen, 1969).

143. Halebid, temple of Hoysalesvara.
144. Halebid, temple of Hoysalesvara, detail of the exterior.

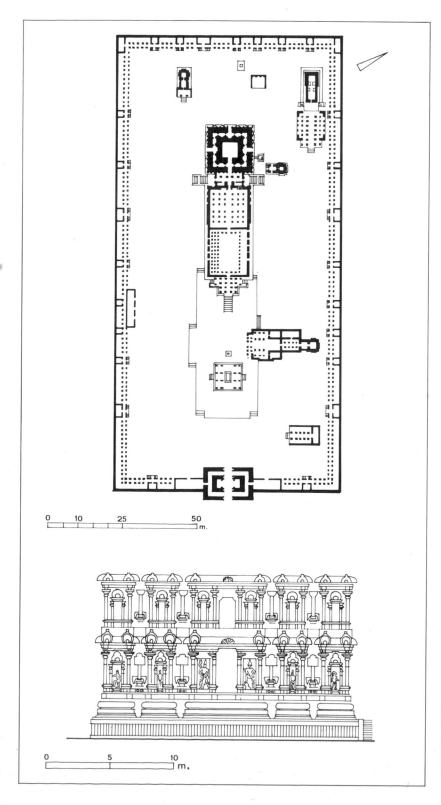

145. *Somnathpur, temple of Kesava.*

146. *Somnathpur, temple of Kesava, section and plan (from Volwahsen, 1969).*

147. *Somnathpur, temple of Kesava.* ▷

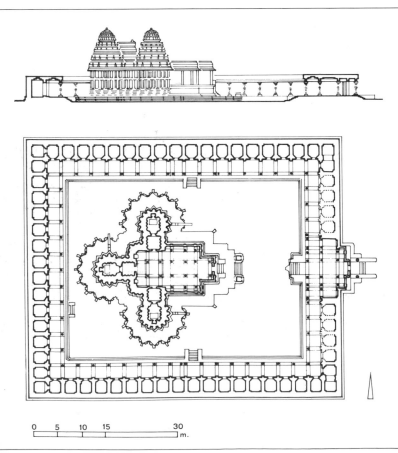

0 5 10 15   30
                      m.

ence, but in essence they mean the northern and southern style, respectively. Such a classification is not entirely justified: French scholars have shown that temples of the *nāgara* type (Plate 114) and sikharas (a word meaning peak, point, or flame) are found not only in Madras but originated in the Deccan region, where we find them at Aihole and Pattadakal. They are present too in Orissa, Kathiawar, and Rajputana—that is to say, in central areas or ones marginal to that implied by the term *nāgara*. Many writers have chosen to keep the stylistic definition found in the Indian texts, eliminating only the *vesara* category that refers to the extreme south. It is preferable, however, to replace these subdivisions with a morphological classification relating primarily to temple roofs, separated as follows: temples with curvilinear roofs (sikharas); temples with pyramidal (or prismatic) roofs; temples with cylindrical (or barrel-vaulted) roofs.

Unfortunately, the destruction wreaked by the Muslims drastically reduced the amount of architectural evidence available in the north. Though this irreparable loss makes it difficult indeed to trace northern developments in style, it is possible to examine these three types of temples.

a) Sikharas

It is possible that curvilinear towered roofs may be related to very ancient bamboo constructions—reed coverings that served to protect Vedic altars.[8] This hypothesis, though plausible, has no true scientific or critical basis. On the other hand, it is certain that the construction of the curvilinear roof—with its superimposed horizontal moldings and its vertical ones, whether rounded in the amalaka fashion or angular, effects which soften the harshness of the transition from the rectangular base to the roundness at the top—is connected with the use of baked bricks. In some cases, a crude brick structure was incised in order to make it more elaborate and definitive, confirming the Indian custom of cutting as a means of achieving architectural form. The roof, rising above the often cubical structure of the base, appears to result from the superimposition of horizontal molded cornices intersected by vertical bands of protuberances and sockets, rounded or with sharp edges. In plan, these moldings show a polylobate motif, approximately cruciform, that perhaps derives—with many modifications—from Persepolitan capitals.[9] The taste governing the sikhara is obviously for a very compact architectural mass, isolated and capable of producing a strong tension on the surrounding aerial space. It is more a plastic taste than an architectural one, and expresses its fancy in a minute elaboration of the enormous ogival dome that rises toward the sky.

The development of the sikhara can be logically summarized as follows. The progressive elevation and narrowing of the ogival dome (generically called the *chapra*) is combined with an interest in the form

151. *Konarak, temple of Surya, elevation and section of the* jagamohan; *plan of the* garbha griha *(a) and of the* jagamohan *(b) (from Vol- wahsen, 1969).*

152. *Konarak, temple of Surya, detail of figured wheels on the socle of the terrace.* ▷

0   10   20   40
m.

◁ *153. Kiradu, temple of Somesvara.*
154. Kiradu, temple of Siva 3.

155. *Kiradu, temple of Siva 2.*
156. *Kiradu, temple of Vishnu.* ▷

itself. This means that the elongation and reduction of the roof are the effect of an upward surge that can easily be related to an increased mystical component and a resulting. perfection in technique. This explanation may be obvious and partial, but it is certain that the multiplication of vertical grooves derives from a clear wish to accentuate the upward direction of the roof. On the other hand, the appreciation of the ogival form as a plastic motif is undeniable; this wish to emphasize the upward effect of the whole is intensified by the addition of smaller sikharas of varying height, joined to and surrounding the central tower and seeming to animate, on various levels, the thrust toward the sky. Once again, we find a demonstration of that characteristic Indian taste, which in the sphere of the figurative arts stops short of true abstraction only through a series of connections that prevent it from fully exploiting the theoretical presuppositions at its disposal. It is this same taste that determines an appreciation for the ogival form and multiplies it at different levels as it rises toward the sky.

It is curious but not inexplicable that the most beautiful temples of this type, with multiple ogives, number among others those at Khajuraho: the temples of Kandariya Mahadeo (Plates 127, 129–31), Visvanatha, and Laksmana (Plate 128), for example, are enriched by a monumental series of sculptures renowned for their innumerable erotic motifs. Their explicitness is not likely to be enjoyed by those who are unprepared for it or are not sufficiently uninhibited. In reality, the ascending movement of these temples, connected with the orgiastic rites practiced by the Chandella rulers, expresses a precise and basically acceptable moral lesson: life offers countless pleasures, among them the predominant ones of sex and love, but it is not infinite; it can be prolonged by magical practices and suitable orgiastic rites, but it is also appropriate, once a certain limit has been reached, to prepare oneself for the last, definitive journey, one that will truly be without return and carry the person to his dispersal in the Absolute. Even the Temple of the Sun at Konarak—which, had it been completed, would have reached a height of over 390 feet—was decorated with erotic scenes. The *mandapa* (originally a hypostyle portico that led into the actual temple lying behind it, and later to become a building in itself, though always subordinate to the temple) attained a height of 230 feet at Konarak (Plates 150, 151). It is conceived as an enormous solar chariot, whose wheels, finely executed and carved, display the figures of amorous couples (*mithunas*) in their hubs (Plate 152). This grandiose solution is in imitation of the *raths* (small temples in the form of processional chariots) erected in various periods and in various forms. Often monolithic, they may also have represented royal chariots, as at Mamallapuram, where the huge boulders with which the site was strewn furnished material that could be artistically transformed into isolated figures and

158. *Vijayanagar (Hampi), temple of Vitthalasvami, view of a mandapa.*
159. *Vijayanagar (Hampi), terrace of the Mahanavami Dibba, council hall.*
160. *Vijayanagar (Hampi), Mahanavami Dibba, detail of sculptured friezes on the terrace of the building.*
161. *Vijayanagar (Hampi), temple of Vitthalasvami.* ▷

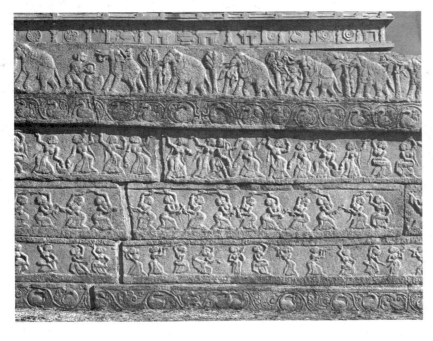

162. *Vijayanagar (Hampi), "underground" temple.*
163. *Vijayanagar (Hampi), Lotus Mahal.*
164. *Chidambaram, temple of Siva Natesvara.*

small temples, the principal one being the Dharmaraja *rath*—the royal chariot (Plates 73, 76).

The lesser towers that form a crown for the main one are called *anga-sikharas*, and can be arranged like isolated structures—almost as foreparts—in relation to the projections of the various faces of the main tower, as we find in the Jain temples of Satrunjaya, dating from the sixteenth century; or else as multiplications of the tower motif and joined to the principal one (a motif known as multiple towers). With this description, we have virtually exhausted this analysis of the sikhara construction, and it only remains to note that the multiple-tower system emerged in the ninth century and immediately proved itself more flexible than the other. Better suited to a wide range of effects, it finally assumes greater aesthetic validity, since it produces a blossoming of curved lines that almost flow from the central amalaka. The motif itself is especially widespread in western regions of India, and according to some scholars can be traced in plan to a complex system of circles inscribed in squares and intersecting among themselves—thus to a geometric basis.

b) Vimānas

Temples with high pyramidal or prismatic roofs are generally called *vimānas*. According to French scholars, there are precedents for the southern *vimāna* in the pictorial images of Ajanta's Cave No. 1, which dates back to the sixth century A.D. (Plate 92), and in the sculptured ones in the *Descent of the Ganges* at Mamallapuram (Plate 74). The first surviving example, however, would be the Dharmaraja *rath*, also at Mamallapuram, which we have already mentioned. The type becomes established about the middle of the eighth century, both with the Kailasanath at Ellora (Plates 86–89) and—for constructed architecture—with that at Kanchipuram (Plate 72). Though it can vary considerably, it is essentially formed by a central structure, square in plan, over which rises the pyramidal roof of steps forming the planes on which what we might call "miniaturized" reproductions of buildings are placed in a rigorously regular fashion. These reproductions slowly diminish in size as they proceed toward the crown (square or polygonal) of the truncated pyramid. On these same buildings in miniature, which assume the form of ordinary pavilions, the *kūdu* (false horseshoe-shaped window) is often represented. This motif, obviously arranged in parallel horizontal rows with regard to the placing of the pavilions, becomes a characteristic decorative element that succeeds in animating the surface. It should be immediately pointed out that an analysis of the lesser ornamental motifs, featuring animals and plants, confirms the significance of these constructions as cosmic mountains sustaining human habitations.

A comparison between the Dharmaraja *rath* at Mamallapuram (36 feet in height) and the *vimāna* at Tanjore, one of the finest examples

167. *Srirangam, temple of Vishnu, detail of the* garuda-mandapa.
168. *Madura, temple of Siva and Minaksi, plan of the whole and section of the southern* gopura *(from Volwahsen, 1969).*
169. *Madura, temple of Siva and Minaksi.* ▷
170. *Madura, temple of Siva and Minaksi.* ▷

and much larger in size, shows the enormous development of this type of temple. At Tanjore, there are thirteen levels instead of three and the pyramidal shape is clearer. The use of the *kūdu* as an ornamental element is infinitely more pronounced, even though far removed, for aesthetic reasons, from the prescriptions imposed by the texts. The Tanjore *vimāna*, known as the Rajrajesvara temple, is a very daring construction: it reached a height of 180 feet and was topped by a single immense stone whose weight has been calculated at 80 tons. The *vimāna* type tends, however, to become heavy and clumsy as a result of the efforts of artists and patrons to increase the proportions of the building excessively. This leads therefore to a progressive aridity in this type, though we must remember that its use was spread over almost the whole of Indian territory. Particularly curious are the mixed types, combining elements of the sikhara with others of the *vimāna*. Primarily to be found in the Mysore region, they are always crowned by an amalaka.

c) Gopuras

Temples with pyramidal roofs, or *gopuras*, form part of the temple enclosure. Originally, they were very simple in form and connected with the gates of ancient cities, but during the medieval phase they became monumental constructions that attained extraordinary height and, in their amassing of materials, took on an isolated grandeur. Their form is distinctly prismatic, with superimposed planes, and slightly tapering toward the top. They constitute a characteristic element in the landscape of southern India and are among the most original constructions of those areas.

In addition, the inventive capacity of southern architects is confirmed by the star-shaped plans of the temples at Halebid (Plates 143, 144) and Belur, commissioned by the Hoysala rulers, in which the sculptural decoration, confined to particular areas, exhibits highly studied effects of light and shadow, calculated for the intense luminosity of the south and even for the leaden light of the monsoon season.

As for the development of the *gopura*, there is not much to say except to point out that it established itself primarily during the thirteenth and fourteenth centuries, and that its extended height sometimes produced an excessively attenuated effect, approaching the simplest form of the tower surmounted by a canopy.

Summary of Indian Architecture

Thanks to the Jains, Indian architecture later discovered the whiteness of marble and the open-work effects that could be achieved with it, but went on to exhaust itself in the more or less successful repetition of created types. The violent crisis produced by the clash with Islam, the historical vicissitudes of this immense world unable to

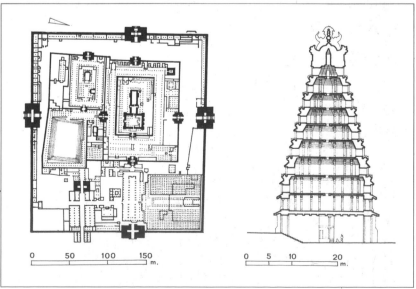

◁ 171. *Madura, temple of Siva and Minaksi, detail of one of the* gopuras.

172. *Anhilvara-Patan, Han Sarovar, installation for an artificial lake or water reservoir.*

173. *Anhilvara-Patan, Han Sarovar, installation for an artificial lake or water reservoir.*

independently express a true capacity for unification (despite the experience of the Mogul Empire), and the increasing contact with Western colonial powers, spread a kind of benumbed torpor over the whole subcontinent. New and daring philosophical and mystical experiments were not enough to rouse a population ill-prepared to recognize the origins and reasons for an oppressive authority (whether local or foreign), and which it did not even think of opposing. Architecture passed into the hands of the Muslim faithful, and the local religious impetus was lost in a thousand streams of individual and group action without succeeding in renewing itself.

Thus, we may consider the great architecture of Hindu India as exhausted by the end of the sixteenth century. Here and there we may still find ingenious insights, advanced solutions, and characteristic geometric patterns. But such examples have no echo beyond themselves. They remain isolated, and are often rediscovered accidentally, or almost so, by scholars or experts in search of secondary monuments or of details that are usually overlooked, or by those who set out to express a different point of view. In the midst of the repetitive monotony, there thus emerged suggestions and incomplete or scarcely realized attempts that nevertheless were not enough to generate a revival: Indian architecture had exhausted itself. In the long period of its prosperity, however, it had accumulated an enormous sum of experience, which—and here we touch on a paradox—is poorly known; the architecture and in general all the artistic activity of India is considered to be "other" than the taste and aesthetic aspirations of the modern world. Its enormous religious content constitutes a sufficient handicap for the majority of contemporary critics and art lovers, while by contrast it is precisely in its complicated symbolism and underlying mysticism that many of those persons well disposed toward it seek the *raison d'être* of Indian architecture. Nevertheless, even granting the relative technical poverty of an art that succeeds in arousing respect despite all preconceptions, we will try to summarize its aesthetic side, expressed in intense and prolonged creative activity, by considering some of its key points.

The architect, the patron, and the public itself for whom the work of art was created virtually constituted an inseparable unity forming part of a solid chain of tradition that went back ultimately to divine inspiration. It was no accident that one of those who had worked on the Kailasanath temple at Ellora, contemplating the miracle of the work just completed, asked himself in wonder: "How was I able to do so much?"[10]

Actually, for the Indian creative intellect, there did not exist any opposition between subject and object. The work, the artist, and those who enjoyed the created forms constituted a unity that, by means of

176. *Vishnupur, temple of Madan Mohan.*
177. *Vishnupur, temple of Jorbangla.*

the visible part, succeeded also in merging with those invisible vibrations (*adrsta*) that had accompanied the creative process. The love for architectural form in itself—always logical and geometric—dominated all the sculptural creations that adorned it and which, deprived of this support, would have lost their full value. On the other hand, the proportions of the architectural structure, rigidly fixed in precise, systematic relationships, constituted the "breath" (*prāna*) of the work itself, which lives—indeed is truly a work of art—only if the rhythm and throb of its lines succeed in being united with the vital movement of its creators. The theoretical units of Indian architecture can practically be traced back to the altar (even the stupa is an altar, in the metaphorical sense), the pillar (and many temples have the meaning and magical function of the pillar), the mountain, cavern (or cave), and finally the door. All are symbolic elements, but in each of them the artist must achieve a point of attraction and concentration in relation to the movement of the pilgrim or officiant obliged to follow a prescribed route. The ideal axis of the stupa, for example, would be the invisible pivot for circumambulation. For this reason, on the strip of the drum supporting the dome, the Greco-Buddhist images of the north take on a perspective that we call rotating, since they tend to remain valid from all vantage points granted to persons performing *pradakshinā* (ritual circumambulation). The relation between vision in motion and architectural and plastic structure is thus a strong one. We find it again even in Hindu temples, where the images are placed in such a way as to offer themselves time and again to the eye of the worshiper.

"In this concentric, concentrating perambulation the devotee sees the piers and recesses of the walls together with their sculptures. He feels their impact, as the buttresses project and display the images. These buttresses are called *ratha*, meaning chariot. It is as though they were being driven out from the center of the monument, each buttress in its respective direction, pulling its own bulk and the images stationed thereon."[11] The structural masses project and carry with them the images found on them. The Hindu temple was created in relation both to a movement toward the center (that of men), and to a monumental space that seems to obey a centrifugal movement with the capacity to explode from the center and dispose the parts of the temple and secondary buildings in such a way as to offer an isolated yet simultaneously total vision. Thus it moves and "breathes" according to the movement of the individual pilgrim and his way of looking, breathing, and thinking. It is, as a well-known French scholar has remarked, a "cinema of stone." And, the fact that the texts sometimes place the construction of ritual chariots side by side with the more complex construction of temples (and vice versa) shows that the aesthetic basis of Hindu sacred architecture is movement. Thus, each Indian architectural creation,

based on geometry and light, on the movement of masses and the real but slow movement of men (Plates 164–167, 169–171), expresses in reality a form that emanates from within, that composes and disposes, to create a *vyaktavyakta* (a form that must exist); in the sphere of culture that created it, this form is the most logical and obvious synthesis of the many highly varied requirements that prompted its birth.

In medieval Hindu architecture, the Indian creative genius reached the summit of its own power and logical rigor. It is now up to us to find a universal aesthetic measure that will allow us to evaluate it more effectively.

Ceylon

The island of Sri Lanka, formerly known as Ceylon (Sēlān in the local language,. but Lankā or Tāmraparnī, in classical Indian designations), lies at the extreme southern end of the Indian subcontinent. As such, it should be classified as part of the Indian world from which it derives, above all for its religious thought. However, in the field of the figurative arts in general and in architecture in particular, the island has had considerable importance and an extraordinary autonomy. It is for these reasons that Ceylon can be considered and studied as an artistic area in itself, even though clearly complementary to India. To begin with, Ceylon still remains a Buddhist stronghold, thus ensuring a linear and prolonged development of the architecture inspired by this religion. Of the island's inhabitants, only the Tamils, who were recently estimated to represent 30 per cent of the local population, were adherents of Hinduism, taking their inspiration—albeit in an independent manner—from forms prevailing in southern India. The peripheral and relatively protected geographic position of Ceylon shielded the island from events that convulsed the neighboring subcontinent, while accentuating to some extent the conservatism characteristic of islands. But these factors are only partly responsible for the independence and originality of Singhalese art. A particular sensitivity to spatial values, and the presence of an unmistakable taste made up of different components (Plate 180), are more notable reasons for Singhalese artistic autonomy and for the influence that Ceylon's architectural forms exerted on centers in Magna India.

The origins of Singhalese architecture, according to tradition, must be traced to the introduction of Buddhism on the island, which local chronicles tell us occurred with the visit of Asoka's son, Mahinda, about the middle of the third century B.C. The ecclesiastical basis of Buddhism (the *samgha*)—that is, the associative essence of a religion that did not originally have transcendental or protective elements suitable for transforming the doctrine into a system and rule of life to mollify the individual in the face of the anguish of existence—required,

among other things, monastic constructions and focal points for the cult. This obviously was translated into an urge to build, to meet the indispensable construction needs connected not only with the very nature of religious life, but also with organizational needs and with the fact that Buddhism alone formulated its possibilities for success on the cohabitation of monks and on continual proselytizing. The activity of Devanam-Piyatissa—the Singhalese ruler contemporary with Asoka and a convert of the missionaries sent by the Maurya emperor—was precisely directed to the building of stupas and monasteries. The Thuparama *dagaba* (stupa) at Anuradhapura would seem to go back, in its original form, to this period. Tradition adds, however, that the Mahiyangana *dagaba* in the province of Uva, and the Girikandi (now Tiriyay) *dagaba* on the northeast coast of the island, also belong to the same time.

In reality, the source of inspiration for the oldest monuments in Ceylon should be sought in the evidence offered by the primitive schools of central India (Bharhut, Sanchi, even Buddh Gaya). Of all such monuments, the most characteristic is the stupa. But Ceylon combines the work commemorating the Buddha (the architectural projection of the whole universe as seen "from outside"; that is, from a dimension, we might say, alien to human sensory experience) with a type of structure that hinges on the cult of the tree of Buddha's Enlightenment—a different approach with a symbolic significance similar to that of the stupa. The building in question is called the *bodhighara*, and though rare, constitutes an interesting alternative possibility for symbolic construction on a Buddhist basis. The *bodhighara*, not unknown in India, must have had a greater importance in Ceylon than in the continental area.

As for the stupa, the persistence of that old Indian form—with its hemispherical dome known as the *anda*—is not due to backwardness. It is, as we have said, the fruit of a spatial sensibility that prefers the tension of the geometrically perfect curved line to the more symbolically charged modifications that evolved successively on the Indian mainland. In addition to its skyline, the plastic volume of the hemisphere attracted and satisfied the taste of Singhalese architects; hence the influence that the stupa of Ceylon (Plate 186) exercised on the bell-shaped, hemispherically topped forms of Magna India from Java to Thailand. Naturally, there are exceptions (for example, a twelfth-century stupa in the form of a graduated pyramid of seven levels; Plate 191), but by and large this influence holds true. On the other hand, that the choice of the hemispherical form was determined by visual taste is proved both by the solutions adopted for the votive rings (the celebrated umbrellas)—which only become heavy when translated into brick, being transformed into a kind of molded conical spiral—and by

the projections or foreparts (*vāhalkadas*) of the enormous stupas of Anuradhapura (Plate 182). Flanked by stelae that are surmounted by animal forms facing outward, they determine the approach to the building for arriving worshipers. These projections are placed at the four cardinal points, in accordance with the pattern of orientation customary for this type of monument. The oldest of these monuments, so far as we know from reliable historical evidence, is the Abhayagiri, north of Anuradhapura. Originally, it was not of great size. It was, however, enlarged by King Gajabahu I in the second century A.D., attaining a diameter of 354 feet and a height that must have approached 347 feet (now, with its cusp broken, it is only 243 feet high). Its *vāhalkadas* are also from the second century A.D., which shows that this distinctive characteristic of the Singhalese stupa was already fully formed in ancient times—a notable divergence from continental patterns.

Lesser stupas were contained within circular sanctuaries called *cetiyāgāras* (Plate 187), covered by a wooden cupola that rested on a perimeter of columns planted a short distance from the edge of the stupa. Two or three wider concentric rings of columns placed around the one upholding the cupola served to support a roof that also rested on a continuous wall placed between the two outer colonnades. An interest in spherical volume and curved lines (or rather in circles and semicircles) is obvious. In more developed examples, the outer wall may be decorated with ornamental motifs that chiefly take advantage of the continuous surface; or it can—as at Madirigiri in the eighth century—be in line with the outer colonnade and assume the form of a stone balustrade (derived from the classical ones at Sanchi). For this type of construction as well, which in Ceylon continues until the fifteenth century, the local development differs from that on the continent.

The cult of the tree of Buddha's Enlightenment led to a strange symbiosis between a living, natural element, conditioned by the needs of its own existence—the tree—and the need for isolation, for making the sacred concrete, for the spatial definition required by the cult. The *Mahāvamsa*, one of the most famous Singhalese Buddhist texts, tells us that the Bodhi Tree (of Enlightenment) in the Mahavihara at Anuradhapura was planted on a raised terrace, surrounded by a *vedikā* (balustrade) with a single *torana* (open gate) on the north side; four pillars, each supporting a wheel, the chief symbol of Buddha's Law (*dhārmacakra*), were placed at the *torana* and the three secondary open entrances at the other cardinal points. From this type—which imitates the celebrated one at Buddh Gaya—derives a hypostyle pavilion with two entrances (north and south), and having a low ornamental roof and rectangular plan, at whose center rose the platform designed to hold the sacred tree, obviously placed under the open sky.

183. Nalanda, Gedige, Tantric Buddhist chapel.
184. Polonnaruwa, Thuparama.
185. Polonnaruwa, sanctuary of Siva in the Chola style.

We cannot verify the truth of assertions in the *Mahāvamsa* concerning the many radical changes that took place with the passage of centuries. We can, however, note the perfect preservation—for this type of construction—of the recently discovered Nillakgama *bodhighara* (in Kurunagala), dating to the eighth or ninth century. The use of "moon stones"—that is, of symbolic semicircles of stones placed before the entrances—is not limited to *bodhigharas*, but constantly recurs as a truly Singhalese characteristic before the outer approaches (passages with symbolic significance) of sacred buildings. We do not know how many *bodhigharas* there were in Ceylon, nor if the alternative that this building offered to the stupa was only a potential one that was seldom exploited. A comparison of the description in the *Mahāvamsa* with the surviving example implies that a slow transformation has clearly detached the original type of the *bodhighara*—very close to the stupa, even though the tree is substituted for the reliquary construction that forms the true stupa (Plate 190)—from that of the stupa itself. The result is that the *bodhighara* takes on an appearance in which the vital needs of the tree—axis of the world, symbol of the Law, and reminiscence of Buddha—prevail over the symbolic values.

The architectural development of the island tends, for several reasons, gradually to abandon the use of wood, whether for royal residences, for monastic buildings, or finally for the superstructures of various buildings whose foundations and access ramps were of stone. Brick constructions, the oldest of which goes back to the eighth century, acquire the name of *gedigēs* (a term, according to the *Rūpas-siddhi-sanne*, equivalent to the Pali form *giñjakāvasatha*, reserved, as Buddhaghosa states, for constructions entirely of brick), a name soon extended to stone constructions with vaulted roofs. The chapels or house-temples for images of Buddha (Plate 186)—called *gandals* from the name of the chamber reserved for Buddha in the garden of Jetavana, or more often referred to as *pilimagēs*—reveal by their growing numbers over the years an ever greater interest on the part of the faithful in the cult of icons (if we may call it so). It is likely that the architects of Ceylon, in planning the first *gandals*, intended to reproduce the pavilion-room of Jetavana. If this is true, it indicates a deliberate local desire to appropriate, so to speak, the holy places of Buddhist tradition. Such an action is typical of outlying areas animated by intense faith. In any case, the *gandal* was originally a square or rectangular building, with a single room preceded by a forepart. Naturally, the type became more complicated with the passage of time, also because of the upsurge in popularity of the cult of images. A *mandapa* was added in the form of an antistructure that acted as a portico but was also a temple in itself (Plate 188). In practice, the *gandal*, having become the classical Buddhist *patimagārā* and a true sanctuary, ended by resuming, at least in its essential lines, the characteristic structure of Hindu temples in India, consisting of three parts: the inner sanctum or true chapel (*garbha griha*);

187. Polonnaruwa, circular sanctuary of Vatadage.
188. Polonnaruwa, Nissanka Lata, detail of mandapa pillars.
189. Polonnaruwa, Royal Palace, the Sannipatasala (public audience hall).

187. Polonnaruwa, circular sanctuary of Vatadage.

188. Polonnaruwa, Nissanka Lata, detail of mandapa pillars.

189. Polonnaruwa, Royal Palace, the Sannipatasala (public audience hall).

the structure that precedes it; and the *mandapa*, a temple structure serving also as a portico.

Naturally, the appearance and size of these structures vary considerably, and—as at Anuradhapura—there is no lack of arrangements of the "quincuncial" kind, in which the major edifice is placed at the center. We thus return to patterns of arrangement that belong to the Indian world. It should be noted that in the late period a particular characteristic of these Singhalese constructions is that they are built entirely of brick (Plate 183). Only the molded stylobates—sometimes also in brick—are, with a certain frequency, of stone, as are the door jambs, which are likewise molded.

In addition, the architecture of Ceylon includes individual and collective dwellings. Vast monastic complexes surround Anuradhapura, to the west of which we find monastic cells (now erroneously called palaces) that were most likely used for meditation. Apart from the remains of the Brazen palace (Plate 181), the amusement garden, and the dam for the artificial Tisavava Lake (built in the third century A.D.), the city included numerous stone baths and its famous sacred buildings. The urban layout, perhaps an involuntary one, thus established a central area for habitation and for political and commercial activity that was virtually encircled by monastic establishments. It has been pointed out, however, that there is a clear difference between official and individual dwellings and community ones. According to the tradition, some of the first monastic dwellings were as severely austere as simple caves, while others were magnificently rich. Such was the case of the residence donated to Mahinda by General Dighasanda, a building that according to the *Mahāvamsa* towered against the sky and was "enclosed by beautiful walls and adorned with superb staircases."

Very probably the so-called Elephant Stables are the remains of a splendid building of this kind, built at Anuradhapura by Kanit-Thatissa (A.D. 167–186), and later rebuilt by Mahinda II (A.D. 777–797) at a cost of 300,000 pieces of gold. The edifice, which included pillars and stylobates of exceptional size, was doubtless capable of vying with the most sumptuous royal dwellings. The habit of donating sumptuous houses continued for a long time, without excluding the presence of hermitages and cave dwellings (later to be adorned by the piety of the faithful) for anyone who sought sanctity in the form of a total rejection of society and the world. Notable examples are the Kaludiyapokuna cave near Mihintale, the Arankale cave, and the group of large caves at Dambulla, all later provided with brick walls or transformed into shrines. As for monasteries, it should be mentioned that the principal part of each complex was the *uposathāgāra*, the large meeting hall where the monks gathered on auspicious days for the ceremony of public

confession and to discuss the proceedings of their order. Important ceremonies and festivals were celebrated in the *uposathāgāra*, whose best surviving example is at Polonnaruwa and is also described in the *Māhavamsa*; its façade was characterized by lanceolate windows. Here the central hall is surrounded by corridors and service rooms (chapels and spaces designed to hold sacred objects and implements). It is polystyle, and at its center has a two-level raised structure for the oldest monk, responsible for the discipline and spiritual order of the entire monastery. A curious fact to be noted is that the monasteries of Ceylon were equipped from the beginning with hygienic facilities greatly superior to those in India; the sewers and water pipes for the large baths constantly appear next to monasteries. The baths, called *pokunas* in Singhalese (from the Sanskrit *puskarani*), are rectangular in plan (though occasionally circular), and were sometimes dug out of the rock. Granite was later used to cover the floors and walls. The best example is the pair of baths (a double swimming pool) situated in the Abhayagiri area, at Vosihara near Anuradhapura, and popularly called Kuttam Pokuna (which means double or twin bath). The two tanks, contained in a single enclosure with six stairways for access, are equal in width, but differ in length and depth (length, 143 feet and 98 $\frac{1}{2}$ feet respectively; depth at center, 19 $\frac{1}{2}$ feet for the larger, 15 feet for the smaller). Both are bordered by a stone parapet projecting over the encased strip of flooring that acts as a frame and edge (or beach) for the two pools. Highly planned in all its details and with hydraulic installations that show great ingenuity, the Kuttam Pokuna is one of the most important architectural works on the island. The Archaeological Department has made significant restorations of the complex, returning it to its original elegant simplicity.

The presence of large hospitals, side by side with the major monasteries, completes the picture of Singhalese architecture. Their existence reflects the diligent civil and social life of the population, which is strongly united by a desire for autonomy and by an effective solidarity that seems to replace the essentially compassionate Buddhist *karunā* by a feeling much closer to active Christian *caritas*.

It is highly probable that Ceylon's geographic position, its formulation of doctrine, and its technical interest in architectural works, were accompanied—in determining the island's wide influence on architectural trends in Southeast Asia—by this activism of its people. It is something easily appreciated by coreligionists who, being more concerned with the contingencies of human life than are the orthodox extremists, likewise wished to react against the inert renunciation suggested by the law of karma.

Mario Bussagli

Introduction

The great span of Southeast Asia and the countries it contains are often referred to as Magna India or Farther India, appellations that serve to underscore the significant influence of India upon the cultures of this vast zone. Contacts with the Indian world directly affected Indonesia and all of Indochina except for the territory of Tonkin and the northern parts of Laos and Vietnam. The gradual result was the transition of the affected regions from levels of culture that were scarcely developed to the plane of complete civilization. As Mario Bussagli has stated elsewhere, "The progressive expansion of Indian civilization, its absorption on the part of populations very different among themselves, and the successive transformation of this foreign influence in the process of its adaptation to various local needs often produced unexpected phenomena, particularly in the field of the figurative arts."[1]

The sporadic penetration of this Indian expansion was peaceful in character, but from the cultural standpoint its impact led to the highly important phenomena Bussagli describes. Archaeological evidence indicates that as early as the first century A.D. the Indians were pushing forward by sea into the areas under discussion, following the coasts and venturing as far as the Sonda Islands. Some scholars believe that this movement was precipitated by pressures exerted by an expanding population or by the missionary vocation of Buddhism; more simply, they can be attributed to the requirements of commerce. The Roman world, especially in the imperial era, exerted a continual demand on the Indian East for pearls, perfumes, silk, precious stones, myrrh, and incense. Consequently, an active trade was established between the Romanized Middle East and India; the Indians searched for gold and spices along the coasts of Southeast Asia, which their special knowledge of monsoons permitted them to reach easily, and here they founded commercial settlements that in time grew into trade centers. A colonization of an economic kind emerged that was supported neither by political aims nor military force; it did not therefore take on the nature of a conquest nor seek to establish hegemony or economic monopoly. Mixed marriages between Indian men and local women likewise contributed to closer and more stable ties between the two populations.

With the introduction of the alphabet and the Sanskrit language, Indian thought became widespread. At the same time there was a propagation of two other elements of Indian life—the organizational model of the state, hinging on the monarchy, and Indian religious beliefs. In the field of art, the ensuing dependence on India is so obvious as to seem a common denominator, albeit within the autonomy and individuality of local styles.

As we have said, the only regions of Indochina to remain outside the Indian sphere were the territory of Tonkin and the northern parts of Laos and Vietnam. These areas experienced, in particular ways, the political and cultural domination of China. Unlike the Indian influence, the Chinese expansion was a true military conquest, obviously hated by the populations who suffered under its yoke. Despite a number of revolts, which generally took place at times of crisis for the imperial government, Tonkin remained a Chinese province until A.D. 938. In Vietnam the Chinese influence was so complete that its imprint remained a predominant factor until the beginning of the twentieth century.

We can summarize the permanent characteristics of the historical equilibrium in the area we are now considering in the following manner: (1) The Indianized states were independent of the political structures existing in India itself; (2) Indian colonization, with its vast cultural effects, was peaceful; it was not supported by precise political aims and was therefore far more acceptable than that of the Chinese, which was essentially political; (3) every crisis of Chinese power was accompanied by a re-emergence of autonomy in the states of Magna India; (4) in the protohistorical phase Magna India was connected with China (or rather with the continent), but with the establishment of Indian influence their relationship changed: this is the point at which the historical phase fully begins and the culture of India is set against the influence of China.[2]

The first information we have on the influence of Indian civilization in Magna India attests to the presence of Indianized states in a period going back at the latest to the second and third centuries A.D. In the case of Indochina we can speak in terms of the third century B.C., the period during which, according to tradition, Emperor Asoka sent two Buddhist monks, Sona and Uttara, to the "Land of Gold" (Suvarnabhūmi), usually identified as the ancient region of Mon in Burma. Sources mention two Indianized states: Lin-yi, the early state nucleus of ancient Champa, emerged in A.D. 192, in connection with the crisis of the Chinese empire that led to the fall of the Han dynasty; Funan, which included part of present-day Cambodia, on the lower course of the Mekong River, is said to have originated from the exploits of the Brahmin Kaundinya and from his marriage to a local princess. We are not presented with documented artistic manifestations until the sixth to eighth century A.D.; by this time, there is already a notable difference between constructions in Indochina and those in the Indonesian archipelago. The process of adaptation and modification must surely have been carried out in wood or other perishable materials, of which unfortunately no traces remain. However, the oldest architectural structures still in existence reveal close ties with their common source of inspiration, being all related to Indian religiosity and to the cult of

193. a) Central Java, plain of Kedu, Candi Pawon; b) East Java, Panataram, so-called Dated Temple; c) Java, Duwur, access gate (candi bentar) (from Hallade, 1954).
194. Java, Dieng plateau, general view of the candis.
195. Java, Dieng plateau, Candi Puntedewa and Candi Sembadra.

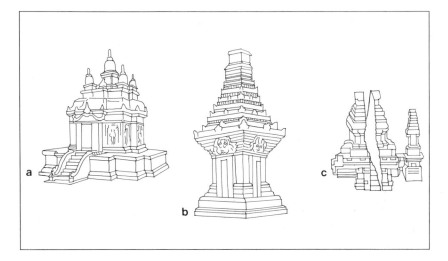

kings who had been assimilated to divinities in the Buddhist or Hindu pantheons (in particular, the cult of Siva). This last aspect is proof that in the world of Magna India as well, architectural production was born of state initiative and connected with religious and royal values, the inspiration for which must be traced back to the Indian world, even though modified by local needs and tastes.

In general, it is not possible to trace the artistic development from any point in time earlier than the sixth century A.D. There are, however, regions for which this date must be moved ahead by at least four or six centuries. In Burma and Laos, for example, each lacking a strong political authority and the concomitant desire to construct buildings destined to endure, perishable materials were in use longer than in other areas. Any reconstruction of the architectural history of these regions is hampered by the disappearance of "lay" buildings, which must have constituted an integral part of local production, though there remains at best only epigraphic evidence of their existence. Equally important, the available documentation is rendered less meaningful by an underlying complexity of symbolism that often defies interpretation.

Indonesia

It is possible to follow the development of Indonesian architecture only from the eighth century on, the period during which the first stone monuments were built there. Nothing remains of the small wooden temples that in all probability were erected in earlier times, nor of the works in pressed brick ultimately destroyed by the region's tropical climate. Andesite, a type of volcanic rock, was the prime construction material, and sometimes stone temples were even demolished so that it could be reused.

Scholars in general distinguish between two cultural periods: the first, called either the Indo-Javanese or the Central Java period, spans the seventh to tenth centuries; the second, the East Java period, spans the eleventh to sixteenth centuries. In the central area of Java, Indo-Javanese culture reached its height under two rival dynasties. One was Buddhist, the Sailendra, and the other, the Mataram, was Saivite. A branch of the Sailendras is credited with the transformation of the kingdom of Sri Vijaya on the island of Sumatra into an empire. The East Java period witnessed a succession of three kingdoms and three dynasties, the last of which, the Madjapahit (1294–1520), extended its rule over other parts of the archipelago and exercised a strong influence on the development of Balinese culture. Buddhism and Saivism coexisted during this phase, merging in syncretic cults that are believed to have been imbued with mystical Tantrism. The conversion to Islam, beginning in the thirteenth century, was fully established on the coasts

196. Java, Dieng plateau, Candi Arjuna.

197. *Java, Dieng plateau, Candi Bima.*

198. *Java, Mount Ungaran, Temple No. 2 of the Cedong-sanga complex.*
199. *Java, Mount Ungaran, Temple No. 1 of the Cedong-sanga complex.*
200. *Java, Mount Ungaran, Temple No. 5 of the Cedong-sanga complex.* ▷

201. *Java, Borobudur, general view.*

202. *Java, Borobudur, detail of the* dagabas *(bell-shaped stupas) on the circular terraces.*

203. *Java, Borobudur, detail of the* dagabas *on the circular terraces.*

204. *Java, plain of Kedu, Candi Pawon, detail of the decoration.* ▷

205. *Java, plain of Kedu, Candi Pawon.*
206. *Java, plain of Kedu, Candi Mendut.*

207. *Java, plain of Prambanam, Loro Jongrang complex, temple in the southern court.*
208. *Java, plain of Prambanam, Loro Jongrang complex, Candi Siva.* ▷

209. Java, plain of Prambanam, Loro Jongrang complex, Candi Brahma.

of Java and on the other islands by the fifteenth and sixteenth centuries.

We know very little about the foundations of Indonesian society in antiquity. It is clear, however, that the most important basic unit of economic and political life was the village, which was largely autonomous and had a mode of labor and production that served the needs of palace-cities and religious establishments and provided an active agricultural commerce. In general, we can assume that the social fabric of ancient Indonesia was largely made up of peasants and princes. Inscriptions going back to the eighth or ninth century, however, show that there was at that time a broad intermediate class consisting of a royal bureaucracy. Priests and monks presided over the sacred establishments (the temples and monasteries), and exercised exclusive control over the sources of revenue for the erection and maintenance of such buildings. The great ceremonies arranged for the king were attended by the village elders, who represented the people, and by groups of local merchants and artisans. We know almost nothing of the activities of these latter groups, which must also have included architects.[3]

It will be recalled that Indian penetration into Indonesia brought with it two religious systems: Brahmanism, especially in its Saivite aspect; and Buddhism, which after an initial appearance in its more simple Hinayana form, became widespread chiefly as the more broadly developed Mahayana, later to be mixed with the aforementioned Tantric elements. Saivism, probably because of its similarity to the autochthonous religious ideas of the Indonesians, appealed especially to the masses, while Buddhism remained the religion of the upper classes and court circles.

It can be assumed that a priestly elite, which initially must have been predominantly Indian, had direct and active access to the court. This elite was dedicated to the conversion of the Indonesian sovereigns, and the conversions they succeeded in motivating were total. It should not be forgotten that the sovereigns were in fact assimilated to the divinities of the new religions. On the other hand, this process of kingly deification, which found antecedents in the indigenous cult of dead chieftains, gave way to an actual faith that identified the royalty of the rulers with the will and protective capacities of the various Indian divinities.

The conception that we describe had, of course, important consequences in the sphere of art. For almost a millennium, major works of architecture and sculpture, commissioned by the monarchs themselves, were inspired by this particular vision. The architectural work became more and more charged with symbolic values, while departing from every functional aspect in the Western sense of the term.

Priests had particular importance in the construction of monuments: they persuaded the reigning monarch of their necessity and

assumed the ensuing organizational burden. An inscription dating back to A.D. 778 makes clear this priestly role. Another inscription, dating back to 842, is equally enlightening. Not only were the priests required to be familiar with Indian treatises (*sāstras*), but some among them specialized as architects (*sthapatis*) or sculptors (*sthapakas*).[4]

From the stylistic standpoint, the Central Java period is the phase more strongly linked to Indian influences. Temple complexes show an ordered and symmetrical arrangement, whereas works of the East Java period are marked by a greater vertical thrust, an absence of monumental buildings, and a less ordered and less symmetrical arrangement. In our attempt to classify these structures, we may single out two fundamental types: the *candi* (the mausoleum or tomb temple), and the true shrine. The *candi*, despite its variations, conforms to a more or less fixed pattern, and is usually divided into three parts (Plate 193): a quadrangular base with moldings at top and bottom (one side being opened by a staircase whose width might vary); a cubic body, often with niches, and with a forepart on the same side as the staircase; the roof, divided into various levels, adorned with horseshoe niches, and with miniature temples, with pinnacles or elements in the form of stupas, surmounted by a cylinder or truncated cone representing the lingam (phallus) of Siva. Inside the *candi*, in a pit dug before construction was begun, there was placed a casket containing the ashes of the sovereign or royal personage. In addition to being much reduced, the inner space had a purely symbolic importance. Among the oldest examples of this type of architecture, we might mention those on the Dieng plateau (ninth century), a center of the cult dedicated to Siva (Plates 194–197).

The most important monument, not only in Central Java but in all of Indonesia, is the stupa of Borobudur (Plate 201), whose construction goes back to the ninth century A.D. It is essentially a colossal stupa built around and over a small hill in the Kedu Valley. Even the choice of the site, like the form of the building, is symbolic, recalling Mount Meru (the mountain situated at the center of the universe) and the complex symbolism of "mountain" and "center" (Plate 203). Borobudur is thus formed at its base by five terraces, approximately quadrangular but actually rather complex. The foundation was decorated with infernal scenes and then covered, since they were not intended to be seen. The first terrace constitutes the true base; the others diminish gradually in size as they ascend to the three last circular terraces, which represent a symbolic celestial plane and show a different kind of decoration (Plate 202). Centrally located on each of the four sides, and corresponding to the four cardinal points, are four staircases leading to the great bell-shaped *dagaba* placed at the top and at the geometric center of the construction. Each square terrace is defined by

213. *Java, plain of Prambanam, Candi Sari.*

214. *East Java, Belahan, "bath" of King Airlangga.*
215. *Bali, Tampak Siring, royal tombs of Gunung Kawi.*
216. *Bali, Bedulu, Goa Gajah (Cave of the Elephant), "bath."*

a wall, which serves as a baluster to the corridor of the terrace above. The walls and balusters are decorated with thirteen hundred reliefs recounting the last life on earth of Buddha (possibly inspired by the *Lalita Vistara*), episodes from his previous lives (*jatakas*), and pious legends (*avadānas*). The circular terraces, which have no walls or balusters, hold seventy-two bell-shaped stupas placed in concentric circles, but which differ from the crowning stupa in that they are pierced in such a way that in each the Dhyani Buddha inside is visible, if only partially. The more than four hundred niches, distributed on the square terraces and containing Dhyani Buddha images, are separated by stupas, each crowned by three other stupas. This whole series of small stupas imparts an elegantly animated outline to the entire construction.

The framing of the doors and niches displays the characteristic motif of the *kālā-makara* arch, a name that alludes to its combination of two stylized animal forms. The first, a terrifying lion's head, is carved on the upper part, while below, on the two sides of the opening or niche, we find aquatic monsters (*makaras*). The combination of these two elements recurs not only on arches but throughout Central Javanese architecture. Symbolically, they represent the two basic aspects of the cosmos—light and darkness, spirit and substance.

The significance of the Borobudur monument is still an open and much-discussed question. Some scholars consider it a place of meditation and edification for the worshiper, who by means of it ascends to the metaphysical level of the supreme Buddhas. It may, on the other hand, be a magical and religious symbol of the rule of dharma over the island and the universe. It has further been suggested that the construction may even be considered a colossal mausoleum.[5] It is even possible that the edifice, besides being a symbolic representation of the universe, is also a dynastic monument of the Sailendras, here seen as Bodhisattvas.

From an architectural standpoint, the three parts into which it is possible to divide Borobudur probably have a twofold symbolic significance: the three worlds (the infernal, natural, and celestial); and the three phases of the epiphany (manifestation) through which the unknowable reveals itself little by little in forms comprehensible to our spirit and perceptible to our senses. On the other hand, the association of a square structure as a symbol of the earth with a circular one as a symbol of the sky would make this work a true mandala. It is indeed a diagram (or psycho-cosmogram) through which the worshiper capable of meditating on and assimilating the value of the teachings expressed by the images proceeds, guided in his long journey until he achieves Enlightenment and salvation; it is not by chance that Borobudur is completely accessible all the way to the top. The edifying character of

217. *East Java, Blitar, Panataram, view of the complex.*
218. *East Java, Blitar, Panataram, Candi Siva, or the so-called Dated Temple.*
219. *East Java, Blitar, Panataram, Temple of the Nagas.* ▷

the work is, in any case, too obvious to be underestimated. The majesty of the monument reveals equally the extraordinary economic wealth of the ruling dynasty, with all the implications to be derived thereby.

As for non-Buddhist works, the most famous and esteemed of Indonesian Saivite temples is the Loro Jongrang complex on the plain of Prambanam. It was probably built between the middle of the ninth century and the beginning of the tenth by the Saivite dynasty descended from King Sañjaya. Reconstruction of the complex shows that it was originally divided into three parts. On one side of the central square three small temples face east; the central temple, dedicated to Siva (Plate 208), is flanked by two smaller ones celebrating Brahma (Plate 209) and Vishnu. In front and parallel to each structure stand three lesser temples designed to honor the "vehicles" of the gods. Each temple rests on a square terrace enclosed by a baluster that forms a gallery. Two other temples, the smallest of all, are placed near the north and south (Plate 207) gates.

In the reconstruction of which we speak, four rows of 156 shrines, probably votive constructions, are symmetrically laid out around the central area. It is believed that structures built of light materials (which have long since disappeared) and intended for monks, women dancers, and pilgrims, were placed outside the encircling wall. It seems that the complex in its entirety was designed for the deification (in the form of Siva) of a king—perhaps Balitung of Mataram, as planned by his successor Daksa (A.D. 910–919). The reliefs that decorate the walls represent scenes from the *Rāmāyana*, and are thus erudite references to Indian culture.

In the second period, that of East Java, the arrangement of temple complexes is much less regular. The appearance of the shrines is altered more by a change in proportions, with a greater vertical development, than by any modification of architectural structures; we find here a transformation of the entrance gates, which now are constituted by a false temple with a pyramidal roof (*candi bentar*) vertically divided at the center. This division allows for a short level corridor that passes between the two halves, and permits entrance by a staircase also contained between the two parts. This sectioning of the architectural structure clearly indicates that it was appreciated for its volume of mass, without any interest in the interior space.[6] Furthermore, a taste for color and the picturesque becomes more developed, with the appearance of painting and sometimes incrustations of ceramic in the decoration of buildings.

None of the shrines of the East Java phase has the grandeur of major Central Java monuments. This diminished interest in the magnificence of architectural structures probably reflects a decline in economic possibilities and a reduction in the labor force.

223. *Plans of temples at Angkor: a) Bakong; b) Baksei Chamrong; c) Mangalartha; d) Ta Keo; e) preah Thkol (from Boisselier, 1966).*

224. *Plans of temples at Angkor: a) prasat (tower-sanctuary), Thom of Koh Ker; b) prasat, Sek Ta Tuy; c) Wat Ek (from Boisselier, 1966).*

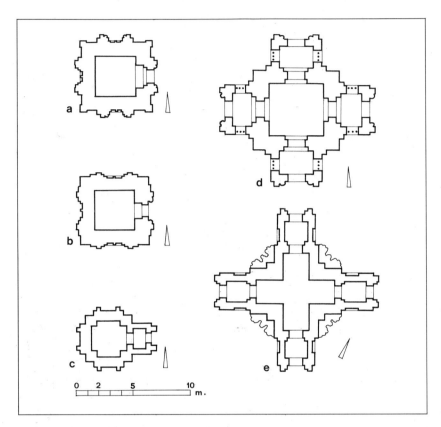

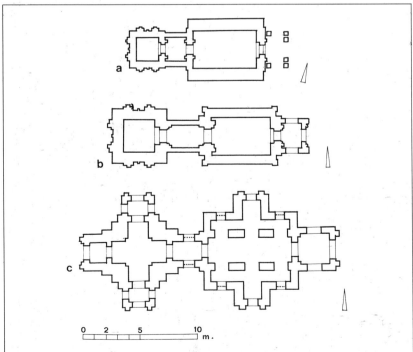

Very little remains of the period of the Singhasari dynasty. We might mention the "bath" at Belahan, probably the sovereign's funeral monument, dated A.D. 1049 and attributed to the reign of King Airlangga (Plate 214), and the royal tombs of Gunung Kawi on Bali, which take the form of *candis* dug out of the tufa (Plate 215). The new Indonesian architectural vision was expressed in such works as Candi Saventar and Candi Kidal (Plate 220; thirteenth century), and particularly in the Saivite complex at Panataram (Plate 217; fourteenth to fifteenth centuries), which clearly manifests the cultural power of the Madjapahit Kingdom. Generally thought to be a state temple (which is doubtful), it is distinguished by its agitated and asymmetrical plan. Important structures in this complex are the Temple of the Nagas (Plate 219; the name refers to serpent gods symbolizing water) and Candi Siva, the so-called Dated Temple of 1369 (Plate 218), whose pyramidal roof appears to be supported by the large grotesque masks of *kālās* placed above the doors.

The fall of the Madjapahit Kingdom in the second half of the fifteenth century marks the beginning of the Islamic period in Indonesia. The decline of Indian culture in this region now begins, at least as far as architecture is concerned. Only the island of Bali would preserve intact the pre-Islamic Hindu culture for any length of time.

Cambodia (the Khmers)

The most important Indianized state in ancient Indochina was Funan, situated in Cochin China between the Bassac River and the Gulf of Siam. In addition to the legends relating to its birth and to the "Land of Gold," certain Chinese sources dating from about the third century A.D. speak of its great wealth in gold, silver, pearls, and spices. Archaeological aerial reconnaissance of these areas has revealed the existence of a dense network of canals, interconnected and laid out in a predominantly northeast-southwest direction. The purpose of these canals was to drain the floodwaters of the Bassac to the sea and "wash" the soil otherwise made saline by drought, thus permitting an intensive cultivation of rice, and to shelter an imposing river fleet. Along the vital points of this canal system traces of cities have been discerned, in which the canals penetrated, dividing them into quarters. This extraordinary complex testifies to the existence of a remarkable economic and political power.[7]

Unfortunately, almost nothing remains of the architecture of the period; the houses must have been built on wooden piles. Durable materials were apparently reserved for shrines, of which there remain only a few vestiges that defy firm identification. What little remains, however, bespeaks a strong Indian influence, though we also find among them some Chinese and Roman objects.

225. *Plans of temples at Angkor: a) Phimai; b) Banteay Samre (from Bois-*
    selier, 1966).
226. *Phnom Bakheng, aerial view of the temple.*

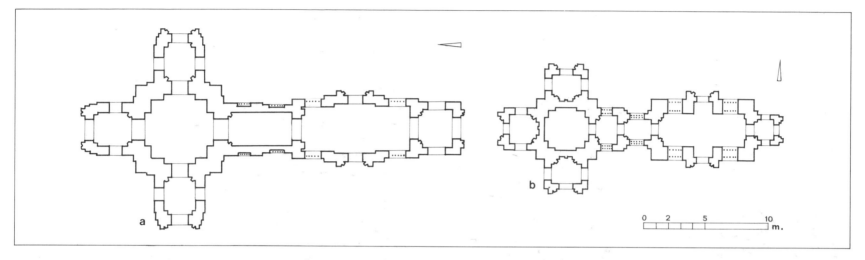

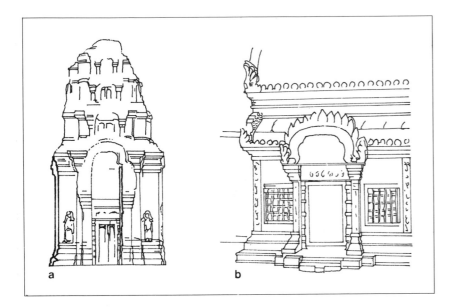

During the same period, there arose in the middle Mekong Basin another Indianized state, also known by the name given it by the Chinese sources—Chen-la. It existed as early as the sixth century, and inscriptions going back to the seventh and eighth centuries testify to the presence in Chen-la of people of Khmer origin. The progressive expansion of Chen-la brought about the almost total conquest of Funan at the beginning of the eighth century. Isanavarman, the king of Chen-la (A.D. 616–635), founded a new capital, Isanapura (today Sambor Prei Kuk), from which the early art of Chen-la—or rather, the first phase of Khmer art—takes its name, the Sambor style.

In this case as well, aerial reliefs allow us to reconstruct the system of urbanization and exploitation of natural space in Chen-la. Its cities were vast expanses of terrain surrounded by earth walls and by a trench that drew water from a permanent waterway; when filled with water, the trench provided irrigation for the rice fields within the enclosure. This technique for supplying water was brought to Cambodia by the Khmers. Though profoundly different from that of Funan, it required from the beginning a centralized society and a single strong authority—precisely the one that was to develop into the structure of Angkor.

The architecture was substantially religious; only inscriptions testify to the existence of lay works of public utility, such as hospitals and "houses with fire" (designed to shelter travelers), all of which were constructed of perishable materials and are now totally destroyed.

The Khmers, like the Indians before them, conceived the temple not as a meeting place for the faithful but as the home of the god it honored; they believed he actually lived there in the form of his sacred image. The Khmer temple was therefore relatively small. The structures of shrines included a tower (*prasat*) for the principal deity and one or more towers for the god's spouse and his "vehicle." Secondary constructions, designed to preserve cult objects and everything connected with the liturgy and exegesis, were added to these buildings. A wall with doors enclosed the complex, and inside a second wall were constructions in perishable materials—the dwellings for priests, musicians, and male and female dancers.

The temples gave concrete form to, and symbolically expressed, the religious beliefs of the country. The sacred building appears rigorously centered and oriented according to the four cardinal points; the façade and principal entrance faced east, the source of life. The main sanctuary was the image of Mount Meru, center of the world, on which the deity has his seat. It was built at the center of the city, close to the palace of the king, who held a mandate on earth from the gods. This organization and arrangement were to remain almost unaltered in the course of the centuries and throughout the changing styles; the static quality of a metaphysical type of structure hindered

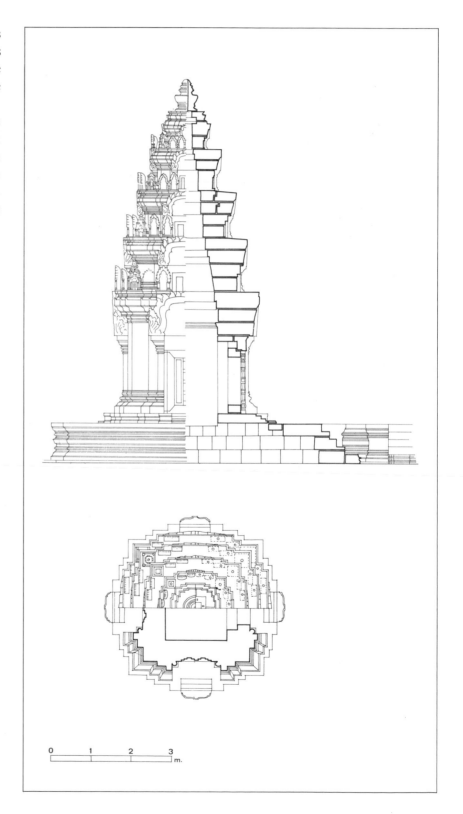

any fundamental alterations. On the religious level, such repetition is not a sign of weakness, but has the significance of a holy rite. This instinct of preservation is also reflected in the persistence, in stone constructions, of building structures and systems much more suitable for wood—the material that had been used for older buildings.

The grandeur of monuments is generally more evident in periods of peace and equilibrium. We owe, for example, the two architectural complexes of Sambor Prei Kuk—one to the north, the other to the south—to the powerful reign of Isanavarman. Nevertheless, under his successor and during a less tranquil time, the Prei Kmeng style flourished. It is a style characterized by sanctuary-towers that are of scant value. Although there was during this period a progressive and strong affirmation of Hinduism, the use of Mahayana Buddhist images spread remarkably. Chen-la found itself in troubled times during the entire eighth century. Only when a new equilibrium was created, coinciding with the founding of Angkor, would they be resolved.

Architecture, as well as sculpture, became impoverished and there ensued an unfortunate period of obvious decline. It was, however, more a political and social crisis than a cultural one; evidently the economy reacted negatively to the interruption of trade relations with India. A new political organization had to be created, as well as a new social and economic one, in order for these arts to be revitalized.

It is probable that the influence of Indonesia, then ruled by the Sailendras, contributed to this rebirth. At that time, the Javanese dynasty exercised a right of sovereignty over the South China Sea and in particular over the coasts of Malaysia, where Mahayana Buddhism was widespread. On the other hand, on the political level, the Sailendras offered Chen-la the example of a great civilization of a monarchical character. It is thought that Jayavarman II, who restored equilibrium and founded the Khmer Empire, spent a long time, either voluntarily or as a hostage, at the court of Java. Upon his return to Cambodia about A.D. 790, he prepared to reorganize the territory of Chen-la by founding a series of capitals, of which the most important was Mahendraparvata. Here he had a lingam built as a symbol of the god Siva and of his own royal divinity; from that point on this would be the emblem of all succeeding Khmer kings. In this way Jayavarman and his successors asserted themselves as universal sovereigns, legitimizing their power by a direct relation to the deity, which in its turn was the essence, order, and mover of the universe. The Khmer territory was again united under a central authority. This political and social order was accompanied by the achievement of a vigorous art, which found expression in a succession of various styles and in imposing architectural monuments.

An innovation of tremendous importance to the establishment of

Khmer power on the political and economic level can be attributed to Indravarman (A.D. 877–889). At Roluos, his residence, this ruler supervised the construction of an admirable hydraulic system that helped to ensure three centuries of extraordinary prosperity for the country. The first step undertaken was the construction of the artificial lake (*barai*) known as Indrataka, which distributed water to the rice fields by means of a network of irrigation canals. The water was then conveyed to the trenches that served the city and defined its boundaries. River navigation, which among other things facilitated the transporting of construction materials, was now possible along the canals. B.P. Groslier has defined the meaning of the innovation and its value to the local economy: "In this way the Angkor city is no longer a simple assemblage of its inhabitants around the temple of the god who protects them. It is the fulcrum of a rational system of soil cultivation, utilizing natural resources in the best manner, and, depending on the case, integrating and replacing them."[8]

The effectiveness of this system, in an area where the fundamental problem remained that of drought, is confirmed by the creation of identical structures in the centuries that followed. Even when, as a result of dynastic conflicts, the Khmer kings abandoned Angkor and moved to Koh Ker, they prepared for settlement in an arid area by setting up a hydraulic system similar to that of Angkor.

It is obvious that it was possible to carry out undertakings of this kind only in an exceptionally strong centralized state, and that the success of these hydraulic systems conferred an almost magical power on the king who constructed one. By providing water in this manner, he gave life. The divinity of the rulers, as well as the veneration bestowed on them when dead, was thus legitimized in the socio-economic sphere. This fundamental view would remain a constant in the sequence of Khmer art. A succession of various styles ensued, with names that derive from the most important centers of the period to which they belong. An examination of the more significant monuments will indicate the basic architectural types of each. An interesting aspect of our study will be the Khmers' admirable use of their network of canals in the construction of shrines by arranging buildings against a background of water in an artistic way.

The basic architectural types used by the Khmers were the tower-sanctuary (*prasat*) and the temple-mountain; the gallery was added later. The more imposing works were constituted by the varied composition of these three elements. The *prasat* is square in plan and built of brick. It opens toward the east, and is surmounted by a roof of superimposed levels that reproduces, on a progressively diminishing scale, the structure of the main body. The temple-mountain is a construction formed by a terraced pyramid (the number of terraces would

vary with time), crowned at the top by five *prasats*, placed quincuncially. This basic structure would be enhanced by the addition of a series of sandstone towers onto the individual terraces.

Both types can be observed in the Khmer architecture of the early style, known as Kulen (eighth to ninth centuries), which at Ak Yom offers our first example of the temple-mountain in its simplest form. The Bakheng style provides other fine examples of the temple-mountain in the pyramid at Bakong (Plate 223) and in the complex at Phnom Bakheng constructed at the end of the ninth century (Plate 226). Compared to the Ak Yom temple, the one at Bakong has a more complicated structure, with a greater number of terraces and towers on the individual levels. Furthermore, the site is enclosed by two successive stone walls that alternate with two wide moats. The Phnom Bakheng complex, in its rich symbology, is an actual calendar in stone, indicating on its various horizons the positions and phases of the planets. Along

233. *Banteay Srei, a portal.*
234. *Angkor, plan of the Ta Keo (from Groslier, 1961).*
235. *Angkor, the Ta Keo.* ▷

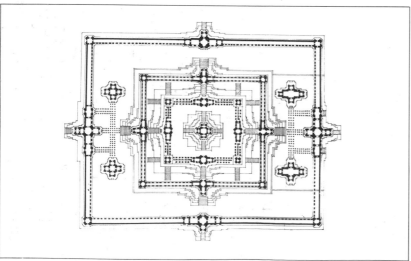

with the temple-mountain, use of the tower-sanctuary continues: the Phnom Krom and the Phnom Bok are each formed by three aligned towers constructed entirely of stone.

Following the era during which Koh Ker was the capital, it was Rajendravarman who initiated the return to Angkor (A.D. 944–968). The tradition of the temple-mountain continued, but other sanctuaries of more modest dimensions were built by the chief vassals of the king. Among these we might mention the Saivite temple of Banteay Srei (Plates 228–233), consecrated by the Brahmin Yainavaraha. The temple, formed by three concentric enclosures, includes three tower-sanctuaries aligned on a terrace. The east gate of the main temple is preceded by a vaulted forepart in brick, while libraries and long halls surround the complex. The forms and proportions that characterize this construction—scarcely verticalized due to a particular wish to achieve balanced effects—are especially elegant and harmonious.

There followed a politically unsettled period during which the Khmers failed to initiate any notable variations in the artistic field. The temple-mountain did not acquire its definitive form until the construction of the Ta Keo around A.D. 1000 (Plates 234–236), which marked the culmination of a development begun as early as Ak Yom.

The entire five-level pyramid of Ta Keo is covered in stone. On the highest terrace, its innovators placed quincuncially five sandstone towers. Around the second level there runs a gallery, which is accentuated at its four corners by roughly constructed towers and enlivened at the center of each side by an access pavilion.

Later builders of the temple-mountain (like those at Baphuon) would emphasize the development of such galleries and erect towers at the corners. The *prasat* of this period, also built of stone, rests on a platform and is sometimes preceded by a forepart. To the sides of the main entrance, we often find libraries. Surrounded by moats and ponds, these sanctuaries, even in their reduced size, have the same quality of refinement as the more imposing monuments.

The fame of Khmer art is largely connected with the Angkor Wat complex (Plates 237–244), the temple-mountain of Suryavarman II (A.D. 1113–1150). This temple, whose main façade looks west, is bounded by a trench that received water from Siemréap via a canal. A road flanked by balusters adorned with serpent motifs leads to the main gate of an enclosure that reproduces on a reduced scale the façade of the temple. The central tower has two lateral wings of galleries; they terminate in a smaller tower. The columns that support the galleries are reflected in the water. Within the enclosure rises the temple, a pyramid with three superimposed terraces, each surrounded by a gallery enhanced by towers and pavilions. Three staircases on the western side lead to three more galleries supported by pillars, and then

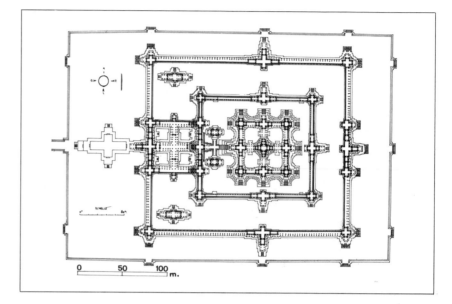

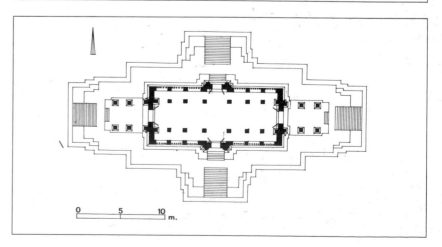

240. *Angkor Wat, axial view of the western part.*
241. *Angkor Wat, aerial view.*
242. *Angkor Wat, southern side of the second gallery.* ▷

243. *Angkor Wat, tower of the central sanctuary (southeast side).*
244. *Angkor Wat, view of the central part.*

245. *Angkor Thom, plan of the Bayon (from Groslier, 1961).*

246. *Angkor Thom, central sanctuary of the Bayon, plan (from Boisselier, 1966).*

247. *Angkor, Baksei Chamrong (from Hallade, 1954).*

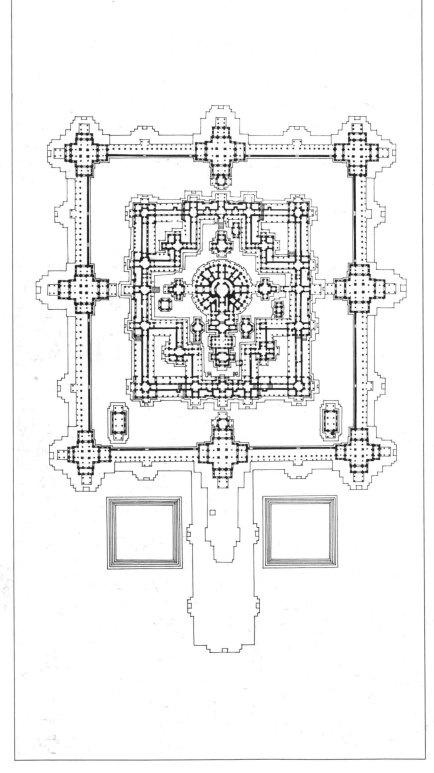

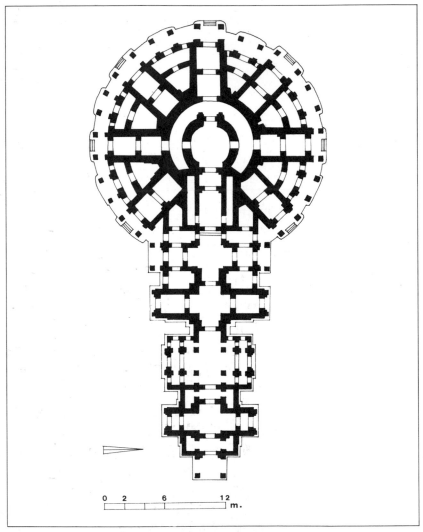

248. Angkor Thom, aerial view of the Bayon.

249. *Angkor Thom, towers of the Bayon.*
250. *Angkor Thom, western gate.*

above to the three staircases of the second terrace. The edifice is constructed in accordance with an extraordinary perspective composition: the height of each of the three terraces seems slowly to increase as one ascends, and each terrace shifts, progressively drawn back, so that the structure as a whole does not give the impression of being inclined toward the spectator about to ascend it.

Angkor Wat is flanked by a series of identical shrines whose plan and structural elements differ from the central complex only in that they are developed horizontally.

The last great creations of Khmer art took place under Jayavarman VII (A.D. 1181–1220), whose powerful motivation and strength of purpose arrested for a time a decadence that later proved to be inevitable. Incongruously, this enigmatic ruler was especially cruel to his enemies, yet was at the same time a deeply religious man. Converted to Mahayana Buddhism, he adopted a new concept with regard to the deified sovereign. In his forty-year reign he devoted particular attention to the ancestor cult, restored almost all the ancient temples, and initiated and dedicated to himself a great number of works, often insisting on changes in the original plans during their construction.

By following this course, Jayavarman VII made Angkor Thom truly his capital, and at its center built his towering temple-mountain, the Bayon. He actually succeeded, with the help of the men he appointed to carry out the work, in surpassing the complex and refined symbolism with which this type of monument had long been charged (Plates 245, 246, 248–253).

The original plan of the Bayon was modified and made more complicated in the course of construction. The initial layout included a vaulted gallery in the form of a Greek cross. Its corners, however, were later closed off by a gallery set at right angles, and the whole was enclosed by still another gallery. At the center of the inner gallery, and on a large base, there stood the sanctuary, circular in plan. Its central chapel was complemented by as many as twelve radial chapels. Each tower was built over the chapels and pavilions and was carved with four faces symbolizing the gaze of the Compassionate Buddha that pervades the universe, placed toward the four cardinal points. The central sanctuary housed a statue of Buddha in meditation, and the radial chapels contained images representing great dignitaries. The colossal faces on the towers served to identify the ruler with divinity and referred as well to the universal sovereignty (a theoretical and wise sovereignty) of the deified king, who looks in all directions and watches over the country, which is represented below by the figures of powerful court dignitaries.

With the death of Jayavarman VII, the process of decadence was accelerated; with him died the last god-king. The world of the Khmers

213

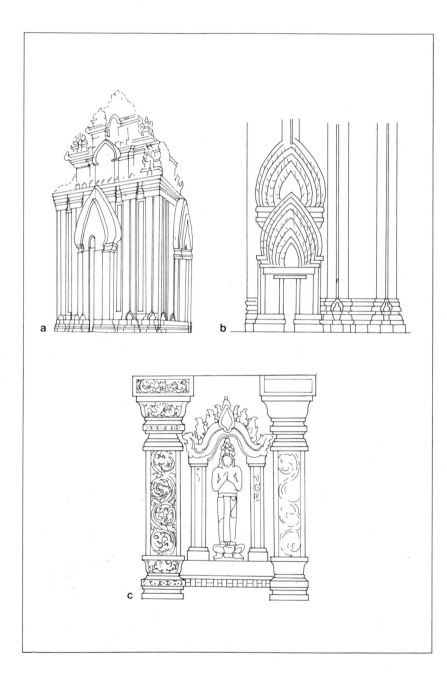

survived only until 1430. Progressive decay of the central power brought about a collapse of the economy and with the disappearance of this central authority, the land that had been wrenched from the desert became arid once again. The devastating attacks of the Thais gave the death blow to a territory that by now was well in decline.

The art that had been inspired by the monarchy and the cult of the king decayed, and the use of perishable materials resumed. It was the sad destiny of the works that followed to have no value beyond that of the historical moment.

Champa

We find that, beginning in the third century A.D., Champa is often mentioned in the Chinese texts, which refer to it as Lin-yi. They describe the ancient kingdom, in direct contact with the Han colonies in Tonkin, as a land formed by warrior states inhabited by the Chams. This was a population of highly expert navigators who, living in a coastal forest area rich in spices, established early connections with Indian traders. The region was later divided into kingdoms or principalities: the most important of these in the beginning were Amaravati, today Quang Nam; Vijaya, today Binh Dinh; Kauthara, on the plain of Nhatrang; and Panduranga, on the plain of Phanrang.

Close relations with Funan, and diplomatic ties and wars with China, brought about a political situation favorable to penetration by both Indian and Chinese influences. We know that at the beginning of the fifth century the sovereign Bhadravarman founded a sanctuary dedicated to Siva in the mountain cirque of Mi-son. Chinese sources note also that the Chams were already masters of brick construction. A more direct knowledge of their art is not available, however, until the seventh century. It appears that after a series of bloody struggles, the Cham Kingdom established friendly relations with Indonesia, an entente that is reflected in the style of the Duong Dong complex (ninth century A.D.). Following some conflict with the Khmers, whose influence is clearly apparent in the style of Mi-son, a very grave threat to the Chams was posed by the hostile expansion of ancient Annam, which had become independent. In A.D. 982 the Annamese succeeded in seizing the capital, and the Chams were forced to withdraw to Vijaya, which remained the center of the country even when, for a certain time, the northern provinces were reconquered.

Persistent Vietnamese pressure, if only with sporadic thrusts in the nature of incursions, had to be dealt with at the same time the country was threatened by the Khmers. In 1145, after fifty years of relative calm, the dynasty and country were overwhelmed by the Khmer armies. The war, which lasted a hundred years, weakened both adversaries to the advantage of the Thais and Vietnamese. In 1417, even the

255. *Duong Dong (Vietnam), Mahayana Buddhist monastery, western wall, southeast corner of the portico.*   256. *Hoa-lai (Vietnam), northern tower, southern façade.*

name of Champa disappears; the territory was completely assimilated by the Vietnamese.

Cham art differs profoundly from that of the Khmers, despite their common Indian model and reciprocal exchanges and influences. This difference is not a question of a natural diversity in taste, produced by diverse cultures and sensibilities, but is rather the result of aesthetic conceptions that diverge because of the radically different functions that the two kingdoms attributed to art.

The essential reason for this divergence is to be sought in the Cham socio-political structure. The system, founded on the division of land, kept the country constantly divided into principalities. Sometimes they were held together by a particularly energetic king, but never with the slightest possibility of reducing his realm to a socially and economically centralized state. Art thus remained the privilege of kings, and had only the dimensions of their power.[9]

Even though—like the Khmers, and perhaps due to Indonesian influence—the Cham kings adopted the cult of the deified king, they never created a temple-mountain, nor any great complexes that can even remotely be compared to those of Angkor. In any case, the Chams' sense of space was not that of the Khmers. Cham architecture possesses no large complexes, with the exception of the Mahayana monastery at Duong Dong. Cham temple structures are constituted only by the grouping of a few sanctuaries, square in plan and enclosed by a wall. At times (but this is rather rare) sanctuaries are preceded by a long hall. In practice, we can say that the only type of building used in Cham architecture is the tower-sanctuary known as the *kalan*, square in plan and always constructed of brick.

The basic structure of the *kalan* is that of a cubic mass topped by a roof of several superimposed levels that tends to become narrower toward the top, imparting to the whole a considerable vertical thrust. Through a succession of stylistic variations, this thrust was to become more accentuated, due not only to the attenuation of the base (no longer cubic) toward the top, but also to the formation of a high socle beneath the base itself; and finally, as a visual effect, to the presence of decorative elements, sometimes strongly projecting, that help to emphasize the vertical effect.

Inside the *kalan*, the covering of the cell is also raised, assuming the form of a fireplace chimney. Of particular importance is the outer decoration, consisting of moldings, fixed (especially plant-form) motifs, and architectural elements. We find, for example, false pillars, often in pairs, or projecting arches of various kinds, but always devoid of any static function. The decoration is always more profuse and elaborate at the lower part of the building.

The roof of the structure consists, as already mentioned, of diminishing planes, which often display at their corners miniature replicas of the building, sculptured in the round. In many cases, it is actually the levels themselves in their entirety that appear as reduced copies of the building below. Diminishing toward the top, in ever smaller forms, they impart to the building a strange effect of flight toward the sky.

Each of the four sides of the parallelepiped of the base has a door (sometimes two of them are false), flanked by small columns and surmounted by a polylobate arch with a characteristically flowing outline. The admirable attention to proportions and the type of decoration itself help to give the *kalan* a particular effect of energy and harmony that constitutes its principal charm.

We are faced here, of course, with only a single type of construction that furthermore remained substantially unaltered. Yet it is possible to follow the development of the *kalan*, for it is marked by a progressive change in its forms, especially the decoration of the arches over the doors and niches. Initially, in the Hoa-lai style of about the ninth century, the arches appear in the form of an inverted U, rising and enlivened by means of a polylobate contour (Plate 256). In the Duong Dong style that marked the third quarter of the ninth century (Plate 255), the arch is decorated by a central flower from which masses of plants fall to the sides, forming rosettes along the entire curve; the garland under the cornice is enriched by ornamental foliage. Such is the case of the main tower of the Duong Dong complex, the great Mahayana Buddhist monastery founded in A.D. 875 by Indravarman II and dedicated to Avalokitesvara, the Bodhisattva of the Compassionate Gaze. Inside the Duong Dong enclosure, whose perimeter is almost a kilometer in length, rises an ensemble of brick constructions, placed in a space divided into successive courtyards oriented along an east-west transverse axis. In the first courtyard, which is the last for the worshiper entering from the eastern side, there are eighteen shrines. On the middle axis, surrounded by other sanctuaries, rises the central tower, open on four sides and containing an altar that no doubt once bore Avalokitesvara's statue, which has since disappeared.

The next style, called Mi-son A 1 (Plate 257), marks the abandonment of the excessive development of plant-form decorations and the return to a simpler and more balanced composition (ninth century). The central tower, characteristically Mi-son A 1, develops its own structure vertically, reduces the superstructures, and introduces more slender pillars devoid of decoration (five in number). The curvature of its arches tends to disappear and be replaced by a linear structure, which may be inscribed in an equilateral triangle. At the corners of the tower rise the typical sandstone spires, a salient feature of Cham monuments.

A time of transition, corresponding politically to the period of Khmer domination, followed the period during which this elegant and harmonious art was created. Then, at the beginning of the twelfth century, the so-called Binh Dinh style (Plate 254) developed, in which the *kalan* ultimately becomes primarily a geometric mass, a parallelepiped with light moldings. Arches assume a lanceolate form, and superstructures are multiplied, repeating the structure of the building. They are, however, reduced in height to endow the *kalan* with a continuous curve in its skyline, imitating the ogival contour typical of the towers of Angkor. It is very likely that the construction of such famous works as the Towers of Copper and Towers of Gold goes back to the end of the thirteenth century. Projecting supplementary arches were later added to the principal arches, some superstructures were multiplied but without any explicit criterion, and corner motifs were stylized to the point of becoming stone hooks. The garland under the cornice disappeared, often to be replaced by zoomorphic friezes.

After the fourteenth century, with the dismemberment of their country, the art of the Chams inevitably declined. Finally, it exhausted itself in the repetitive aridity that marks such works of the period as the *kalan* at Po Romé, which is formed by a cumbersome complex of four brick structures, awkwardly constructed and decorated with heavy and illogical niches.

Burma

The art of Burma reflects more than any other in Indochina the cultural influence of the Indian world. The first certain evidence of this Indianization appears in fifth-to-sixth century fragments of gold leaf on which sacred Buddhist texts are incised in the Pali language. The Indians, however, also introduced Hinduism into Burma along with Mahayana and Hinayana Buddhism. Only the latter religious form would maintain a position of importance in the history of this region.

The earliest populations of the area, those whom we might theoretically consider autochthonous, were probably Mons and Pyus of Mongolian stock. In the ninth century, however, groups of people of Tibetan origin emigrated south from their original lands along the borders of Tibet and China and entered northern Burma, where they took control of two regions: Kyaukse, economically important for its abundant rice production; and Pagan, a key region because of such attributes as a strategic position, a natural road network, and commercial possibilities. Under Anawratha (A.D. 1044–1077), the Burmese were converted to Hinayana Buddhism and extended their rule to include most of the country. Anawratha's capital city of Pagan, where Mon prisoners captured during the invasion were concentrated, became, also because of their presence, a center for the spread of Buddhism, and it was here, during the reign of Kyanzittha (A.D. 1084–1112),

that the great building period began. The tolerance of the new king permitted the coexistence of different religions, and under his successor a truly Burmese style began that was destined to triumph for two centuries. Extremely friendly relations were established with Ceylon, and it was perhaps in this period that Tantric Buddhism arrived in Pagan. In 1287 Burma was invaded by the Mongols, who under the leadership of Kublai Khan seized the capital and ended the Burmese dynasty. Not until the fifteenth and sixteenth centuries, when political conditions were more favorable and new dynasties arose, were there signs of a rebirth and encouragement of the arts.

An exhaustive study of Burmese art and architecture, one that would enable us to follow their development over the centuries and attempt a classification by styles and schools, has yet to be made. Of civil architecture, nothing remains. Numerous monuments of a religious nature survive, however, although they are often in a considerable state of ruin due to war, pillage, and careless restoration. Fortunately, the dry climate of the area has helped to preserve a much greater number of works than in any other part of Southeast Asia. Except for a few Hindu constructions and some others deriving from Mahayana Buddhism, all the monuments of this period were inspired by the Hinayana Buddhism of the Theravadin sect (whose stronghold was in Ceylon). Since it is not possible to trace the artistic phenome-

260. *Prome (outskirts), temple of Lemyethna.*

261. *Prome, temple of Payatan.*
262. *Prome, stupa of Payagyi.*
263. *Pagan, stupa of Sapada.* ▷

264. *Pagan, temple of Ananda, elevation and section (from Griswold, 1963).*
265. *Pagan, temple of Ananda.* ▷

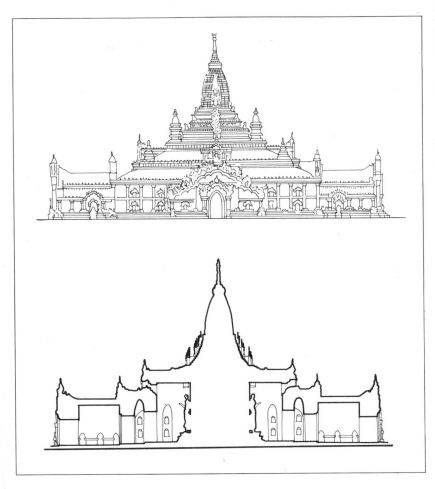

nology of this region with sufficient certainty, we will proceed by examining construction techniques and the various types of buildings.

A typical feature of architectural construction is the use of rib vaults, obtained by the close positioning of flattened arches, which may be erected without centering by utilizing a connecting element. The question of whether this building system originated in India or China is still to be resolved.[10] The material employed, except for certain small works built of stone, is generally brick, covered by thick stucco in which decoration was incised. Colored tablets of enameled terracotta were often used for decoration; or, inside the monuments, carved wooden panels. Stupas and sanctuaries remained massive in appearance, with interior spaces looking as though they had been excavated from the rock. The Indian technique of cut or excavated architecture left traces even in the constructed architecture of a foreign country.

Specialists have followed different systems in the classification of Burmese buildings. Some distinguish ten types of monuments (De Beylié); others, nine (U Lu Pe Win); still others indicate only two types as being fundamental. They are the stupa and the building that includes a hall for the cult or habitation; the others are considered to be simple variations of these basic types (Parmentier and Marchal).[11] We will follow this last criterion, examining particularly those types and subtypes of which important examples survive.

Traditionally, the Burmese stupa is composed of four parts: (1) a masonry terrace, square in plan; (2) a very high plinth, by preference polygonal in plan; (3) the bell-shaped body of the actual stupa, ending in (4) a conical spire—often formed by rings—crowned by a parasol (*hti*). Variations are infinite. Hemispherical domes are rare, and are always flared at the bottom so as to introduce the bell shape; cylindrical bodies that replace the polygonal form of the so-called plinth are more frequent. There are even conical stupas, knob-shaped structures with concave contours that result from a widening at the base, and bulb-shaped ones.

The Burmese bell-shaped stupa, especially frequent in Pagan (Plate 263), can be a very elaborate architectural type. The terrace, which is square, has in these cases superimposed levels that diminish toward the top and act as ambulatories. At the four cardinal points, staircases connected by ramps permit passage from one level to another. The body of the bell-shaped stupa rises directly from the highest level of the base. In addition, there are enough other, equally complicated, forms to justify the more elaborate classification systems of which we spoke.

However, the Burmese stupa does display two characteristics that distinguish it from the Indian structure: (1) the absence of a terrace with baluster (*harmikā*) surmounting the dome from which the spire

rises; (2) a greater development of the base, composed, as we have mentioned, of superimposed square platforms that constitute a kind of ambulatory to which one ascends by means of axial stairs. Furthermore, the Burmese stupa tends toward progressive verticality. The form of the older stupas can be cylindrical, like the Bawbawgyi of the seventh century near Prome (Plate 258), or, like the Payama and Payagyi (Plate 262), be shaped like a giant sugar loaf. The Pagan dynasty preferred the bell-shaped form, which perhaps brought with it certain Singhalese components, whose number has still not been satisfactorily determined.

The latest Pagan edifice that we know of is the stupa of Mingala-zedi (Plate 270), begun in 1274. The construction is formed by three terraces surmounted by a stupa with a molded circular base; it is topped by a bell-shaped drum ending in a conical spire. False *kalasas* (vases for ambrosia) are placed at the corners of the terraces, while at the four corners of the level from which the actual stupa rises there are four small stupas that reproduce in miniature the structure of the central one. At the center of the four sides of the terraces, staircases lead to the upper levels. This monument at Mingalazedi is the most characteristic Burmese stupa. The type of building with an inner hall, very widespread at least until the Pagan period, offers various subtypes, though it always has the appearance of a compact mass of bricks in which chapels

and corridors have been dug out. Buildings of this type are generally known as cave-buildings. A vaulted cell opens at the center of the mass, and over it is raised a block that supports an imposing crown of the sikhara type.

The most important monuments of this kind are the Ananda, consecrated in A.D. 1091 (Plates 264, 265), and the Thatbyinnyu (A.D. 1144). The Ananda, built by King Kyanzittha (A.D. 1084–1112), marks the triumph of the style known as Mon. According to legend, this sanctuary was intended to reproduce the form of the cave of Nanda-mula, where Indian monks who had been received at the Burmese court had once lived.

The plan of the construction is that of a Greek cross. In it the arms are formed by massive porticoes placed around the central square. The latter consists of an immense and solid block of brick that rises to support the tower structure, which is modeled after a sikhara and thus gives the building its religious significance. The two narrow concentric corridors inside enable the worshiper to perform a circumambulation around the 30-foot statues of Buddha, placed in niches on the four walls of the central block. The outer roof is formed by a series of diminishing platforms, from the last of which rises the cupola-tower. The corners of the platforms bear repetitions, on a reduced scale, of the central dome.

The Thatbyinnyu, built in Pagan in A.D. 1144 by King Alaung-sithu, is similar to the Ananda. It does not, however, possess the four wings that give the latter its cruciform structure. The square plan is very obvious, and the central construction constitutes a dado around which an enormous basic mass is developed, similar in various ways to the base of the Ananda. The shape of the monument can best be described as a stupa that by its base terraces rises on a wide platform in the form of a cube, which in its turn is supported by enormous base terraces. In all, the monument includes five levels, of which the highest is crowned by the sikhara, while the two immediately below it form a kind of vihara.

Siam (Thailand)

The actual history of Siam begins only in the thirteenth century, when the Thais of the middle Menam Basin succeeded in freeing themselves from Khmer domination and founding their first king-dom, at Sukhodaya. Archaeological evidence nevertheless enables us partially to reconstruct the previous period as well, which is of no small importance for the formation of Siamese art and civilization. It would appear that at least as early as the sixth century A.D. there existed in the Menam Delta an Indianized state, Dvaravati. The bronze images of Buddha created by Dvaravati artists (discovered at Korat and Nagara

Pathama) show in fact a clear Indian influence of the Gupta period. It is probable that the expansion of this kingdom is related to the dismemberment of Funan, but though we can reconstruct the historical situation little is known of Siam's artistic development in this period.

Later, in the ninth to tenth centuries, the country underwent a process of progressive "Khmerization" (in the sense of an absolute hegemony of Khmer culture at the expense of local traditions), which reached its height in the eleventh century, when Suryavarman I, a Siamese Mon, ascended the Khmer throne to become one of the greatest rulers of this multinational empire. However, despite the preponderant Khmer influence, Siam remained the most orthodox center of Hinayana Buddhism, which was so strong a faith that it asserted itself even at Angkor when the conquests of the Khmer kings led to the integration of Siamese territory with their other possessions. Unfortunately, we know very little of the art of this period (eleventh to twelfth centuries) as well, aside from the undeniable fact that it was an art inspired by Buddhism. Only recently has research in the vicinity of Nakhon Pathom (Nagara Pathama) brought to light the remains of a few large brick complexes (Plates 286, 287).

In the architectural sphere, the existence of stupas of obvious Indian derivation has been ascertained, as well as that of a kind of reliquary-monument or chaitya, consisting of a brick cube surmounted by a full roof with molded levels. Chaityas were decorated on the outside by Buddhist images under arcades, and temple complexes were surrounded by ambulatory galleries. Often the chaityas were erected on imposing terraces. The two most interesting monuments of this kind are Wat P'ra Pathama and Wat P'ra Men.

The Thais, a people of the same stock as the Vietnamese, succeeded during the thirteenth century in dominating the Siam region. The extended exposure of the Thai people to the Mon-Khmer civilization had already left its mark in their embracement of Hinayana Buddhism. Once they had conquered the country, the Thais limited their efforts to spreading their own feudal organization and the Thai language (formerly called Siamese). Meanwhile, they were, of course, assimilating the Indianized culture of their new subjects. Increasingly, the Thais asserted themselves feudally at the expense of the Khmer Kingdom, which by now was well in decline, and they finally founded a new nation with its capital at Sukhodaya. History links its beginnings and growth to the name of Ram Kamheng (1281–1300), the monarch under whose rule the process of unification began. Later, the Thais of the Lop Buri region, the center of which was Ayuthia, succeeded in annexing Sukhodaya and conquering Angkor (1353). They would rule Siam until 1767, when they were finally defeated by the Burmese, who had been attacking them sporadically since the fifteenth century.

The earliest style we find in the Siam region is the Lop Buri, a

233

272. *Sajjanalaya, Wat Suan Geo Udyana Yai.*
273. *Sajjanalaya, Wat Cetiya Jet Teo.*
274. *Sajjanalaya, Wat Chang Lom.* ▷

twelfth-to-thirteenth century development of the Khmers. One example of the Lop Buri style is the Brah Prang Sam Yot (Plate 285), a Khmer sanctuary formed by three towers frontally aligned, located in the province for which this innovative style was named. Two interesting elements of this structure are the stucco decoration and the presence of human masks at the bases of its columns. In the Wat Mahadhatu (Monastery of the Great Relic) at Lop Buri (Plate 284), the principal sanctuary is still inspired by the ogival tower at Angkor Wat, but displays considerable vertical thrust and rests on a high pedestal. An unmistakable desire for surface movement is apparent in the reduction and fragmentation of the structures; the interior cell has also become smaller, and its unique position on a very elevated pedestal makes it a true reliquary, inaccessible for direct worship.

The Wat Kukut at Lamphun, completed in 1218, more faithfully maintains the appearance of the Indianized art of the Dvaravati phase (Plates 282, 283). It is a brick construction erected on a square base; and the five cubic bodies, progressively reduced in size, that rise in levels above this base are decorated on their faces by three niches containing images of Buddha. Furthermore, they display at each corner a bell-shaped structure that perhaps reproduces, on a reduced scale, the pinnacle in which the building must originally have terminated.

The socio-political structure of Siam was transformed under Thai domination, and inevitably the change was reflected in the artistic sphere. In the feudal society of the Thais, the chief—besides being lord and head of his family, of his vassals, and of the free men who owed him military service—had a religious authority that reinforced his political power, since it made him the ruling figure in the cult of the earth spirit, the *phi muong*. This tradition remotely echoed the Chinese system, and led to a form of royal cult very similar to that of the deified Khmer kings. It was not by accident that Ram Kamheng had placed on a hill near Sukhodaya the sacred image of a "Lord of the Summit," who rose above "all the spirits of the kingdom."[12]

The architecture of the Sukhodaya period abandons stone as its prime construction material and makes use of stucco-covered brick. A preference for two characteristic buildings is now manifest as well: the *prang* (or shrine), derived from the Khmer tower, is preceded by a hall with columns, which is covered by an imposing roof of wood and tiles. This hall, which contains the statue of Buddha, may even be large enough in size for use as a meeting place for monks. The second type is the stupa, often placed next to the sanctuary, in a form that either recalls the bell-shaped Indian structure transmitted from Burma or else imitates the tower-sanctuary of the Wat Kukut type. The structures and variations of the *prang* and the Thai stupa have their origin at Sukhodaya.

276. *Sukhodaya, Wat Srisvaya.*

280. *Ayuthia, Pu-kao Tong (Golden Mountain).*

Among the other kinds of monuments we find, those of the commemorative type are exemplified in the Wat Mahadhatu at Sukhodaya (Plate 275), characterized by a slender tower terminating in a bulb.

Before the total unification of Siam was completed, the Thai kingdoms produced various regional schools, among which the Lan Na, which imitates Singhalese examples, should be mentioned. The founding of Ayuthia and the unification of the country marked the merging of the two artistic traditions on Siamese territory—the Thai and the Khmer. From the beginning, the most important characteristic of this long phase was a return to Khmer models. Furthermore, the Thai rulers themselves would largely assimilate the organization of the Khmer court, an investiture that assumed, as we have noted, almost the nature of a deification. Of their old capital of Ayuthia, there remain today only slight traces of the foundations and brick walls of the palace. Still standing, however, are some of the ancient city's five hundred pagodas, which are scattered over the entire urban area. The southern part of the city once contained the royal chapel, or Wat P'ra Si Sanpet (fifteenth to eighteenth centuries), its nucleus formed by three large brick stupas in hemispherical form, covered in stucco and containing Buddhist relics (Plate 279); all three stupas had been placed on a terrace surrounded by a gallery.

In 1782, some years after the destruction of Ayuthia, a new capital was founded at Bangkok; the intent was to have it reproduce the appearance of the capital city that had been destroyed. The royal palace allows us to verify the survival of certain architectural forms elaborated by the Thais. The Wat P'ra Keo, a Buddhist temple of precious stones (Plates 288, 289), is formed by a sanctuary with a rectangular plan, with concave roofs and pronounced slopes, covered in brightly colored tiles. This type of roof is common to any meeting hall, whether it be the one intended for monks (*bot*) or that built for laymen (*vihan*); inside there may be only one nave or three. The statue of Buddha was placed at the end opposite the entrance. The Wat P'ra Keo is surrounded by a cloister; to the northwest a *chedi* (cetiya) was erected, in a bell form derived from the Singhalese stupa. It rises from a base surmounted by a small colonnade and a bell-shaped structure, on which rests the spire, composed of diminishing concentric rings. To the north, we find a *mondop* (mandapa), square in plan and formed by a cubic mass crowned by small diminishing levels and topped by a spire. Finally, to the northeast, there rises the temple where the statues of kings were preserved. It is a *prasat* derived from the Khmers, similar in its plan to a Greek cross, surmounted by superimposed roofs and enclosed by a slender *prang*—the final, stylized, Siamese result of the Khmer tower.

283. *Lamphun, Wat Kukut.*
284. *Lop Buri, Wat Mahadhatu (Monastery of the Great Relic).*

285. *Lop Buri, Brah Prang Sam Yot.*
286. *Nagara Pathama, Brah Pathama.*
287. *Nagara Pathama, Monastery of Brah Padona.*

◁ 288. *Bangkok, Wat P'ra Keo, Royal Chapel of the Emerald Buddha.*

289. *Bangkok, courtyard of the Royal Chapel of the Emerald Buddha.*
290. *Bangkok, Jetavanarama (Wat Po).*

Laos

The first great Laotian kingdom was Lang Ch'ang, founded in the fourteenth century by Fa Ngum (1353–1373), who had grown up at Angkor and was the son-in-law of the king of Cambodia. Fa Ngum summoned a group of Khmer monks and craftsmen to his court immediately after his coronation, and the stable political order of the country that followed was the result of his initiative. A state emerged that hinged on two centers of culture: Luangprabang in the north, where the influence of the Chiengmai Thais and later of the Burmese was to prevail; and Vientiane, the southern city where the Khmer heritage would predominate and the artistic impact of Ayuthia would be most felt. The geographical structure of the region, constituted by the narrow Mekong Valley, hindered the formation of a truly unified society, and as a result the Thais of Laos never progressed beyond the stage of small feudal mountain principalities. The harsh realities of incessant internal struggles, particularly violent at the beginning of the eighteenth century, and wars with Burma and Siam, left little time for the development of art. We might say that the fall of Vieng Chan in 1778 and later destruction at the hands of the Siamese in 1828 constituted a blow that would still it for the time being.[13]

The art of this area is very akin to that of Siam, as is only natural, given the similar origin of the two peoples and their common religion—Hinayana Buddhism. The absence of a central political authority is especially reflected in its architecture, wherein the use of light and easily perishable materials predominated. As a result, remains are very scarce and do not allow us to follow in any complete fashion the development of this particular art. We can note, however, that its chief architectural types are: (1) the Buddhist monastery or wat, in which the essential construction is the cult hall or meeting hall (*bot* or *vihan*); (2) the *th'at*, which replaces the stupa and is a reliquary connected to the wat; (3) the chapels and libraries similarly connected to the wat.

The tower-sanctuary (*prasat* or *kalan*), so widespread in Khmer and Cham art, is practically nonexistent in Laos; the divinity is offered to the devotion of the faithful in a building that combines the characteristics of a temple open to the worshiper and a shrine with walls and roof of brick. Moreover, while constructions in Java, Champa, and Cambodia are often very ancient, the oldest pagodas in Laos generally go back little more than two centuries. As for the absence of the tower-sanctuary, it seems strange that only Laos, among all Indianized countries, did not make use of this type of architecture. Parmentier[14] believes that the tower-sanctuary could not have been lacking in the Laotian wooden architecture of ancient times. It is his opinion that political conditions in the country prevented its being translated into stone, and that this is

291. *Luangprabang, Wat Chieng T'ong.*
292. *Vieng Chan, Wat P'ra Keo, meeting hall.*

293. *Tran Ninh, Wat Ban P'ong.*
294. *Vieng Chan, P'ya Wat, perspective section (from Groslier, 1961).*

why no traces remain unless perhaps in the Wat Th'at in Luangprabang and in the *th'at* of the Wat Xtaphon at Muong Kuk.

Those constructions that have come down to us testify to the use of brickwork cut in large blocks, with the bricks being joined by means of a lime mortar. The vaulted roof was frequently used for small constructions; the saddle roof and the four-slope roof are characteristic of Laos. The so-called keel of the saddle roof is placed in accordance with the main axis of the hall, and the slopes descend to protrude beyond the walls. In the roof with four superimposed slopes, the two lower ones—which project considerably with respect to the four walls—rest on columns that form an actual gallery or veranda. Inside, the hall (or *vihan*) is divided into three naves; here the columns act to support the roof directly.

The *vihan*, which constitutes the basic part of the monastery, can be any one of the following: the simple hall, enclosed by a saddle roof; the hall with veranda, covered by a four-slope roof; and finally the hall with a circular nave, whose roof is supported by the outer wall. One or three approaching doors give access to the hall, which contains on an altar at the rear the statue of Buddha; an interior space was necessary for meetings between monks and the faithful. The *th'at*, which takes the place of the stupa or the chaitya, displays an extraordinary variety of solutions, but always the presence of common characteristics is easily discernible. The *th'at*, which is fully constructed in masonry, contains between its socle and top an element derived from the stupa that may vary in form from hemispherical to bell-shaped or bulbous.

The other architectural types that appear in Laos are chapels in masonry, and libraries, built of wood or sometimes of wood and brick, raised on a high socle.

The three styles that can be distinguished correspond to the three provinces into which the country is divided: (1) the Tran Ninh style, easily identified by the enormous lateral development of the roof and scant height of the walls (Plate 293); (2) the Luangprabang style, distinctive for its lesser use of masonry and less imposing roofs (Plate 291); (3) the Vieng Chan style, characterized by high walls, roofs that are not especially ample, and vast halls (Plates 292, 294).

We might examine in particular the Th'at Luang in Vieng Chan, which is also important for its antiquity (it was founded in 1586). The temple, which imitates contemporary structures in Siam, is erected on an enclosed base. The mass of the stupa, constituted by a hemispherical section on a square base, ends at its four corners in elegant spires, supported by a band of lotus petals. The base of the stupa is surrounded by buildings on a reduced scale, reproducing the base of the stupa, which develops outward. The enclosure is constituted by a cloister, opening on each side into chapels, with the southern one serving as an entrance to the gallery. The outer cloister of the full perimeter wall opened on its four sides into four pavilions.

Vietnam

Archaeological findings in Vietnam begin from around the fourth century B.C. with a wealth of bronze art. Its most important traces, bronze drums that show an obvious Chinese influence, have been found in the Dong-Son area. The Tonkin Delta was a Chinese colony until the tenth century, a subjugation that not only gave the country its social and economic structure but also profoundly influenced its art. According to Vietnamese tradition, two kingdoms—both partly legendary—existed at the beginning of the country's history. The first, known as Xichquy, extended northward as far as the Blue River; the second, Van-lang, more or less corresponded to the actual Tonkin. The first historical kingdom, Au-lac, falls between 257 and 208 B.C. Its capital, Co-lao, has been unearthed, in the form of an immense enclosure whose imposing vestiges have not yet been fully explored.

From 214 B.C. to A.D. 938 Tonkin, divided into three border regions, formed part of the Chinese Empire and felt its influence not only politically but culturally as well. The official language of the area was Chinese, which contributed decisively to making its culture even more Chinese. When a system of dams (built in a series of successive divisions) was created in the delta to encourage agricultural development, Chinese rule was thus established *ense et aratro*—by the sword and the plowshare. This irrigation system, with its series of diminishing basins, and its canals dividing the land geometrically into units and hamlets, indissolubly bound the Vietnamese to the needs imposed by this means of exploiting the soil, since such installations had to be constantly controlled. It also determined the structure of the Vietnamese village, a unit complete in itself, and capable of drawing all its subsistence from the rice fields.

There persisted, however, a deeply rooted cult of earth spirits, a fundamental religious element on which official Confucianism had little effect. The political structure of the country was that of a pyramid, with the Chinese emperor at the top; the least sign of weakness in the central power was accompanied by a breakdown in the political-administrative structure of the territory itself. The history of Vietnam is thus not the history of an empire or an ideology, but of small cells of farmers in search of arable land, who are prepared to move for that purpose with the support of the soldiers of the central power.[15]

In the tenth century the national Dinh dynasty (A.D. 868–980), taking advantage of the decadence of the T'ang emperors, seized power. One of its characteristics, as was true also of later dynasties, was a push toward the south, a drive that arose from Vietnamese cultivation of the

295. *Hoa-lu', den (dynastic temple) of Dinh.*
296. *So'n-tay, dinh (temple of tutelary deity) of Chu-quyen.*

lowlands. The people remained tied to the aforementioned cult of earth spirits, but since they were cut off from the sphere of Indianization, the king and the aristocratic class devoted themselves to Confucianism and Taoism.

At the beginning, there was no architecture to speak of—even though luxury objects worthy indeed of the name of art were produced —until the great fervor of Mahayana Buddhism spread into Vietnam from the China of the Six Dynasties and the T'ang. This new development gave rise during the ninth century to important monasteries, of which unfortunately almost nothing remains today. The terraced tower of Binh Son (Vinh-yen) was built under the Li dynasty during the twelfth century. It is adorned with terra-cotta coverings and medallions inspired by Chinese models of the period.

By 1225 the Vietnamese had begun to prevail over the Chams. Although they were arrested first by the Mongol menace, then by the Ming annexation of Tonkin, they finally succeeded in reasserting themselves as an independent force and annexed all of Champa. Under the Le dynasty (fifteenth to eighteenth centuries), they were truly successful in creating an empire. The Nguyen dynasty that was established in the year 1801, once it had resolved problems of internal opposition and resistance and unified the country, turned against the Thais. The French conquest of Indochina put an end to Vietnamese attempts at a total encirclement of Indianized Indochina.

Architecturally, the period of the Le dynasty proved to be the richest, and fortunately a great many of its works remain to attest the Vietnamese reworking of Chinese themes and elements. The most important of these are the royal tombs at Lam-so'n and the buildings at Hoa-lu' (Plate 295).

Of the art of the Nguyen dynasty, which begins in the nineteenth century with Gialong, its founder and first ruler, numerous architectural works remain. Except for the palace halls in Hué, they are all of a religious nature. Four types of buildings can be distinguished: the *dinh*, or temple of the tutelary deity of the village; the *chua*, or Buddhist temple; the *den*, or Taoist dynastic temple; and the *van-mieu*, or temple of Confucius. Each building is of wood, with a framework supported by columns that rest without being embedded on stone socles fixed in the ground. Their fundamental characteristic is their natural setting, the framing of the work by the landscape.

The *dinh*, built on piles, appears to recall the houses represented on the Dong-Son drums mentioned earlier. In this building the notables received visitors, deliberated on questions of common interest, and sacrificed to the tutelary deity; here literary contests and social life took place.[16] It is generally composed of two parallel wings—the rear one constructed with a forepart at its center that holds the altar of the

297. *Hué, royal tombs of Nguyen, detail.*

298. *Hué, mausoleum of Emperor Tu'-du'c.*
299. *Hué, tomb of Emperor Minh-mang.*

300. *Hué, tower of the Linh Mu pagoda.*
301. *Hué, eastern gate of the imperial city.* ▷

302. *Hué, imperial city; in the background, the Throne Room.*
303. *Hanoi, the Van-mieu (Temple of Literature).*

guardian spirit—and large halls for banquets and meetings. Adjacent buildings contain kitchens and a place for animal sacrifice.

The form of the *chua* can best be described as that of an H lying on its side, surrounded on three sides by loggias and by a courtyard on the fourth. The H-shaped part comprises the actual sanctuary, the incense hall, and the hall where the faithful assemble, while the loggias and courtyard contain statues of bonzes (Buddhist monks). Outwardly, the *den* is similar to the *chua*, but inside a statue or symbol is enclosed in a shrine that is impossible to enter. The *van-mieu*, dedicated to Confucius, is a vast complex of buildings arranged within an enclosure.

The imperial palace complex in Hué, built by Gialong and showing a strong Chinese influence, deserves particular mention. The Hué complex (Plates 297–302) is constructed in obedience to all the geomantic rituals that were thought to ensure the presence of beneficent influences for the dignitary whose home it would be. Surrounded by hills to protect its gates from evil spirits, the palace is a series of enclosures that increasingly diminish until one reaches the Throne Room, heart of the construction and of the empire itself. Each courtyard contains a reconstruction in miniature of the entire universe, a microcosm of rocks, trees, and lakes. The architectural structure of the Hué complex does not allow itself to be deciphered; to gain knowledge of it would be tantamount to controlling it magically. We are indebted to Groslier for his excellent interpretation: "In fact the imperial residence would seem to be an ideogram written on the earth by the Emperor-Organizer of the world, for the eyes alone of the Emperor of Heaven, from whom he has received his powers."[17]

Arcangela Santoro

Introduction

We wish to point out, first of all, that our title, "Himalayan Region," does not correspond in any way to the present political situation of the region we are about to consider. It has instead been chosen for geographical and historical reasons. Kashmir, Nepal, and Tibet occupy within the Himalayan chain a position that has endowed them with common characteristics, and they have shared for more or less brief periods similar vicissitudes. We must take into account also that from the religious and artistic standpoint these three countries—at least upon their emergence on the plane of civilization as we know it—found a common matrix in historical India.

Obviously, the Indian influence did not prevent the Himalayan world from developing independently the plastic and figurative arts, but constitutes instead the model to which we will have to refer often if we are to understand the historical and artistic events of Kashmir, Nepal, and Tibet. In the architectural sphere, this phenomenon is particularly evident in such religious monuments as the stupa, monastery, and Hindu temple. Since these structures were intended to discharge a given function—precisely that of the cult—a display of determined elements of construction is inevitable. We will thus have similar structures in a world where, unlike the West, the symbolic value is much more important than the aesthetic one. Of course, artistic sensibility and religious symbolism change from region to region due to different influences and varying geographical and historical conditions; there exists also a local substratum that does not always spontaneously allow a transition to the claims and conditioning effects of new cultures. We cannot, therefore, expect these similar structures to be identical.

On the other hand, the panorama of so-called lay or civil architecture is more varied, even though it too—and perhaps to the same degree—is governed by elements extrinsic to pure aesthetic value and is subject to laws that keep it closely tied to political, economic, and/or military factors.

In this chapter, which is proposed essentially as a history of monuments in the Himalayan region, we will therefore follow the two strands representing religious and civil constructions—given the limits (unfortunately still fairly narrow even today) set by present-day archaeological research and scientific studies.

Kashmir

The name Kashmir (*Kasmira* in Sanskrit) indicates the region comprising the valley of the Jhelum River and its tributaries, as well as the inner slopes of the mountain chains that determine its boundaries. The geographical position of Kashmir, a pleasant and fertile valley

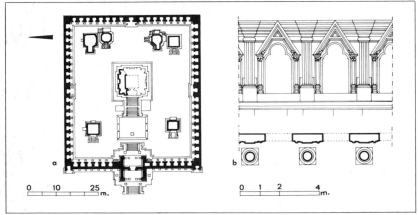

completely surrounded by mountains, helped in the past to protect it from all-too-frequent aggression, and at the same time to isolate it partially from the outside world. Its fortunate physical situation had considerable importance in the course of the historical vicissitudes through which the country passed. Insofar as architecture is concerned, it contributed to no small degree to the creation of works that in some way seem to reflect the serenity enjoyed by the country and the magnificence of the natural environment in which it is immersed.

The history of the "Happy Valley" of Kashmir has its roots in legend, but the folktales related by its people are echoed by a number of respected chroniclers of ancient and recent times. The story of its origin was thought believable even by the Chinese pilgrim Hsüan-tsang, considered by many, because of the prestige he enjoyed, a highly authoritative source. In remote times, say the Kashmiris, their valley was submerged by an immense lake in which a monstrous dragon lived. The good spirits sought to destroy the creature and eventually they succeeded. When they drained the lake that had been his home, they brought to light the verdant valley that we know today as Kashmir.

The chronicler Kalhana, in compiling the *Rājataranginī* (the dynastic chronicle of Kashmir), places a series of fifty-two kings, who must also be considered of legendary origin, at the beginning of Kashmir's history. Historical outlines begin to emerge more precisely with the appearance of a ruler by the name of Gonandiya III. The Gonandiya dynasty was destined to survive until the later advent of the Karkota dynasty; its duration is not specified by Kalhana and cannot be deduced from other sources. It appears, however, that Kashmir was part of the Maurya Empire during the reign of the great Asoka, and of the Kushan Empire; Kanishka, the most famous Kushan ruler, is reported to have sponsored in Kashmir the second great Buddhist council recorded in the sacred texts. Unfortunately, it would later fall into the hands of the Hephthalites, the people Buddhist sources blame for huge massacres and destruction in the whole northwest territory of India, which suffered harsh domination under these so-called White Huns.

Finally, in A.D. 622, Durlabhavardhana founded the Karkota dynasty, whose most illustrious representative was to be Lalitaditya Muktapida (A.D. 724–c. 760), a ruler whom the German scholar Hermann Goetz places in the ranks of such great men of history as Alexander, Charlemagne, and Napoleon. Lalitaditya's reign marks an important turning point in the history of Kashmir: its territorial expansion during his tenure was astonishing. The *Rājataranginī* mentions conquests in India as far as the Deccan, in Afghanistan, Tibet, and up to the northern confines of the Central Asian caravan routes at Kucha and Turfan. Lalitaditya's greatest contribution, however, was the impulse

he provided in his homeland for the development of all activities, among which those of an artistic and cultural nature occupied a privileged place.

His death, amid the snows of Manchuria, where he is said to have been overwhelmed by enormous enemy forces, was perhaps a historical reality; certainly it is in accord with the myth that grew up around his person.

As so often happens, after the death of Lalitaditya the dynasty languished. The Utpala dynasty that followed was, however, distinguished by two strong and purposeful rulers, Avantivarman (A.D. 856–883) and Sankaravarman (A.D. 883–902). With their passing, however, a slow but inevitable decline set in, both political and cultural, which was to make possible the Muslim conquest of 1339, which the Karkota dynasty in its beginnings had so brilliantly avoided.

The effects of the historical events here summarized are apparent in the various phases of Kashmir architecture. The chronological sequence of the monuments that have come down to us is anything but certain, and scholars—while finding themselves in agreement in attributing a particular group of works to a given historical period—place each monument differently with respect to the supposed line of development of the Kashmir architectural style. We will therefore limit ourselves to a subdivision along general lines (following the criterion already adopted by Percy Brown) and progress through the most significant historical phases.

Local Kashmir tradition would have it that King Asoka himself had gone to the valley and founded the first Buddhist complex on the outskirts of the present Srinagar. But since nothing has been preserved from the Mauryan period, we will consider first that span of time from A.D. 200 to the rise of the Karkota dynasty, which is indeed characterized by monuments inspired by Buddhism. From this first phase of the Kashmir past, only the ruins of Ushkur and Harvan remain today. In these cities, it has been possible to single out a group of buildings connected with the cult: a stupa, a chaitya or sanctuary, a monastery, and other religious structures.

Two highly interesting conclusions can be drawn from a study of the remains at Harvan: the first regarding the structure of the Kashmir stupa in the first centuries of the era under study; the second concerning construction techniques.

The Harvan stupa has not been entirely preserved. All that remains is the base with three successive orders and an access stairway, erected at the center of a quadrangular space. Nevertheless, it is believed that it resembled the numerous images of stupas found on stamped terra-cotta plaques. The dome was thus crushed at the center, and the traditional "umbrellas" of Indian models were replaced by a pyramidal structure

with thirteen levels. The chaitya, on the other hand, was closer to the Indian type, preserving the apse plan illustrated so magnificently in India at Karli and Bhaja. It is evident, however, that this plan did not enjoy excessive favor on Kashmir soil for no further trace of it is found in the medieval period.

The construction technique differed from the methods employed in neighboring regions, but was simple enough in its use of pebbles mixed with a mortar of mud. Later, in the sixth to seventh century, the pebbles were replaced by larger, unsquared stones, and the interstices thus created were filled with small stones. To obviate the appearance of a surface decidedly disagreeable to the eye, both walls and floors were covered by decorated terra-cotta panels, which were often little masterpieces of applied art. Much as the use of such coverings may produce the impression of a well-developed art, the building techniques of this period were obviously still at a rather archaic level.

It is thus surprising to discover that only a century later local architects were such masters of the technical method of constructing buildings with perfectly squared and well-finished blocks, held together by cement mortar or even by the help of metal hooks. This change in building technique was accompanied by an intensification of construction activity. Between the seventh and the tenth centuries the Buddhist complexes of Parihasapura and Pandrenthan were built, as well as the temples at Loduv, Narastan, and Martand, and finally those at Vantipur and Patan, to mention only the most noted.

To what do we owe this exceptional renewal, and what were the stylistic elements that characterized the second phase of Kashmir architecture? Undoubtedly, Lalitaditya's conquests—whose effect was a sudden increase in the national wealth and in the possibilities for more heterogeneous contacts—played an important role. Equally influential was the sovereign's wish to erect monuments that would be both votive offerings to the divinity and tangible signs of his own glory.

The great Karkota ruler, in the course of his expeditions, had seen the monuments adorning the capitals of conquered kingdoms, and certainly many artists must have joined his retinue, bringing with them to Kashmir a rich store of knowledge and experience. The problem is thus one of discerning in the various monuments of the medieval period what has been borrowed and how much is an original contribution by the local culture.

When we compare the Buddhist monuments of Parihasapura and Pandrenthan to those of the previous phase, certain structural changes are discernible. The Cankuna stupa—which takes its name from Lalitaditya's Tocharian prime minister, formerly a functionary at the T'ang court and an intelligent collaborator in the expansionist policy of his king—has a square base and two terraces, with differentiated levels

310. *Patan (Kashmir), temple of Sankaragaurisvara.*

311. *Pandrenthan, temple of Siva Rilhanesvara, section, elevation, and plan*
(Enciclopedia Universale dell'Arte).

for the ritual circumambulation (*pradaksinapatha*). The chaitya (also at Parihasapura) has now abandoned the apse plan and adopted a square one, even for the inner cell designed to hold the sacred image. The progressive relinquishing of the geometric figure of the circle as a basic structure, in favor of the square, must also have occurred in the sphere of Brahmanic architecture. One notes in fact that the Sankaracarya temple, which may be among the oldest of the Lalitaditya period (though scholars are not in full agreement on this point), is square on the outside and circular within, while later temples are definitely oriented toward the quadrangular form. While it cannot be excluded that some of these modifications should be attributed to changes in ritual, most of them certainly came about for aesthetic reasons.

It has been pointed out that medieval Kashmir architecture took Gandhara architecture as its model, in particular such important Buddhist monuments in the Swat Valley as the Guniyar monastery and the Takht-i-Bahi stupa. It is sufficient to compare the latter with the Temple of the Sun at Martand (Plates 304, 305) to be convinced of this. The general arrangement—that is, the open quadrangular space surrounded by chapels—is the same. In the center, the stupa is to one side, and the cell or *garbha griha* to the other. An examination of the individual structures, however, reveals some differences. At Martand, in fact, we already find the three elements that can truly be considered intrinsic to Kashmir architecture: the trilobate arch, the triangular tympanum (sometimes broken), and the pyramidal roof. The first two embellishments were also known to Gandhara artists, and it is to the credit of the Kashmiris that they were able to bring them together in such a way as to form a decorative element of refined taste.

Reduced to such terms, the differences would seem minimal and would serve to support the assertions of those who are convinced of a more or less direct Gandhara derivation. But, apart from the fact that several centuries lie between the two monuments cited—during which time such events as the invasion by the White Huns surely brought about an interruption in cultural exchanges between the two regions—it seems to us that the Temple of the Sun at Martand is of a completely different order from the Takht-i-Bahi stupa.

In fact, both Percy Brown and Hermann Goetz maintain that a Classical derivation is to be seen in Kashmir architecture, not one borrowed through Gandhara, as has hitherto been held, but adopted directly. At this point, however, the positions of the two scholars diverge, with Brown putting the accent on the contribution of Greco-Roman art, and Goetz on that of Syriac-Byzantine art. The second hypothesis is to be preferred, not only for obvious considerations of chronology, but also because Kashmir architecture never achieves Classical levels of harmony and equilibrium. Its Classical elements rest in

312. *Pandrenthan, temple of Siva Rilhanesvara.*

313. *Perspective sketches of Nepalese architectural elements: a) Bodhnath shrine, elevation; b) type of multiple wooden roof for Saivite temple (Enciclopedia Universale dell'Arte).*

314. *Chabahil (Patan), stupa of Carumati.* ▷

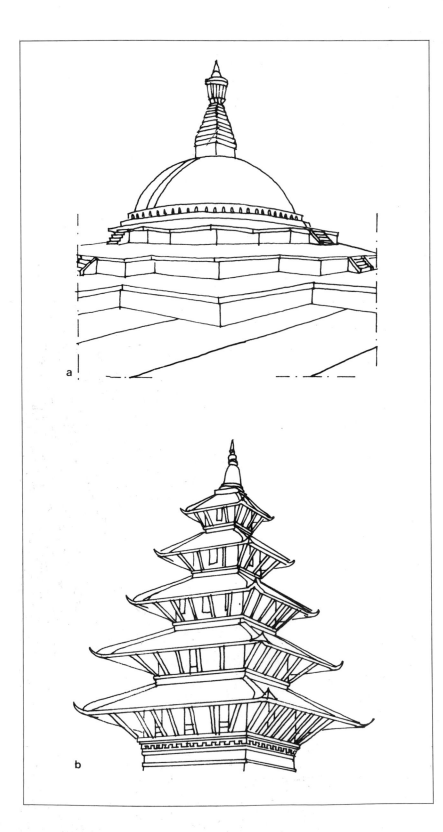

a

b

its technique of construction and use of an "almost Doric" capital, whose presence gave rise to the first doubts about a direct derivation from Gandhara, which favored the Corinthian capital. The Martand temple, in fact, is not free of imbalances and imperfections. The local artists themselves must have been aware of these flaws, for in a later period they were partly eliminated. The Avantisvami temple, for example, is a less imposing but undoubtedly more perfect work. Avantisvami (Plate 307)—the temple at Vantipur dedicated to Vishnu—and the Sankaragaurisvara (Plate 310) and Sugandhesa temples at Patan represent the moment of perfect equilibrium, the crystallization of the theoretical ideal of Kashmir builders.

The design of the Avantisvami temple is similar to that of Martand, but here an inner and an outer colonnade enrich the sixty chapels surrounding the central courtyard. The outer colonnade runs along the perimeter wall and harmoniously connects the outer façade of the building, which acts as an entrance, with the sacred enclosure (placed slightly to the rear). The central open space of the sanctuary contains a pool for ritual ablutions, and at the corners four small lesser temples.

Later temples—except perhaps for the twelfth-century one of Siva at Pandrenthan (Plates 311, 312), which is characterized by the "lantern" dome typical of Central Asia—wearily repeat the same motifs and remain to attest a process of decadence that becomes progressively more evident up to the moment of the Muslim conquest.

Nepal

The present independent state of Nepal includes a good part of the southern slope of the Himalayas. It is bordered on the north by high mountains and extends southward toward the *tarai*, a plain still largely covered by jungle.

But the heart of Nepal, the area inhabited since antiquity and which until the advent of the Gurkhali dynasty also corresponded to the political confines of the state, is the basin formed by the Bhagmati Valley. Nepal, like Kashmir, was favored on diverse occasions by its geographical position in the pursuit of an isolationist policy that shielded it from the military ambitions of the two colossi pressing against its borders—Tibet and India.

Local tradition relates that Asoka, the "sovereign dear to the gods," was the first illustrious visitor to the land that was the birthplace of Buddha, the Enlightened One: the discovery of a column with an inscription by this ruler in Lumbini Park on the outskirts of Kapilavastu would seem to support this version. Nevertheless, it remains difficult to establish whether Asoka's journey took place solely for devotional reasons, or rather, as seems more likely, these were simply a screen to conceal the king's intention to inspect his distant dominions.

We have no other information on events preceding the rule of the Licchavi dynasty except that concerning the court of the Sakya princes. It was from this line, which had its capital at Kapilavastu—present-day Tiraulakot, where excavations have recently been carried out—that Prince Siddhartha Gautama, called Sakyamuni or Buddha, was born; he spent part of his earthly life nearby (sixth to c. fifth centuries B.C.). The city soon fell into ruin, and the Chinese pilgrims Fa-hsien and Hsüan-tsang, respectively of the fifth and seventh centuries A.D., already found nothing but the foundations of a few houses and a number of holy buildings, stupas, temples, and monasteries. Today, on the supposed site of Buddha's birth, one can see a chapel and the Asoka column that we have already mentioned.

Certain Buddhist monuments on the outskirts of Patan would also seem to belong to the third century B.C., the most notable being the Piprahva stupa and the Chabahil complex, where today it is still possible to admire the great stupa named for Carumati (Plate 314). The legend of Carumati describes her as a daughter of Asoka who settled in Nepal, where she gave considerable encouragement to the religious activity of the region and promoted the construction of numerous holy buildings.

The Chabahil stupa provides a point of departure for describing Nepalese variations on this type of monument, so important in the history of Indian architecture, even if there is some question whether the stupa should not be considered a work of sculpture rather than of architecture. In the beginning, the Nepalese stupa adhered sufficiently to its Indian prototypes. It was dominated by a great hemispherical dome —with chapels at intervals—on which a plinth (*harmikā*) supported the final pyramidal part with its thirteen steps (as a variant we also find thirteen diminishing circles). The *harmikā* is characterized by the presence of an outline of a human face, in which the large painted eyes are especially conspicuous.

These additions are not accidental and correspond precisely to Buddhist symbology; the thirteen levels surely stand for the thirteen heavens, the long path that one must pursue to reach enlightenment. As for the meaning of the painted eyes on the *harmikā*, opinions are not always in agreement. They are generally held to represent the Buddha as "he who sees all," an aspect of the Enlightened One especially felt by the local population, since it had been grafted onto a previous sun cult. There is, however, Volwahsen's suggestive hypothesis, according to which this usage would derive from an exact representation of the stupa as Purusa, the primordial human being. In Indian architecture, in fact, the relation between the structure of the human body and architectural structure is extremely evident and is referred to in the texts. The stupa would thus not be an exception to this rule, and in this case

◁ 317. *Katmandu, temple of Taleju Devi.*

318. *Patan (Nepal), temple of the Mahabuddha, detail of a tower.*
319. *Patan (Nepal), temple of the Mahabuddha, detail of a tower.*

the presence of a human face on the four sides of the plinth can be logically explained.

Thus, with its initial structure remaining fixed, the Nepalese stupa may articulate itself differently, both in the base and in the cupola. In the Bodhnath stupa, for example (Plate 315), the base is constituted by two large terraces with differentiated levels, while in the so-called Five Stupas in Patan the dome is not perfectly hemispherical; it bulges at the point of juncture with the lower wall, itself curvilinear, which acts as a connecting element between the *anda* (cupola) and the base. Finally, the Svayambhunatha stupa (Plate 316), in addition to the enrichment of its *harmikā* by metal and ivory inserts, displays four pointed panels placed in such a way as to correspond with the four cardinal points, with sculptured images of the five Dhyani Buddhas.

Nepalese history in the first centuries of our era is marked by the progressive rise of the Licchavis, who must have enjoyed a certain prestige even beyond the national borders, since Chandragupta, the founder of the Gupta Empire in India, asked to marry one of its princesses. Amsuvarman (A.D. 585–650), the founder of the succeeding Thakuri dynasty, was in close contact with the famous Tibetan sovereign Sron-btsan-sgam-po, to whom he had given his daughter in marriage. This Thakuri princess is an important figure in Tibetan history, since some of the credit for spreading Buddhism in court circles has been attributed to her. The fact is all the more significant when one remembers that in Nepal, contrary to what might have been expected, it was Hinduism that prevailed over Buddhism.

The country's political history also indicates the path to follow in singling out major artistic trends; indeed, in the period we will call Licchavi-Thakuri, a strong Indian influence made itself felt, especially in the eastern regions dominated first by the Pala dynasty and later by the Sena. Moreover, we know that during the following century the country passed under Tibetan rule, which was prolonged for a period of time that still cannot be clearly specified. There occurs almost a historical void, an obscure period in Nepalese history lasting virtually until the thirteenth century and yielding only fragmentary and sometimes conflicting information.

Around 1200 a new dynasty, the Malla, rose to power. It was destined to last until 1768, when the country was shattered by the conquering impetus of the Gurkha sovereign Prithvi-Narayan-sah, who founded the dynasty that is still in power. As we see, Nepal remained untouched by the Muslim expansion, and to this distinction it owes the preservation of that predominantly Hindu character, unchanged over the centuries, that still imparts great fascination to the country.

The Malla dynasty encouraged the formation of large urban

320. *Patan (Nepal), temple of the Mahabuddha, detail of a tower.*
321. *Patan (Nepal), façade of a Hindu temple.*

322. *Patan (Nepal), view of Darbar Square.*
323. *Patan (Nepal), view of Darbar Square.*
324. *Bhadgaon, temple of Bhairava.* ▷

centers, as is attested by its three great capitals, Katmandu (Kantipur), Patan, and Bhadgaon, erected at a short distance from each other and dominating the communication roads with the interior and with India. These three cities have in common not only their function, but also their arrangement of the principal buildings and quarters. The center of Patan, for example, is constituted by a public square, around which rise the royal residence and the administrative offices. The square, which was used for religious and civil ceremonies, was often embellished by columns with sculptural groups representing rulers or divinities of the Hindu pantheon. It thus became the crossroads, the true center of convergence for all city life. It would therefore be obvious that the streets diverged from it, extending themselves radially to divide the various quarters of the city. This urban structure is extremely interesting sociologically as well, especially when one considers that each quarter was inhabited by a particular social class and all converged toward the Darbar Square (Plates 322, 323) almost confusedly, as though the builders' single concern was to maintain the connection with the center.

In any case, the city as a whole is picturesque, as is the individual building. The typical house of the Newaris, the ancient ethnic group that originally dominated the region, is built around an inner courtyard, where all domestic activities took place. The building, in brick, generally includes three stories. Each story serves a different function and is therefore articulated in a different way. The façade displays a use of full and empty spaces that—though chiefly dictated by technical requirements—does not lack aesthetic effects. The first story is usually lightened by the presence of a portico that creates an area of shadow, while the second, in its compactness, reflects the light in full. The flat surface is interrupted, however, by the window element, typical of Nepalese architecture and justly renowned for the exquisite delicacy of its execution. The very wide outer frame is worked in wood, with projecting jambs, an upper cornice of considerable dimensions, and a much smaller lower one. A curvilinear fillet, sometimes further embellished by carved figures, may be added to these elements. The window space is filled by a metal grating. Another area of shadow is created at the third story, and is defined by the slope of the roof, supported by a series of richly carved beams.

To conclude the subject of civil architecture, one might say that in Nepal a taste for decoration clearly prevails over structural considerations, and it is the effect of light and plastic form that is chiefly sought. Thus, extreme care is sometimes reserved for details, as can be seen in the windows or the splendid doors of principal buildings such as, for example, the Golden Door of Bhadgaon (Plate 326); or even in constructions created for eminently practical purposes, such as fountains.

Religious architecture clearly complies with different requirements, and is, as always, conditioned by its function. The element common to all temples is the square cell containing the divine image, surrounded by a dense colonnade (which partially hides it from view) and erected on a series of diminishing plinths. One approaches by a staircase flanked by zoomorphic and anthropomorphic figures. The distinguishing element, on the other hand, is the roof, which may be either of the sikhara or pagoda type.

Both of these terms require a word of explanation here. The sikhara roof, borrowed from India, consists of a very accentuated elevation of the upper part following a curvilinear tendency, and probably derives from an ancient roof obtained by the joining of four long rushes laid over a quadrangular structure. The pagoda is the well-known system requiring a series of roofs of decreasing size supported by oblique beams. This type is especially characteristic of Far Eastern regions, but its origin may well have been in India. Some scholars maintain that it is derived from the succession of umbrellas on the stupa; and others, as Percy Brown has shown, from Indian models in the Malabar and Kanara regions. Worthy examples of one and the other type still adorn the sacred buildings of the three capitals. The Nyatpola temple in Patan (built in the first years of the eighteenth century during the reign of Bhupatindramalla) and that of Vatasaladevi in Bhadgaon are two examples.

A study of Nepalese architecture is not complete without mention of the Krishna Mandir temple in Patan. Relatively late and constructed in stone (it should be remembered that the material primarily used here is brick, in the most varied dimensions), it is composed of three spacious superimposed colonnades, enlivened by the presence of chapels that help to impart to it a sense of airiness. It possesses an almost "classical" rhythm that the architecture of the region had never known before.

The Gurkhali architecture of the nineteenth and twentieth centuries, while remaining within the fold of tradition and thus maintaining the archaic atmosphere that pervades the royal cities, often avails itself of the influence of Western architects, particularly French and Italian.

Tibet

Tibet's geographical position as the highest country in the world has often been the inspiration for such poeticisms as the "roof of the world," the "country of snows," and others equally appropriate. Indeed, Tibet is an extended plateau averaging about 16,000 feet and covered with snow for long periods. The country's economy is based essentially on cattle raising, since agriculture is profitable only in the valleys adjacent to the great rivers—the Indus, the Sutlej, and the

◁ 328. *Bhadgaon, Nyatpola Deval, temple of Isvari.*

329. *Spiti Valley, Tabo monastery with its eight temples: a) gtsung-lag-k'an; b) dkyil-k'an; c) gser-k'an; d) aBrom-ston lha-k'an; e) sgo-k'an; f) Byams-pa'i lha-k'an; g) aBrom-ston lha-k'an; h) dkar-abyun* (Enciclopedia Universale dell'Arte).
330. *Spiti Valley, Tabo monastery, view of the temples.*
331. *Spiti Valley, Tabo monastery, view of the temples.*

Brahmaputra. In short, it is a land that offers its inhabitants scant possibilities for survival, one that chiefly lends itself to the nomadic or semi-nomadic life of its shepherds and livestock breeders.

Obviously, such an economy involves suitable social structures. The archaeological and literary sources are not of much help in reconstructing Tibetan history, but it is not unlikely that the early Tibet of our era was based on a feudal society, the heritage of a more ancient division into territorially settled clans or tribes.

Tibetan religious activity plays an equally important role in the country's history, and to some degree it too has been favored by the Tibetan economy. Primitive Tibetan religion (Bonpo) hinged in fact on shamanistic practices, linked to propitiatory rites involving the magical powers of the celestial and infernal worlds. It was a religion that often went over into superstition, but it was followed by the Tibetans for many centuries even after the introduction of Buddhism.

The beginning of the seventh century A.D. brought to Tibet the demise of the existing political order and the rise of the monarchy. This new concentration of power in the hands of a single individual permitted the realization of undertakings (such as national reunification and territorial expansion) that would have been impossible for the extremely divided local potentates. The realities of the situation would indicate that the first two sovereigns, K'ri-slon-brtsan (A.D. 590–620) and Sron-btsan-sgam-po (A.D. 620–649), worked hard to keep the feudal aristocracy under control; the struggle between the monarchy and the local aristocracy, sharpened also by the religious factor, remained one of the salient characteristics of Tibetan history.

Meanwhile, Buddhism had penetrated Tibet with the advent of Sron-btsan-sgam-po's marriages to two princesses, one Nepalese, the other Chinese, who were followers of this faith. Although it was at first limited to the sphere of the court, Buddhism received considerable impetus from another famous ruler, K'ri-sron-lde-brtsan (A.D. 755–797). It was he who declared it the state religion, promoted the creation of monastic centers, and invited the magician Padmasambhava to Tibet. This thaumaturge from the Swat Valley founded the sect of the Red Caps (later to be opposed by the Yellow Caps). K'ri-sron-lde-brtsan's next step was to embark on a wide-ranging expansionist policy abroad, which eventually led to his occupation of Changan, the T'ang capital. With his passing, the monarchy began to decline, and we have only the vaguest information about the period from the middle of the ninth century through all of the tenth. A rebirth—a religious one, but religion and politics are often difficult to distinguish in Tibet—occurred from the eleventh to the twelfth centuries, as a result of missionary work by Atisa, a scholar from the Indian university of Vikramasila, and his disciples. The subsequent Mongol invasion deprived Tibet of its

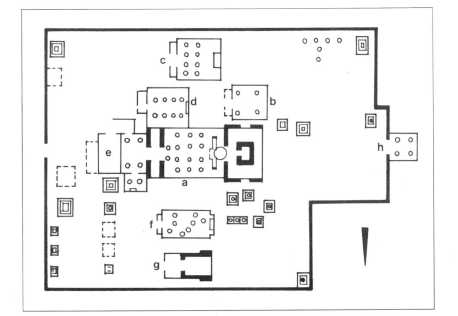

332. *Spiti Valley, Tabo monastery, stupa.*
333. *Spiti Valley, Tabo monastery, façade of the Du-vong.*

334. *Yarlung Valley, upper part of a chorten.*

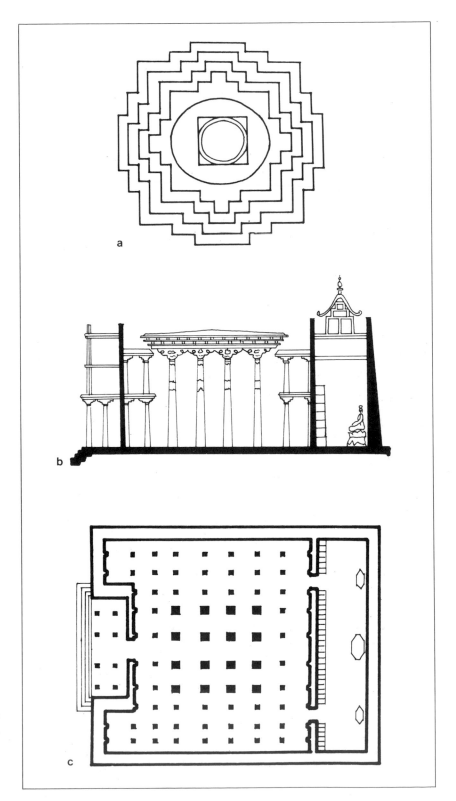

335. *Buildings in the Tibetan area: a) Gyantse, the kumbum; b) and c) Tibetan temple, longitudinal section and ground plan* (Enciclopedia Universale dell'Arte).

independence and tied its destiny to that of a foreign power, whether of the Mongols themselves or of China proper. In the sixteenth century, the Dalai Lamas created the so-called Lamaistic state, which was to last until the 1950s, when Tibet passed definitely into Chinese hands.

The conclusion that can be drawn from this very brief historical panorama is that life in Tibet hinges on the religious factor. If it is true, as Petech says, that Tibetan chronicles are "stories of the clergy, and biographies are hagiographies," then architecture and the figurative arts are no exception.

Tibetan religious architecture looks principally toward two types of monuments, the chorten and the temple. The chorten derives from the stupa but, compared to its model, involves modifications in structure and function (Plate 334). It has a square base (throne), four steps, and a pot-shaped cupola of modest size, on which is superimposed a pyramidal structure composed of thirteen umbrellas or wheels, then a half-moon, a sun, and a pinnacle. These five elements can be schematized in five geometric figures that correspond to the five elements of Vajrayana mysticism, the five mystic syllables, the five colors, and the five mystic parts of the human body.

The chorten (a term that Tucci defines as "a receptacle, a support for offerings") emerges as a funerary monument and as an actual receptacle for sacred objects, placed there at the moment of consecration, or even later by whoever wishes to be rid of them without committing sacrilege (a special opening was left for this purpose). Later, the ritual character was accentuated (the rites necessary for consecration involved circumambulation of the stupa while repeating the phrase *om mani padme hūm*), and finally the chorten acquired a salvational significance.

There are eight types of chorten, and they repeat substantially those of Indian stupas, which take their names from events in Buddha's life. Thus, for example, we have the "great enlightenment" chorten, the "preaching" chorten, the "descent from heaven" chorten, the chorten "of many doors" (or "victorious" chorten), and so forth. The visitor to Tibet can observe along the most frequented routes of the plateau many such structures, connected by low walls on which the words *om mani padme hūm* appear. Later changes in the initial pattern involve the chorten's proportions and its base—the latter, in the largest examples (called *sKu-abum*, the hundred thousand images), is articulated in successive planes, designed to contain a series of chapels sheltering various divinities. These divinities change from plane to plane in relation to their greater complexity with respect to the initiatory revelation that will take place at the top. It is thus a pyramid that aims to express the process by which the worshiper is brought from multiplicity to the summit of the One.

279

336. *Gyantse, monastery, terminal drum of the kumbum.*
337. *Gyantse, monastery, the large stupa.*

338. *Tashilumpo, monastery.*

The symbology connected with these sacred buildings is extremely complex and is related to the mandalas reproduced on *tankas*, the renowned silk paintings typical of Tibet; however, it is not our task to explore it here. We might simply point out once again the clearly subordinate relationship existing between architectural structure and religious requirements.

The temple, too, shows a development of its own (Plates 329–331, 335). The archaic type, found primarily in western Tibet, consists of a quadrangular cell with a *pronaos*, or covered veranda. Inside, on the back wall, there was generally a niche to hold the statue of the divinity, and a corridor for circumambulation. One finds, however, even in temples older than the eighth to ninth centuries, more articulated structures. At Samye, a site famous for its monastic complex because of its connection with the figure of Padmasambhava—who may have been summoned to Tibet precisely to exorcise this place—there rises a three-story temple, square in plan, and with four stupas at the sides. Here the height is justified by the cosmic symbolism of the monument, since it is intended to represent the holy mountain and the person of the king, in his quality of Dharmaraja. This notwithstanding, the tendency toward elevation is clear. At Iwang the building is enlarged only by its two side chapels, but at Samada we already find two stories; and, passing through the aforementioned Samye temple and the later Lha K'an at Tholing, we slowly arrive at the nine stories of the Ushando temple. The dimensions of the building also increase proportionately, the atrium becomes wider—at Gyantse (Plates 335–337) it actually functions as a meeting hall for the monks—and the courtyard before the sanctuary is surrounded by a covered veranda with chapels at intervals. The outer façade is distinguished by the veranda, supported by pillars, and by the outer band of the roof, richly decorated with sculptural elements representing animals or particularly significant symbols. In more complex examples, the interior appears as a large hall subdivided into three naves by a double row of columns with painted capitals. The roof is flat and has a central opening; at times the latter is replaced by side openings that run the whole perimeter of the hall between the walls and roof.

The temple constituted the center of monastic activity, but around it rose actual cities in which convents, libraries, and meeting halls eventually took their place.

Civil architecture is rather uniform. The typical house is trapezoidal in form, resting on a somewhat massive stone base, on which walls of sun-dried bricks are built that decrease in thickness and tend to taper toward the top. The roof is always flat. The whole decorative aspect, the pillars adorning the façade, the trapezoidal windows, and the balustrades are of wood, variously painted. Depending on the economic

340. *Lhasa, view of the Potala.*
341. *Spiti Valley, view of the Kye monastery.*

assets of the owner, the building may reach a height of two to three stories or even more; some castles, or dsongs (Plate 339), and royal palaces—such as the Potala, the former residence of the Dalai Lamas in Lhasa (Plate 340), or the palace in Ladakh—are as high as nine stories. The Tibetan fortress departs from the austere and imposing model of the civil building, and adds elements characteristic of military architecture: towers, fortified walls, bastions, and drawbridges.

We may conclude by saying that Tibetan architecture must be considered an artistic activity of minor importance in the country, and therefore one in which external suggestions are accepted without any critical evaluation on the aesthetic level. Thus, it is not unusual to find buildings in which each story follows a different style: Indian, Chinese, Khotanese. One distinction can be made on the basis of function: civil architecture readily indulges a taste for color (the wood of the windows, the red band running along the walls under the roof) and folklore; while religious architecture accepts the patterns dictated by tradition and turns primarily to Indian models.

In short, architecture in Tibet becomes a noble art when it is charged with symbolic meanings, when it is sacred art, when "to construct" (if we may borrow Tucci's expression) means "to remake the world" by following the pattern of a mandala.

Chiara Silvi Antonini Colucci

Chapter Four   CENTRAL ASIA

Introduction

In our study of the architecture of Central Asia, we will concentrate on the present Soviet Socialist Republics of Turkmenistan, Tadzhikistan, Uzbekistan, and Kirghizia, southern Siberia, and Chinese Turkestan. From proto-historical times until our own era, Central Asia has been the theater of countless historical vicissitudes—from the nomadic migrations of the centuries that straddle the beginning of the Christian Era, to Iranian and Chinese domination, and finally to the formation of local empires or of small independent states. These are circumstances that make it extremely difficult for a discussion such as ours to observe criteria of classification based on present geo-political realities. A historical-cultural subdivision that takes into account the structure of Central Asia in more ancient periods will be far more suitable for our purpose. We will therefore divide the territory into western Central Asia, comprising the regions that gravitated politically or culturally toward the empires of the West; and the east-central area, known as Serindia, which, as its name indicates, flowered, culturally speaking, under the influence of India and China. In addition, so many monuments have been brought to light in all the decades of excavation and exploration that we cannot possibly approach our subject from that perspective. To resolve this problem, we will instead set forth the essential lines of the process of urbanization and architectural development, beginning with the most ancient of the Central Asian settlements.

Western Central Asia

For twenty years, Soviet archaeologists have been studying the remains of local cultures dating as far back in time as the Neolithic period (fourth to third millennium B.C.). It is now possible to locate the beginnings of these civilizations in time and space, and simultaneously to appreciate the high level of social organization achieved by the earliest groups of sedentary settlers in the region. The first of the two oldest settlements, which was found in southern Turkmenistan, shows important analogies with the organization of contemporary cultures of the Iranian plateau. The second such settlement was discovered in Khwarizm, the region lying between the two tributaries of Lake Aral, the Oxus and the Jaxartes (present-day Amu Darya and Syr Darya), and the protohistorical home of the Kel'teminar culture of the ancient Persian province of Chorasmia. Here we already find the nucleus of the two fundamental types of dwellings, which in modern language might be called "community" and "one-family."

According to an ethnographic definition still valid today, community villages belonging to the Kel'teminar culture are house-villages. We find that they are reduced to a construction, ovoidal in plan and large enough to shelter over one hundred people, with a wooden framework composed of three concentric rows of vertical poles and a series of horizontal beams that support the roof of rushes. The central poles reached a height of 26 to 33 feet, and at the top a circular opening was left for light and air, and especially to allow the escape of smoke. The numerous hearths inside the house were assigned for domestic use, except for a large hearth about 3 feet in diameter that was presumably of a religious nature. The interior of the house-village was thus divided into two sectors: one for domestic life and the other for community life, the latter centering around the cult of fire (Plate 342).

The other type was undoubtedly more complex and showed a remarkable capacity for urban planning. The village was divided into two sections, western and eastern, separated by a large central artery. Dwellings, formed by a single room sheltering several "families," were placed in the western part; in the eastern section, isolated buildings served a religious and social function in a broad sense. The sites of Akca-tepe, Jalangac-tepe, and Mullali-tepe, all belonging to the Geoksjur culture, are laid out according to this pattern. The last two localities, at a higher level, show an important innovation: a canal-wall, interrupted at intervals by circular spaces, surrounded the entire village.

Archaeological evidence for the second millennium is supplied by Khwarizm, which in these later centuries saw the flowering of the Tazabag' jab and Surjargan cultures. Their settlements show that in the meantime notable changes had occurred, such as the use of clay and the introduction of the rectangular house. This progress can no doubt be ascribed to climatic variations and probably also to the advent of a new population that constructed its dwellings in a different way.

In the first half of the first millennium B.C., the Neolithic cultures of Margiana (Jaz-tepe), Bactria (Kobadian), Fergana (Cust), Sogdiana (Afrasiyab), and Khwarizm (Kjuzeli-gyr), all presenting a similar cultural appearance, emerged and developed. The inhabitants of these regions introduced innovations in building techniques that may seem of little importance—among them the use of raw clay bricks—but which in reality were destined to be taken up again, perfected, and to have great significance in the period immediately following. New needs arose later, for no longer did agriculture wait passively for the earth to produce its crops, but endeavored instead to obtain the maximum yield from its fields. More or less rudimentary canal systems were built, while security for the community was provided by the erection of stockades or defensive walls.

A little later, and almost simultaneously in the various regions of Central Asia, a movement took place that, in accordance with Childe's definition, we may call an "urban revolution"—the birth of true cities. From this moment on, Central Asia was on the road to becoming that

342. *Collective hut of the protohistorical culture of Kel'teminar. Recon-struction on the basis of archaeological data verified at Dzanbas-kala (Khwarizm) (from Tolstov, 1948).*

343. *Dzanbas-kala, center of the Kangjuj culture. 1. Plan | 2. Recon-struction | 3. Arch with arrowhead embrasure | 4. Reconstruction of a portion of perimeter wall, with arrowhead embrasures and relative vertical section (from Tolstov, 1948).*

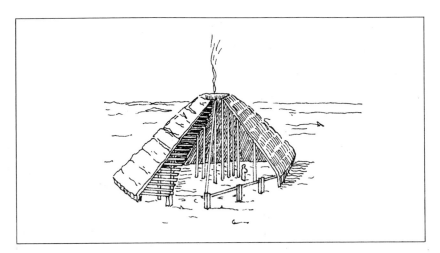

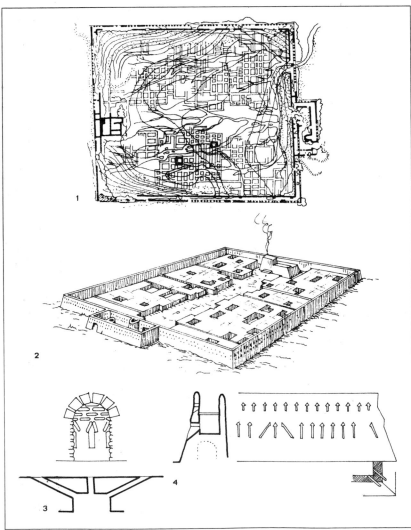

"country of a thousand cities" that classical and Chinese chroniclers recorded in their writings. Fortunately, the work of modern archaeologists is now bringing its kaleidoscopic past to light.

Schematically, we might say that in this period there are two types of cities, the city of inhabited walls and the city of continual construction. Both seem to have had antecedents: the first in the houses of the Amirabad culture (Khwarizm, eighth to seventh centuries B.C.); the second in the protohistorical villages previously mentioned.

The more characteristic model, and one peculiar to Central Asia, was without doubt the city of inhabited walls. As one can easily imagine, it consisted of an enclosing wall built around a quadrangular space left completely free of constructions. The walls, of considerable thickness, were subdivided within into numerous small rooms for use as dwellings, arranged in double or even triple rows; from the outside the walls appeared as actual bastions, reinforced by towers and provided with embrasures. The city was entered by four gates, furnished with a forepart in the form of a labyrinth that constituted a kind of enforced passage. The free space of the interior very likely served to shelter livestock during the night and in the winter months. This type of city is primarily attested in Khwarizm, at Kjuzeli-gyr and Kalaly-gyr (sixth to fourth centuries B.C.), and indeed left a lasting stamp on the region, destined to be reflected in the great defensive structures that characterized the cities and castles of later periods.

Cities of continual construction, on the other hand, took the form of a complex of dwellings grouped in two different sections, sometimes opposite each other and surrounded by the enclosing walls. The type of house it contained might vary from a simple one-room structure to a group of rooms arranged around an inner courtyard. Compared to the plan of previous urban settlements, the structure of these cities showed a notable variation: public buildings (including those for the cult) were grouped inside a fortified citadel—whose function seems to have been quite similar to that of the acropolis in Greek cities—placed at one of the corners of the city.

We must keep in mind that the period in which this exceptional urban development took place corresponds to that of the expansion of the Achaemenid Empire toward the east. There is no doubt that contact with Iranian civilization had profoundly beneficial results for Central Asia. It stimulated cultural enrichment and encouraged trade to a remarkable degree, thus giving local populations new sources of revenue and contributing in particular to the development of the urbanization phenomenon.

The cities of the sixth to fourth centuries B.C. were vast in extent, with houses that were comfortable and at times even elegant; we note particularly the introduction of columns as supports for the ceilings.

There was at that time an unfailing market into which flowed the goods of the West and those of the nomadic East. The material exchange of products was accompanied by meetings and cultural interminglings that in time led to a relatively easy transmigration from one world to another. Different as they were from each other, the peoples of the steppes and of the settled populations nevertheless participated in and profited from this intercommunion.

Bactria, Margiana, Khwarizm, and Sogdiana had in the meantime become territories with an advanced agricultural economy, made possible by a dense and highly efficient network of artificial canals for irrigation, complete with dams. It is precisely this technical perfection and efficiency that has prompted attempts to formulate the hypothesis of a common political structure for the whole western Central Asian area. According to some scholars, a confederation may have emerged of more or less independent states, joined together by a pact of alliance for the maintenance of the canals. Others claim that one of the regions (Khwarizm or Bactria) may have assumed leadership over all the others, imposing a common political order and organizing the distribution of water. Whatever the situation was, it is certain that countless cities flourished during this period. Besides those already mentioned in Khwarizm—to which we can add Dzanbas-kala (Plate 343), Sah-Senem, and Bazar-kala—we might cite Kalaj-mir and Balkh (Bactra) in Bactria, Gjaur-kala in Margiana, Maracanda (the ancient Samarkand) in Sogdiana, and Surabasat in Fergana.

The more southern areas of this territory were successively involved in an event of enormous historical importance: Alexander the Great's victorious march from Greece to India. In reality, from the military and political standpoint, only Bactria can be included among the territories conquered by the Macedonian army, but it is obvious that events of such importance could not have taken place without provoking a whole series of repercussions in the neighboring territories. Moreover, Alexander left behind him armed garrisons, later fortresses; he created cities and erected triumphal arches and altars to the gods—in short, he left tangible traces of his passage. Most of the cities, however, are known to us only from information furnished by his biographers, and modern archaeologists are still striving to retrace this or that city said to have been constructed by him. At the outset of this research, there was little that could be attributed to Alexander and to the period immediately following (during which the so-called Greco-Bactrian kingdom was formed). Such architectural elements as ornamental friezes, columns, and capitals (found in ancient Termez), and some splendid silver coins with the heads of sovereigns, comprised the lot, a paucity that has led to the conviction that the period of the Greco-Bactrian Kingdom had not produced anything in the sphere of plastic and figurative art. Fortunately, the findings of recent years have come to disprove this hypothesis, and today, in addition to Termez, we know of several Greco-Bactrian cities along the banks of the Oxus: Dal'verzin, Kej-kobad-sah, Kuhna-kala, and Ai-Khanum, newer sites that have yielded more or less recognizable vestiges of urban settlements.

Much of the work is still in progress and the data in the process of being interpreted. It is obvious, however, that the Greco-Bactrian city was composed of one-story houses, divided into two principal quarters by a wide street, and characterized by an acropolis and thick defensive walls. In practice, it was extraordinarily similar to cities of the continual-construction type.

There is considerable discussion of the genesis of this urban structure in Central Asia, namely whether it should be considered the natural development of the agricultural villages in the Geoksjur oases of Namazza-tepe or, still farther west, of the lower strata of Anau. It may, on the other hand, have been determined by the Hellenic example that was brought onto Central Asian soil by the first Greeks to arrive there, colonists and war prisoners whom the Achaemenids thought it safer to transport to the eastern regions of their empire. We will restrict ourselves to tangibles and consider only such decorative elements as the stucco moldings, of which remarkable fragments have survived, and the Corinthian capitals long imitated by local artists as being of clear Classical derivation in architecture.

Other important centers thrived outside Bactria. Afrasiyab in Sogdiana, of which the architectural particulars are still not known, must certainly have been a large city, and the site of Koj-krylgan-kala in Khwarizm bespeaks a city so unusual that it deserves to be examined in detail (Plate 344). Koj-krylgan-kala emerged in the fourth century B.C., in the period that Tolstov calls Kangjuj (an approximate transliteration of the name given to Sogdiana in the Chinese sources), and survived until the fourth century A.D. It shows two successive phases: from the fourth century B.C. to the first century A.D., and from the first to the fourth century A.D. The peculiarities of this locality are essentially two: first, its circular plan, and second, the simultaneous function of the monument as a tomb and as an astronomical observatory. As for the plan, it has been observed that cities with a circular plan are attested among the Assyrians, the Medes, and the Parthians, and from this the logical conclusion has been drawn that the builders of Koj-krylgan-kala were inspired by Western models. It cannot be overlooked, however, that the form of the construction is related to the function of the monument itself, which, though surely built for cult purposes, was also utilized as an observatory. It is thus possible that the origin of this plan was inspired by a precise reason, one to be sought in the sphere of astral-funerary symbology.

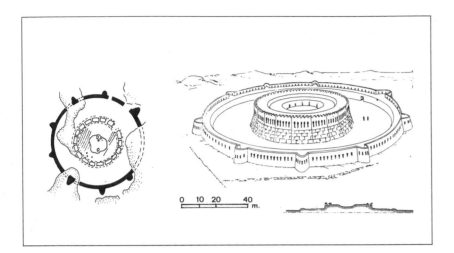

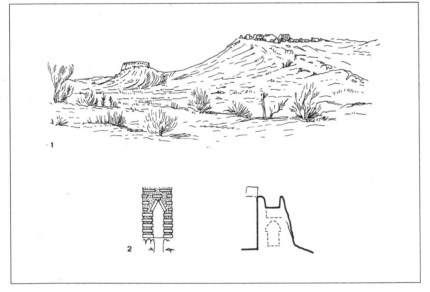

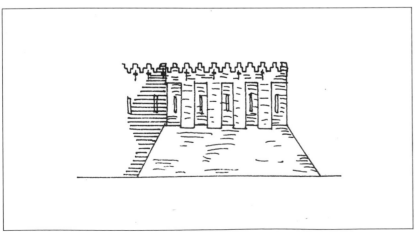

Koj-krylgan-kala, in its latter phase, appears as a large construction, 286 feet in diameter, and consists of a central two-story edifice and fortified defensive walls with eight towers and a monumental entrance gate, facing east. The complex is surrounded on the outside by a rampart that is 49 feet wide and 10 feet deep. Originally, the space between the central building and the walls had been conceived as an open courtyard. Later, it was used for the construction of dwellings intended to house persons attached to the cult and engaged in the observation of the stars. Finally, little by little, its defensive character was emphasized—the bastions were reinforced, and embrasures appeared on the outer side of the walls and rampart. Here we can already glimpse the transition, soon to be observed on a broad scale, from the fortified city to the fortress-castle of post-Kushan times.

From the first century B.C. to the sixth century A.D., this area was in fact subject, directly or indirectly, to the Kushan Empire, which was so important to the history of India. The Kushan presence in Central Asia assumed a significance that went well beyond the limits of mere political domination. To be part of this empire meant in effect to be connected with a militarily strong state, one whose international relations placed it simultaneously in contact with Han China and imperial Rome. It included the benefits of a very extensive trade network, and finally, an exposure to the early teachings of a new creed, Buddhism, which the Kushan rulers had welcomed and were prepared to spread over all the territory they governed. In short, the cultural atmosphere of the Kushan Empire was of the greatest possible breadth, merging as it did the artistic and ideological influences of various fully developed civilizations.

The Kushan period in Central Asia is usually subdivided into "ancient" and "late," in order to make the distinction between two substantially different phases. The first is represented in Bactria, where the Kushan clan began to emerge, coin money, and erect monuments that were already an expression of its sovereignty. Halcajan, the oldest Kushan locality so far discovered, is located on the banks of the Surkandarya and dates as far back as the first half of the first century A.D. The most important edifice of the site is the royal palace, rectangular in plan, and including a richly decorated throne room and various other rooms connected by corridors. The architectural layout of the building seems to be of Iranian derivation, as is suggested by the hexastyle ivan and other lesser elements that correspond exactly to those at Surkh Kotal, the city within whose acropolis a temple has been found dedicated to Mithra by the Kushan emperor Kanishka. In both localities, however, the Iranian element has, broadly speaking (we find some components properly belonging to Kushan culture), been overlaid by the Hellenistic one, clearly distinguishable in the decoration.

At the same time the Kushans ruled in Central Asia, the Parthian Empire thrived in the territories of Parthia and Margiana. The splendor of Parthian civilization in the first period of its empire, when the Arsacid rulers succumbed to the fascination of Hellenism, is reflected in the great quantity of objects of exquisite taste found in the city of Nisa. Nisa emerged as the principal center of the small Parthian kingdom in the middle of the third century B.C., but, with the growth of the dynasty, it progressively increased in importance and size. The city is divided into two parts, old and new. The first is probably an imperial city and includes fortified castles, temples, and a necropolis for dead sovereigns. Two buildings seem to have had a particular significance: the Square Hall, a room adorned with numerous columns with capitals of the Doric, Corinthian, and Iranian kind, where presumably ceremonies connected with the cult of the dynasty were performed; and the Round Hall, also decorated with columns, which in all probability served as a temple.

The new Nisa substantially represents the true city (going back to the first century B.C.) and includes a fortress, temples with columns, an acropolis, and numerous dwellings. The thick walls of pounded earth covered with brick that surrounded the city had reinforcement towers that today have been largely lost.

Khwarizm has a history of its own within the context of these regions, in that it almost always remained independent or at least autonomous from foreign empires. Nevertheless, both for convenience in classification—and because, as we said, the Kushan presence was a determining one for the whole Central Asian territory—here, too, the period following the expansion of Kangjuj culture is called Kushan. Besides Koj-krylgan-kala, such important centers as the city of Toprak-kala (Plate 346), as well as the fortresses of Kavat-kala, Anga-kala, and Ajaz-kala (Plate 345) all belong to it.

Fortress-cities may be said to follow the tradition of the "cities of inhabited walls," in that they appear as isolated complexes with one outer and one inner enclosure wall. In the intermediate space, small separate rooms were built, the so-called dwelling-corridors. The plan is usually quadrangular, and the difference between one fortress and another is reduced to the greater or lesser perfection with which the defensive bastions are constructed. Thus, the one that seems to be the oldest of all, Ata-tjurk-kala, has walls of unbaked bricks and is totally devoid of towers; Kurgasin-kala, on the other hand, has rectangular towers, placed without order and at irregular intervals. A new development appears, however, at Ajaz-kala and Anga-kala: the towers, semicircular or square, are disposed systematically along the walls. It should be noted that these fortresses constituted the centers of agricultural complexes that extended all around them. Here the peasants lived and attended to the work of the fields, having recourse to the protection of the fortress—where an armed garrison was permanently established —only in case of danger.

Toprak-kala, as we have indicated, was a true city and falls within the previous vein of urban tradition, consisting as it did of a citadel, the fortified residence of the local rulers, and of an inhabited center, symmetrically divided into two parts by an artery about 26 feet in width. The city was entered through a labyrinth-gate, itself amply attested by tradition. The whole city was enclosed by walls furnished with embrasures and fortified by numerous towers.

It would be worthwhile at this point to examine briefly the different types of embrasures to be found on the outer walls of the city during various periods. In the ancient period—at Dzanbas-kala, for example—they are arranged in two continuous rows, interrupted at regular intervals by a group of three, of which the two side ones are placed obliquely. With the development of supporting towers, the use of triple embrasures is abandoned; the walls become animated and the alternating rhythm between full and empty spaces is emphasized by the introduction of projecting pilaster-strips. Embrasures are then employed on the rear part. Still later, the embrasures are transferred to the pilaster-strips and grouped almost to form a decorative motif. In addition to the arrangement of this important element of defense, it is also worth noting the form of embrasure employed in Central Asia: it is called an arrowhead embrasure from the particular shape of its outline (Plate 343).

To return to Toprak-kala, we may add that its fortification was completed by a moat encircling the outside along the entire arc of the walls. The citadel consisted of three towers placed in the northwest corner, and a royal palace that included a deputation hall, rooms for the sovereign and his harem, inner courtyards, an armory, and above all a fire temple standing directly before the entrance gate of the citadel. Adjoining the acropolis, and thus in the northeast corner, there was a broad open area that in all probability contained the market; then came the twelve residential quarters (six on each side), each of them composed of a certain number of one-room houses, sometimes arranged around an inner courtyard.

Fortunately, Toprak-kala, the royal residence and as such certainly the most important city of the period, has been only partially damaged by time. Not only has it been easy to distinguish its plan (Plate 346), but it has also been possible to recover fragments of the mural paintings that adorned the halls of its buildings, as well as other findings of considerable merit. The cities of Eres-kala, Kyrk-kyz-kala, and Kurganci-kala, which have come down to us in a much worse state of preservation, must have been quite similar.

The archaeological findings for cities emerging in this period in other Central Asian regions are still far from numerous, or at least are not such as to merit particular attention. Tali-Barzu, for example, a city in Sogdiana a short distance from Samarkand, founded around the second or third century of our era, is reduced to a few dwellings and the remains of fortifications.

With the advent of the fourth century, the decline and subsequent fall of the Kushan Empire created a power vacuum in Central Asia, and led to the formation of two different but parallel phenomena: on one side, there existed a consolidation of the supremacy of local lords, who from their castle strongholds ruled over the surrounding territory and supervised the regular functioning of the irrigation canals; on the other, there arose a succession of new migrations by peoples from the east, who were attracted to this vacuum and tried to fill it, though in many areas their rule was nominal at best.

In the fifth century the Hephthalites, considered by Buddhist sources (which perhaps exaggerate their ferocity) a true calamity, overran Sogdiana and Bactria in the course of a relentless march to the south. Later, it was the turn of the Turks (T'u-chüeh), who, being much less barbarous than their predecessors, were open to many of the influences that the local culture was prepared to give them. Finally, the Muslim conquest produced a clear break with the past and brought Central Asia within the sphere of a civilization based on entirely different presuppositions. Added to all this was the interference in the area by the two great powers pressing on its confines: to the east, T'ang China, and to the west, Sassanid Iran. The latter had long considered these territories an integral part of its sphere of influence.

Clearly, the historical circumstances were hardly conducive to the existence of large urban agglomerates, and in effect what we see in the fifth century is a progressive decline of cities. On the one hand, they would have been too easily subject to pillage and destruction, and on the other, there would seem to have been less reason for their existence; in such tormented and insecure times, commercial activity was reduced and an agricultural economy once again prevailed. Thus began the so-called medieval period, which saw the emergence of a feudal society. The process that led to feudalism is quite clear: the agricultural districts, which, as we have previously seen, were already protected by a fortified construction, were transformed into fiefs. The fortified construction thus became a fortress-castle for the local lord and his retinue. The power of the feudatory was in direct proportion to his capacity or possibility for providing prosperity to the agricultural community, and in the final analysis was closely tied to the success of natural or artificial irrigation.

The castles generally show an identical structure. At the center there was a quadrangular tower on a high stylobate or artificial podium; there follows a first enclosing wall, reinforced by semicircular towers, within which runs a continuous series of rooms for habitation. A second enclosing wall is very similar to the first except that it has no towers; a third wall is placed at some distance from the other two. The castle and the first ring of walls were inhabited by the lord and his family, the second by his servants. The space between the second and third circle of walls, left free of constructions, was reserved for agricultural activities useful to the whole community. The only possible variation in this type of plan was one whereby the central edifice was shifted toward the walls or to one corner of the fortress. The subdivision of the castle-tower's inner space assigned for habitation nevertheless undergoes various changes with the passage of time. In an early period the dwelling rooms take the form of long narrow corridors, with a single opening on the side of the outer wall (as in the Mount Mug castle in Sogdiana); then these same corridors are provided with a central opening, to be transformed little by little into a passageway of greater or lesser width. Moreover, the corridors were also widened, becoming actual rooms that, disposed along the outer wall, served for the various members of the family. At Yakke-Parsan, for example, a space was left free at the center, assuming an importance, as the focal point of the building, that was subsequently emphasized by a domed roof (Plate 348). A further development is shown by the castles of Ak-tepe in the Tashkent district (with two levels), of Kyrk-kyz (Termez), and Akyrtas (Semirec'e), of the sixth to seventh centuries A.D. Here the proportions are considerably increased, and the building would seem to have been divided into four distinct parts with separate entrances; the parts are connected by corridors and galleries converging toward a central space, either the domed room previously mentioned or an inner courtyard to which everyone had access.

According to the earliest Arab sources, castles numbered in the hundreds. We have tried to indicate their general characteristics, as drawn from the more or less recent findings of the Soviet archaeologists in numerous localities: Tesik-kala (Plate 347), Berkut-kala, Kum Baskan-kala, Yakke-Parsan, and Tok-kala in Khwarizm, Kala-i-Bolo in Fergana, Kalai Mug and Batyr-tepe in Sogdiana, Zang-tepe and Chairabad-tepe in Bactria, and others. Numerous as they were, these castles were clearly not all of equal importance. Gradually, as they grew and developed, the complexes that were favored by their situation along the more frequented trade routes once again assumed their role as cities. They were joined in this transformation by those cities that held positions of particular political and administrative importance either as seats of local justice or because they were in direct contact with the capital of the state to which they belonged.

347. *Tesik-kala, Afrigidian culture. 1. View of the ruins / 2 and 3. Reconstruction and plan of the complex / 4. Reconstruction of a fragment of the walls of the central fortified building (from Tolstov, 1948).*

348. *Yakke-Parsan, reconstruction of Afrigidian center (from Tolstov, 1948).*

349. *Kafyr-kala, vertical section of the rock-cut cupola, covered in stone and bricks. Note the wells for the transition from the square plan of the base to the round one of the cupola (from Litvinsky-Zeimal, 1971).*

The names of the cities of this period sound much more familiar, since often they were centers that continued to live and prosper even after the Arab conquest—Samarkand, Bukhara, Merv, for example. Thus, it will not be to these that we will turn in order to describe the typical city of the seventh to eighth centuries, but rather to those cities that soon ceased to exist and that therefore convey an exact image of both the building techniques and the urbanistic conceptions of the period. We find that the Central Asian city of the seventh and eighth centuries is divided into two distinct parts: the citadel and the *sahristān* (the actual city). A ring of walls generally surrounded both, but whereas previously, as construction of the castle proceeded, all vital urban activities were concentrated in its interior, if not actually within the fortress-tower, now little by little political and social life passed beyond the walls of the citadel and were transferred to the *sahristān*. In the space reserved for the latter, temples and administrative buildings were constructed, and here economic and cultural life took place. Two main arteries passed through the complex, connecting the four entrance gates. The position of the citadel was not fixed; it might occupy a corner, or be at the center, or even lie outside the walls (as in the case of Isfidzab-Sajram). The two principal streets were usually perpendicular to each other, and the building for the cult was often erected at the point where they met.

Widespread as this pattern was, it was nevertheless not the only one adopted. As we have observed, some of the buildings that should have formed part of the complex enclosed by the walls—the citadel, the temple, or the market, for example—might be placed outside. The plan itself of the whole might vary. If it departed from a more or less quadrangular shape—as at Merv, Hiva, Termez, and Isfidzab-Sajram— it was possible to arrive at that of Balkh, formed by ten wall segments of varying length, or at asymmetrical plans that would actually be difficult to define by any precise geometrical term. The regions of western Central Asia were rich in centers of this type, and it would be pointless to supply the reader with a lengthy list of them. Instead, we will note some particulars of a city that, while certainly not the largest or richest of its time, offers us the inestimable advantage of being archaeologically better documented: Pjandzikent in Sogdiana.

The plan of this city does not depart from the usual pattern. Inside its high walls, which were reinforced by ten oval towers built of unbaked bricks, were the citadel and the *sahristān*. Houses in the latter were distinguished from each other according to the degree of culture, importance, or wealth of the owner. The most magnificent were of vast size, with two stories, and included a reception hall with walls adorned by painting and sculpture, benches of pounded earth that ran along the walls, and a staircase ascending to the upper story. There

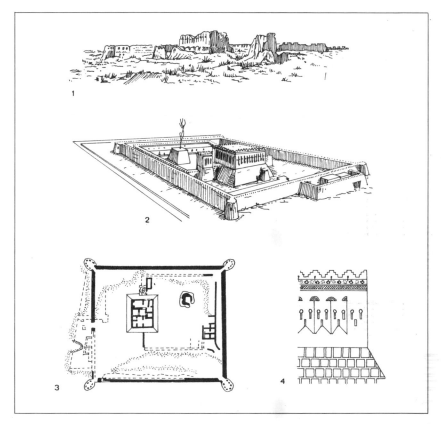

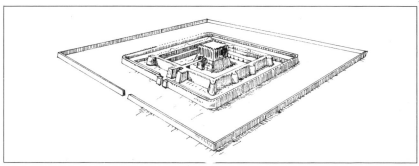

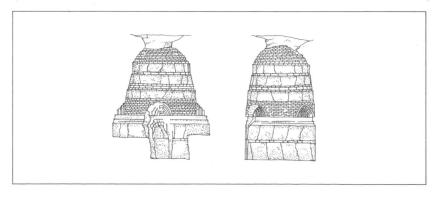

350. *Adzina-tepe, axonometric reconstruction of a complex with vaults and domes (from Litvinsky-Zeimal, 1971).*

351. *Adzina-tepe, arch with keystones of cut bricks (from Litvinsky-Zeimal, 1971).*

352. *Adzina-tepe, plan and elevation (partial) of the so-called northeast façade of the miniature stupa in Room XXXI (from Litvinsky-Zeimal, 1971).*

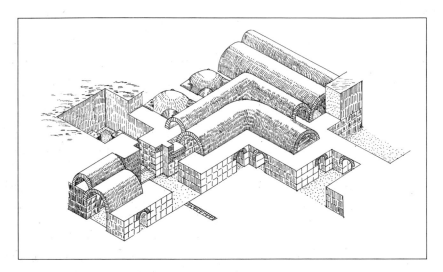

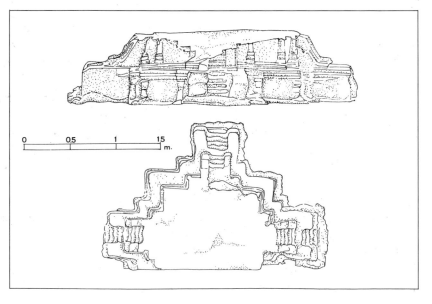

might also be special rooms devoted to the cult or to cultural manifestations (perhaps theatrical and dance spectacles). Outside, extreme care was lavished on the façades, which were provided with an arcade or a loggia. The roof system might be of the vault, cupola, or lantern type. In the latter, characteristic of the Central Asian area and frequently adopted by local architects, the vault was closed by means of a structure of wooden beams arranged in squares that progressively diminish in perimeter. These squares follow each other symmetrically in such a way that the corners of the higher square are diagonal to the sides of the one beneath. The preferred construction materials were unbaked bricks (measuring approximately 20 x 10 x 5 inches) and wood. Two temples have also been found at Pjandzikent, consisting of a central hall, its roof supported by columns, two side rooms, a courtyard to the east, and a cell (with no communication to the outside) to the west. Around this central structure there were other rooms, assigned to various uses.

So far we have often spoken of cult buildings, but we have not paused to consider one very important sector in the sphere of Central Asian architecture, that of Buddhist edifices and religious architecture in general. It was in the Kushan period that Buddhist architecture evidently emerged, with the spread of this creed beyond the confines of its country of origin. This period also saw the flowering, in India, of the Gandhara school of art, which produced works of great merit by expressing the values of Buddhist thought through forms inspired by the Classical world. This definition is surely simplistic and inadequate, and indicates only two components of the school in question, but it would be inappropriate here to go into the controversial subject of Gandhara art. We have mentioned it only because all scholars agree that the religious painting, sculpture, and architecture of Central Asia have each felt its influence to some degree.

At Kara-tepe, a Buddhist complex carved out of the rock (second to fourth centuries A.D.), the Gandhara influence is obvious, but only in the fragments of sculpture and in the stuccowork, since this type of rock-cut construction goes back to Indian examples that precede the flowering of the artistic school of the northwest. Closer to the Gandhara model—albeit modified by substantial Iranian elements—would seem to be the monasteries and sanctuaries of Bamiyan (northern Afghanistan), a very active Buddhist center of the fourth to seventh centuries A.D. Though the site is famous chiefly because of its mural paintings and its two colossal rock-cut statues of Buddha, some architectural elements are worthy of note, such as the domes of the square-plan caves, and the lantern roof previously mentioned.

Finally, Central Asian monasteries and stupas of the seventh to eighth centuries show that they had assimilated not only the Gandhara example, but also those of Gupta India and Sassanid Iran, and above all were able to rework these suggestions in keeping with their own designs. Two localities dating from this period have recently been brought to light: Ak-Besim and Adzina-tepe. The first site has revealed two important Buddhist sanctuaries—one rectangular in plan, the other square—as well as a Nestorian church with a cruciform plan; the second site has yielded a vast sacred area divided into two square adjoining and communicating courtyards within which numerous temples and stupas were constructed (Plates 350–352).

These findings in the Ak-Besim and Adzina-tepe complexes testify to the full vigor of Buddhism in the late period, while their coexistence with religious buildings pertaining to Zoroastrianism, Manichaeanism, and Nestorianism would indicate a climate of broad tolerance or even of religious syncretism.

Serindia

The link between China and the western regions had been made possible since antiquity by the formation of commercial centers near the oases at the foot of the T'ien-Shan Mountains and along the waterways that supplied the Tarim Basin. Through them passed the great "silk route" used by the Chinese merchants to transport their precious commodity to the West. The caravans, however, not only conveyed Chinese merchandise to India and Iran, and across them to the eastern Mediterranean, but received in exchange products that were distributed throughout their own domestic market. Exchanges took place that only the temporary incursions of nomads from the steppes (always attracted by the material well-being of the settled populations and eager for plunder) were able to disrupt.

The silk route thus attracted the attention of all the empires that were formed in the adjoining regions, from the Kushans of India to Han China, from the Arabs to the Turks, from the Hsiung-nu to the Hephthalites. The rulers were interested, however, in conquering the territory without jeopardizing the specific function of the city-states—they had no desire to interrupt the flow of trade—and limited themselves to controlling and exploiting these sources of revenue. The centers along the caravan route, on the other hand, were small autonomous entities having no practical possibility for making common cause against the invader; they were instead easy objects of conquest. The desert separated one from another, ensuring that each developed in accordance with its own particular nature, more often in conflict than in union with the neighboring cities. At most it was a question of cities joined more by their capacity to receive foreign influences than by reciprocal exchanges.

The silk route set out from the city of Kashgar, into which flowed the caravans coming from the West, and proceeded along two different paths: a northern one passing through the cities of Tumshuq, Kucha, Shorchuq, Qarasahr, and Turfan; and a southern one that went through Yarkand, Khotan (or Yotkan), Niya, and Miran to link up with the other at Tunhwang on the Chinese border. The first information we have on the city-states of Central Asia appears in Chinese sources of the Han period, and allows us to trace their existence back to the second century A.D. Another highly important source for the history of these cities consists of the travel diaries of Buddhist monks who went on pilgrimage from China to India across the deserts and oases of Central Asia. They accurately described the chief characteristics of the kingdoms they encountered—their climate, agricultural and craft production, customs and costumes, and—naturally—religious institutions, with particular reference to Buddhism. For example, Hsüan-tsang, the most famous of Chinese pilgrims, was able to observe and thus report on many monasteries that in the seventh century were in full activity in Kucha, Aqsu, Karghalik (south of which a large mountain contained a "multitude" of cells and niches for monks), and Khotan. When we remember that by that time no few historical vicissitudes had already disturbed the tranquillity of the Central Asian oases, it is logical to suppose that there had been in previous centuries an even greater number of Buddhist monuments.

The commercial contacts to which we have referred help us also to single out those cultural areas that influenced the artistic development of the various centers and the evolution of thought, transmitting not only figurative models to be reproduced, but above all such religious experiences as Buddhism, Zoroastrianism, Manichaeanism, and Nestorianism.

The sands of the desert, wind, erosion by water, and the hand of man have caused irreparable damage to the structure of these cities, and only the patient work of such illustrious scholars as Stein, Grünwedel, Von Le Coq, and Oldenburg has made it possible for some part of the art treasures they contained to come down to us. Stupas, monasteries, fortresses, and especially wall paintings and stuccowork remain to testify to a high level of civilization. As for architecture, we can explain its essential substitutive elements, in both the religious and civil spheres, by deducing them from the few surviving monuments that still preserve visible traces of their original structure.

Buddhist architecture can be divided into two large groups: cave temples and open-air constructions. The origin of the cave temple or monastery is undoubtedly Indian, and is connected with the desire of architects of that country to abandon wood as a construction material in favor of something more durable. A natural cave offers the possibility of achieving this purpose, and the enormous patience of the

Indian *silpin* smooths the walls, models the vault, and carves all the figurative elements necessary for the cult. But in Central Asia, in most cases, the geological situation is quite different. The rock does not have the granitic consistency of that in India; on the contrary, it crumbles easily, lends itself poorly to the stonecutter's chisel, and may often collapse. In addition, the Central Asian area is frequently subject to seismic disturbances. Given therefore a desire to reproduce Indian models, the cave monasteries of Central Asia were necessarily more modest. We can distinguish four types of caves according to the kind of roof adopted. The first type includes two rooms and a vestibule, and has a ridge vault or a cupola; the second generally adopts only the cupola; and in the third type, the ceilings have false incorbelled beams. Finally, there is a simpler roof system that provides a flat roof with fluting, in imitation of the wooden beams used for houses.

Open-air constructions have obviously survived to a much lesser degree, and often nothing has been found but the remains of foundations. The two most frequent types of monuments are, however, as in all the Buddhist world, the vihara or monastery and the stupa. One of the oldest centers from which conspicuous building ruins remain is Miran, where there stood a monastery within which a cell with a domed ceiling held a large stupa. The complex, like that of Ravaq in the Khotan oasis, has been shown to relate to Gandhara prototypes; and while in the case of Miran the relationship is confirmed by an examination of the paintings, which clearly show the influence of the Indian school, at Ravaq the composition itself recalls the monuments of Gandhara. The vihara in the Khotanese city contained a stupa, protected by a wall built in a square around it and adorned inside and out by stucco statues of considerable size. The wall is reinforced at the corners; the stupa, cruciform in plan, was erected on a base with three steps.

Unfortunately, the scarcity of archaeological evidence does not even allow us to determine a precise line of development for the stupa. We can only say that the base seems to assume an increasingly important role, with two or three steps (as in the stupas of Endere, Niya, and Ravaq); the cupola either becomes thinner by elongation and replaces the classic umbrellas with a series of superimposed diminishing planes (as in the case of Miran), or is reduced to a very modest size. In general, there is a tendency toward elongation and a vertical development for the whole monument.

As for civil architecture and city planning in general, we have very little to go on. A few beams still fixed in the soil have led to the supposition that houses and palaces in the city-states were composed of a wooden framework and walls of pounded earth that have not withstood the particular climatic conditions of the region. This is too little to give us an idea of what the caravan cities must really have been like, though we know them to have been rich and to have provided a stimulus for every kind of cultural activity. In a few cases, literary and artistic evidence makes up for the archaeological gaps. Thus, since Chinese sources extol the ability of musicians and dancers from Kucha and Khotan, we must suppose that these arts enjoyed great favor in the two cities, and that the artists had at their disposal buildings especially constructed for this kind of spectacle. Similarly, the stories of pilgrims or certain details of frescoes introduce us to the interiors of the royal palaces, whose splendor we can imagine.

Naturally, the cities also provided for constructions of a military nature—bastions, fortifications, and ramparts. It was necessary to prepare a system of defense in order to avoid eventual surprise attacks. As we have seen, however, the inhabitants of the oases were more inclined to peaceful activities than to martial exploits, and for this reason the models for their fortifications were probably borrowed from peoples thought to be more expert in this field. It is not surprising that the forts of Endere and Miran (seventh to eighth centuries) respectively show a clear T'ang Chinese and a Tibetan stamp.

Because of our lack of data, the total picture we have sketched is far from being exhaustive, but it is encouraging to know that archaeologists are persistently continuing their work of extracting from the desert any slight trace of the past. Perhaps someday soon the physical appearance of the ancient cities of the silk route can be more fully reconstructed.

Chiara Silvi Antonini Colucci

Chinese architecture, it is often said, contains no clear stylistic differences, but only a slow evolution from simple to more complex forms. This opinion can be attributed to the predominantly wooden nature of the buildings—a technique ill suited to revolutionary developments; and to the establishment since earliest times of certain essential characteristics for the most widespread type of building—the pavilion (*tien*), with its tripartite structure consisting of the base (*chieh-chi*), the columns (*chu*) that support the system of corbels (*tou-kung*), and the roof covering (which immediately takes on an overriding importance in the structural harmony of the whole building). All of these factors lend credence to this idea. At the same time the complicated geomantic, ritual, and sumptuary regulations that link all new constructions with a past viewed as perfect in the Confucian sense would seem to confirm the common impression.

Even the way in which the buildings are laid out is typical and does not seem to change much through the centuries. The monumental conception of a building complex, seen only in the horizontal sense—that is, with broad but not especially high structures, placed in an orderly fashion in accordance with a particular rule of proportion by which no element can exist apart but is completed by a similar and opposite one—goes directly back to the Chou dynasty.

These basic characteristics, together with a love for nature and the desire not to disturb it by works that might upset its balance—interference that would have grave consequences on the magical level—form part of Chinese humanism and are prompted by the sociopolitical and religious forces that help to shape it.

Actually, Confucian pragmatism is directly responsible for the rigid standards of axiality and symmetry that made it possible to arrive at a graduated and hierarchical order in the city. The royal palace was placed at the center of the urban system: the network of streets, the dwellings, the directional complexes, and the service areas. This hierarchical process is also found in the countless sumptuary regulations that determine colors, materials, installations, and the structures of dwellings in relation to every step in the social ladder.

The other aspect of Chinese religion (and philosophy), Taoism, is instead responsible for the ecological sensibility by which Chinese architecture is related to nature and the surroundings: walls follow the contours of hills, even so colossal a work as the Great Wall (Plates 353, 358), and splendid imperial gardens include lakes, rivers, and hills. If, as is often the case, these elements are artificial, they are nevertheless carried out with wonderful naturalness. The rocks, pebbles, and plants in small gardens, though laid out in accordance with mysterious rhythms and well-defined magical relationships, give the marvelous impression of having been put there by the whim of Nature, even when they are simply the fruit of a refined sensibility. These architectonic poetics, applied but neither codified nor recognized—since architecture has never been a true art for the Chinese and thus, aside from a few technical construction manuals, there are no adequate treatises on the subject—would seem to be extremely valid, given their successful diffusion throughout the Far East, which began in the Han period and was later extended.

The interest aroused by modern Japanese architecture among artists and critics all over the world confirms this validity, since many poetic canons of ancient China still underlie, in re-elaborated forms, the works of the best contemporary masters.

It is precisely this undoubted validity and its consequent duration over the centuries that have suggested the idea that Chinese architecture is totally lacking in stylistic variations. Only our Western taste prevents us from noticing at first sight the profound differences between a T'ang building and a Liao building, so bedazzled are we by the exoticism of these works and ill prepared to grasp their cultural foundation and variations.

To demonstrate that constant innovation, changes in style, and revivals exist in the development of Chinese architecture, we will try to adopt, in this very different field, the nomenclature employed in the West to describe the progress of our own architecture.

It is an ambitious attempt, which errs first of all by the rigidity and arbitrariness inherent in any system of classification. On the other hand, since architecture is singularly linked to the social factor that directly gives rise to it, it may seem impossible to employ correctly terms conceived to define phenomena that have manifested themselves in a completely different world. Nor would this seem suitable for the purpose of clarifying a stylistic evolution that, whatever our sentimental esteem for it, is in a certain sense alien to our way of considering architecture. Nevertheless, it is my belief that correspondences exist (almost undefinable, but real all the same) between artistic phenomena belonging to two such diverse and distant worlds, which are historically related despite the fact that they lie at opposite ends of Eurasia. Thus, it is not absurd, after an archaic period that creates long-lasting building and structural prototypes—the Shang and Chou dynasties (Plates 355–357)—to recognize a classical period, in which the emphasis is on spectacular and monumental effects, but also on balance and harmony. So-called classical styles exist in India, flourishing when the local culture rejected suggestions from the Greco-Roman world and reached its own full splendor. After this phase, which corresponds to the four centuries of the Han dynasty, there follows a medieval period that produces elongated forms in sculpture similar to those of our Gothic (Plates 366–368), and which many, even historically speaking,

have considered the exact equivalent of our Middle Ages. This is the period of the Six Dynasties.

The attention paid by the T'ang dynasty to the rediscovery of the classical at the time of the Han phase, together with a typical sense of measure, strength, and harmony (Plates 373–378), amply justifies equating the new period of imperial splendor with the European Renaissance. Moreover, the spread of Buddhism had already created in wide areas of Asia the conditions for an Asiatic humanism that profoundly altered and exalted the value of man. Certain Sung works, especially those of the Northern Sung, still show Renaissance traits, despite the brief interruption caused by the period of the Five Dynasties. Under the Southern Sung and in the barbarian Liao reign (Plate 403), however, we see the appearance of elements of plasticity in decorated surfaces and a concern for chiaroscuro, a variety of architectural features that would pass from a kind of Mannerism to the strong volumetric and chromatic contrasts of the Yüan (Plate 409)—and to a certain extent also the Ming—"Baroque." This pseudo-Baroque, simplified in line and enriched by minute and even colored ornamentation, delicately painted flowers, birds, and plants, will change in color from the Ming to the Ching periods to produce a "Little Baroque," a light and fanciful Rococo; in some Ching buildings, particularly the royal palaces, it is even possible to note, as Soper[1] has already done, a kind of delicately structured Neoclassicism (Plates 460, 461).

We can, therefore, assign the essential phases of artistic evolution in general, and of architecture in particular, to various dynasties, which for diverse reasons promoted different architectural trends. It is important to consider these daring but by no means arbitrary correspondences with traditional Western categories before returning to the customary classification by dynasty. The divergence in chronology between China and the West for such classifiable phenomena with the same name is sometimes considerable, but this hypothesis has been drawn primarily as an answer to all those critics who have too hastily judged Chinese architecture as monostylistic. They unwittingly approach absurdity in suggesting a fixed view of an architecture that has undergone three thousand years of development.

Prehistory and Protohistory

Chinese literary sources, thought to be of the late Chou period, refer to a very ancient time when men lived in "holes and nests," presumably caves or dwellings dug in the earth and similar to those still used by certain populations living at a primitive level in such northernmost areas of Asia as Korea. In an infinitely more remote period (possibly five hundred thousand years before Christ) the earliest hominid so far discovered on Chinese soil—the *Pithecanthropus* of Choukoutien (*Sinanthropus pekinensis*)—undoubtedly sought shelter in the natural caves and grottoes near Peking, for it is in these caves that remains of skeletons of *Sinanthropus*, already with slight Mongoloid characteristics, have been found. He produced hatchets, knives, and disk-shaped stone scrapers, knew what fire was, and practiced burial rites and probably cannibalism.

In addition to Choukoutien, traces of more recent Paleolithic sites have also been found at Ting-ts'un in Shansi (Ting-ts'un man), at Sjara-osso-gol in the great bend of the Yellow River, in Honan and Szechwan. But it is only in the Neolithic period—that is, from the beginning of the fourth millennium B.C., with the introduction of agriculture and thus of stable settlements—that we have finds of any architectural value. Excavations carried out between 1950 and 1955 at Pan-po-ts'un near Sian in Shensi (Plate 354) have revealed the existence of an agricultural village, datable to the middle of the third millennium B.C., of already defined characteristics. It has been assigned to the middle phase of the so-called Yangshao, or painted pottery, culture that seems to have developed in the loess lands of the northeast.

The huts are surrounded by a wide ditch, used for drainage and defense, which separates them from the burial grounds. The latter are arranged in a circular or quadrangular fashion, and sunk about a foot and a half into the earth, with a hearth at the center. Four holes around the hearth indicate the presence of wooden columns designed to support the roof, probably consisting of a wooden framework of small beams and completed by straw, branches, or woven reeds, then covered with clay. The conspicuous nature of the roof (which must almost have touched the ground), the custom of having the entrance face south, the wooden pilasters, and above all the presence of the so-called clan house (a spacious rectangular structure situated almost at the center of the village), are significant. They represent the germs of certain characteristics of traditional architecture and urban planning that were to prevail in future centuries, even though the idea of a pounded earth floor dug lower than ground level was discontinued in the historical period.

The villages of the Lungshan, the other great contemporary Chinese Neolithic culture (in some cases superimposed on the Yangshao), show nearly the same configuration. They are, however, often situated on hills and surrounded by a wall of pounded earth, which at Ch'eng-tzu-yai is rectangular in shape and very similar to those of later Shang cities. The tombs, which lie within the wall, consisted of trenches where the body was placed supine along with such funerary trappings as vases, axes, and arrows. This differed from the custom in the northeast, where—for example, at Pai Tao Koi Ping in Kansu—the corpse, again surrounded by funerary offerings, was buried in the fetal position.

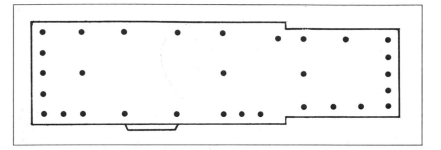

Shang Dynasty (1766–1122 B.C.)

Confucianism, with its cult of the antique, contributed to the origin and preservation of a number of historical works dealing with the most archaic phases of Chinese history. According to the oldest sources, Chinese civilization begins with a series of mythical emperors, true cultural heroes, who are said to have invented agriculture, ways to control the flow of rivers, and writing. But no traces of these mythological rulers—or better, of the historical phases to which they correspond—nor of the successive Hsia dynasty, which according to traditional chronology would seem to have lasted from about 2205 to 1766 B.C., have been found by archaeological excavation. The Shang dynasty, which apparently extended its dominions along the middle and lower course of the Yellow River in the regions of Honan, Hopei, Shansi, Shensi, and Shantung, is considered on the basis of archaeological and stratigraphic evidence to follow immediately on the heels of the Neolithic period. Here Chinese history begins. Here the ancient legends are confirmed, if only in part, by archaeological finds.

Of the numerous capitals to which, according to tradition, the Shang rulers moved, two at least can be identified—one near Cheng-chow, which would be the ancient Ao recorded in the *Bamboo Annals* and by Shih-chi, thought today to have been begun around 1500 B.C.; the other at Hsiao-t'un near Anyang. This latter is considered to be the last and most famous capital, the so-called Great Shang, founded according to the *Bamboo Annals* by P'an-Keng in 1300 B.C. It is primarily on this site that the discoveries made by Japanese scholars up until 1937, and later by the Chinese themselves, have made it possible to discern nearly parallel rows of square or rectangular dwellings, presupposing a chessboard pattern of streets, and, more important, spacious terracings of pounded earth for temples, palaces, and other major buildings. These structures had stone foundations (occasionally covered by a surface of bronze) into which wooden pillars must have been inserted, as in the case of the rectangular great hall, some 98 feet in length, in which we find two of the three essential components of Chinese architecture: the terraced foundation, and the supporting structure of wooden columns, securely linked by a series of wooden architraves, and placed—regularly spaced and with a central row—slightly behind the edge of the terrace.

It has even been possible to recognize the outlines of a certain development in Shang architecture. In the older capital near Cheng-chow, the terracings of buildings were lower and less frequent, while the houses, often with rectangular foundations of from 9 by 5 feet to 52 by 25 feet, had pounded earth floors sunk about a foot and a half below ground level.

Near Anyang, on the other hand, the pounded earth pedestals of the buildings are higher and much more numerous. Though the old type of Neolithic dwelling with its sunken floor survives in many examples, round or square in shape, we nevertheless find buildings that were obviously at ground level; these may mark the moment of transition from the sunken dwelling to that raised on terracing.

The walled city, however, already appears to have taken definite shape: at Ao, near Chengchow, the remains of the wall measure 1 by 1.2 miles in perimeter. At Anyang, the streets form a chessboard pattern and the most important buildings must have been similar in appearance to the future Chou city, even if the roofs most certainly were different, since we find no trace of roof tiles.

The urban structure corresponds to a highly distinct society, a kind of sacred monarchy that extended its rule over the feudatories of other cities and villages, and in which both slavery and human sacrifice were practiced. Indeed, almost all the important buildings exhibit traces in their foundations of human or animal sacrifice. The large royal tombs, along with their rich bronze and ceramic trappings, their chariots and the skeletons of horses, in particular contain numerous remains of decapitated human victims, testifying to a religion that provided for both human sacrifice and the survival of the spirit after death (Plate 357). The skeleton of a dog (a chthonic and demonic animal) has been unearthed from the deepest part of the foundations, sure evidence of a special propitiatory or apotropaic rite.

These royal tombs, mainly in the vicinity of Anyang, also show the magical and religious significance that the Shang builders were already attributing to the orientation of their structures. The large tomb of Wu-Kuan Ts'un (Plate 356) and the royal necropolis near Hsi-pe Kang reveal the existence of a precise scheme for funerary constructions in which greater importance is given to the southern side, where the funeral cortege entered on the occasion of the burial. The sepulcher consisted of a quadrangular chamber, dug deeply into the earth, with two access ramps on the northern and southern sides, sometimes almost 66 feet in length. In the more complex examples, two shorter ramps were added on the eastern and western sides, giving a cruciform shape to the whole. The coffin was placed in the funerary chamber under a wooden structure about $6 \frac{1}{2}$ feet high, outside of which lay the bodies of the numerous sacrificial victims. The grave was then filled in with earth and leveled with the surrounding terrain. No traces of any particular elements that would have revealed the presence of the tomb from the outside have been discovered.

Chou Dynasty (1122–255 B.C.)

The advent of the Chou dynasty, which succeeded in expanding its frontiers until it eliminated the former Shang rulers, did not con-

stitute a real cultural or artistic break. On the other hand, it was precisely during this period (the longest ever ascribed to a Chinese dynasty) that political changes occurred that were also to have a marked influence on architecture. Unfortunately, only a very few Chou sites have so far been found, and it is hardly possible to trace a difference between the buildings of the first period of relative internal peace (roughly coinciding with the so-called Western Chou reign, which lasted until 771 B.C.) and those of a later period in which the struggles among various feudal states became increasingly acute—to such a degree that the monarchy was obliged to transfer its capital from the outlying Changan to Loyang (Eastern Chou period, 771–255 B.C.). Thus we are unable to follow the changes in any proper sequence. We can, however, note the results.

Many other changes took place in the period that Chinese texts call that of the "Warring Kingdoms" (480–222 B.C.), when the monarchy was no longer able to control the centrifugal forces of its individual vassal states. This was a time of considerable unrest, but also of great cultural and artistic achievement. The two most influential Chinese philosophers, Confucius, who wrote commentaries on the Chinese classics, and Lao-Tzu, author of the *Tao Te Ching,* are thought to hav elived during this period.

Generally speaking, the Western Chou period represents a continuation of the structural and artistic models of the more refined Shang type. The texts mention the transfer of craftsmen from the last Shang capital to the Chou capital, situated near Changan. The plan of the walled city was continued, as well as the custom of burial in underground sepulchral chambers laid out according to rigid geomantic and ritual rules. One notes only the greater importance assumed by garrison towns, the military centers of the time, and an attempt to locate urban centers in proximity to the great traffic arteries, a feature that does not hold true for the previous phase. A lesser interest in fortification works is apparent, indicating a temporary feeling of greater security.

As for the tombs, the custom of burial in a sacrificial pit was preserved, as we discover from the tenth-century B.C. tomb excavated near Changan, and those of the necropolis near Loyang (tenth to ninth centuries B.C.).

For the Eastern Chou period and that of the "Warring Kingdoms," the documentation at our disposal is a little more ample; first of all, there are numerous references in the texts to architectural facts and data. As far as theoretical urban planning is concerned, the *Chou Li*[2] contains a highly explicit description of the "ideal captial." It is formed by "a square nine *li* [about 3.6 miles] on each side, with three gates on each side, and nine longitudinal and nine transverse streets,

each sufficient in width for the passage of nine chariots. To the left the Ancestral Temple, to the right the Altar of the Earth, to the front the Court, to the rear the Marketplace." The greater complexity of the Chou urban plan as compared to the Shang city is obvious, and there is no doubt that the *Chou Li* anticipates the urban layout of the later imperial capitals. But what is rather indicated by the archaeological evidence from this period is a freer general outline, probably due to the conditions of the terrain and also to the form of pre-existing sites.

Of the capital of Chengchow, near Loyang, there remain only traces of the pounded earth walls, from 10 to 20 feet in width. But the imposing scale of the fortifications found in the capitals of the various kingdoms, especially in the regions of Hopei and Shantung, testifies to a later phase in which there was a serious need for defense. Hsia Tu near I-hsien (Hopei), in the northwestern state of Yen, exhibits a surrounding wall almost 33 feet at the base, with an irregular perimeter, far indeed from the canonical square shape and enclosing a very broad area. This suggests that within the walls, in addition to major buildings (of which some fifty foundation platforms have been discovered) and houses, there must also have existed agricultural fields. The plan mentioned in the texts seems to have been more closely executed in the city of the Chao kings, near Han Tan in Hopei; here the quadrangular layout of the colossal walls (about 66 feet at the base and 49 feet in height), and the axial position of the ruins of the major buildings (of which foundation terraces and column bases still remain), contrast nevertheless with the greater proximity of the most important complex to the southern side. This is a marked divergence from the canonical orientation.

Clearly, the *Chou Li* is a theoretical text that does not correspond to the actual situation in the area of urban planning. Similarly, its allusions to the structures and shapes of individual buildings, which turn up also in other texts, in many cases cannot be taken literally. It is certain that, along with the phenomenon of a gradual development of buildings along a central axis leading to the royal palace, the traditional courtyard arrangement of private dwellings also begins at this time. A ballad in the *Shih Ching*[3] mentions the basic parts of a residence —entrance gate, courtyard, frontal portico of the reception hall—and emphasizes the importance of the courtyard. The texts also point up the magnificence of sculptured and painted decorations, and of brick tilework, the use of which, judging by these sources, would seem to have been widespread from the beginning of the eighth century B.C. The archaeological evidence suggests that such ostentation did not develop prior to the fourth century B.C.; it thus constitutes one of the most significant innovations with respect to the Shang period.

What stands out is the monumental size of carved, painted beams and columns, of the foundation platforms, extensive gardens, and high watchtowers. At the same time, that complex of sumptuary and structural regulations requiring the architectural decoration of each house to correspond to the social rank of its occupants begins to be stabilized.

We can study certain structural characteristics of Chou buildings more closely by examining the incisions on bronze vases. The most important such representation is found on a bowl from a Honan tomb in Hweihsien, though the archaic nature of the rendering raises a number of problems in itself. The two-story building it represents exhibits the typical supporting framework of wooden columns, topped by a tile roof, which does not, however, seem to have the excessive importance in the overall structure of the building that will occur in later constructions. It lacks entirely the characteristic curvature of the slopes of later roofs. The corbel system here seems simplified and reduced to a single block, almost to a wooden capital. On the upper roof, acroteria in the form of goatlike heads may be the prototypes of the very widespread "owl-tailed" acroteria of much later times.

Certain structural details are more difficult to interpret: the foundation platform does not seem to be indicated, perhaps for lack of space, while the upper floor seems to rest on lateral columns rising from a kind of platform, in its turn supported by smaller pillars that rest on the roof of the lower story. It is an anomalous structural solution and hard to explain, unless we ascribe it to a mistaken representation by the engraver, or even to an attempt to show two adjoining buildings in perspective.

Other evidence providing us with direct documentation of the Western Chou period are its tombs, which in general are still close to those of Shang times. However, the practice of sacrificing a dog in the foundations seems to have disappeared, and we can distinguish variations in form and dimension corresponding to the social rank of the deceased, and above all, to local customs. A divergence from the normal scheme is found in the tombs of Tangshan in Hopei, where the wooden coffin is replaced by stone slabs, perhaps foreshadowing the later stone sepulchers of the Han period.

Other burial grounds have been found in southern regions, where the penetration of northern culture is evident, as at Tung-sun-pa (Szechwan) and at Changsha (Hunan). Here the elaborate design (in wood) of the modestly proportioned funeral chamber (depth, 23 feet; length, 6 to 10 feet; width, 3 to 6 feet) shows the degree of acculturation in this area to currents from the north.

Contrary to the statements of Soper[4] and other scholars, no tombs of the Chou period show traces of the tumuli that were to constitute the characteristic feature of Han burial grounds. Examination of the

necropolis situated near Ku-wei-ts'un in Honan—where three tombs of enormous dimensions but similar in shape to the Shang type have been found—has shown that in this period the practice of marking the presence of a sepulcher externally on the surface of the soil had scarcely begun. Tumulus No. 2, in fact, is topped by a layer of pounded earth rising about 20 inches above the level of the terrain, and with a border of large stones placed at intervals; this may constitute a distant prototype (as a surface marker) of the later tumuli.

On the other hand, it is difficult to ascertain the structure of sacred buildings, to which the texts refer often but unclearly and of which the excavations have still not yielded sufficient traces. Probably there were throughout the region altars of pounded earth, square in form and dedicated to the soil in which the victims were buried; or, round and dedicated to the sky under which the victims were burned. But the primitive characteristics of the Ancestral Shrine and of the Ming T'ang (Shining Pavilion), which seems at first to have been the king's residence and later to have become a royal temple, have not been sufficiently reconstructed. Even the Han rulers, anxious to establish the firmest ties with the ancient past, had tried to determine the traditional plan, without, however, being entirely successful. The memory of it had been lost.

It is certain that the shape of the shrine must have been connected with complicated geomantic and ritual rules. And, since the texts mention that the seat (throne) of the emperor was shifted around in the various rooms according to the season, it must surely have been based on astrological requirements as well. But for these ancient shrines, the texts permit us to glimpse only the use of structures and models common to both dwellings and sacred buildings; this is a characteristic feature of all Far Eastern architecture as applied to royal residences intermediate between the temple and the house.

Ch'in Dynasty (255–206 B.C.)

Though this phase covered only a very brief span of time, it marked the unification of Chinese territory and the foundation of the Celestial Empire and made a clear break with the past in social, economic, and political areas. There were obvious repercussions for architecture as well. Shih Huang Ti, the First August Emperor (259–210 B.C.), and his minister Li Ssu to an even greater extent, pursued a centralizing and unifying policy that sought to annul completely the centrifugal forces of the old feudal states. While trying to eliminate all ties with the past—hence the persecution of Confucians and the burning of a large portion of the ancient texts in 212 B.C.—they strove to create a truly homogeneous China through the adoption of a single script, a single system of weights and measures, and a great network of roads to facilitate exchanges and contacts as it converged toward the capital, Hsien-Yang in Shensi.

The individual regions were obliged to adopt a single gauge for the wheels of carriages, which so far had differed from state to state and constituted a more serious obstacle than one would think to contacts and exchanges. The deportation of the feudal nobility with their families to the capital (the texts speak of more than one hundred thousand persons) brought interregional characteristics to Hsien-Yang. Thus, the isolation that made the architecture of one state different from that of another came to an end. As Soper rightly states: "It was for the first time possible to compute a sum of Chinese architectural achievements. The next step must have been the fusion of regional differences into what was intended to be a single imperial style."[5] Unfortunately, archaeological excavations have not yielded many traces of this "architectural revolution." Hsien-Yang was in fact burned by the rebels led by Liu Pang, founder of the Han dynasty, and the texts record that the fires lasted for three months. Nevertheless, by examining the artistic production of the successive Han dynasty, we will be able to complete the picture. But the taste for the monumental and the imperial splendor that the texts ascribe to the constructions of Shih Huang Ti is likewise clear from the excessive dimensions of certain buildings. The palace of A-fang, for example, is described by the sources as an immense complex placed among gardens, ponds, and rivers, with its great central hall "five hundred paces from east to west and five hundred feet from north to south."[6] This same taste can be discerned in the emperor's great tomb near Hsien-Yang.

Here the tumulus appears for the first time. It is of colossal dimensions: its square base measured about 980 feet on each side, and the height, according to tradition, was 492 feet.

Another innovation is shown by the presence around the tomb of stone animals about 12 feet high; they seem to have connected the funerary garden (which, according to the texts, extended for more than five li around the tomb in the layout of the Han imperial tombs) with an avenue of access or shên tao (Road of the Spirits), which was flanked by large stone sculptures. It should be mentioned here that the Chinese li is equivalent to about one third of a mile. It has been thought that Shih Huang Ti mobilized all the working resources of the nation for such colossal architectural works in order to avert the danger of new civil wars and secessions.

The texts mention the thousands of workers employed on the Great Wall, another of Shih Huang Ti's grand achievements and one that has come down to us, albeit through later reconstructions (especially the almost total one carried out in the Ming period). Erected along the northern confines as a bulwark against the nomadic tribes that

359. *Sepulchral tile representing a monumental gateway of the Han dynasty. Chengtu (Szechwan), Hsi-ch'eng Museum (from Sickman-Soper, 1956).*

360. *Small terra-cotta model of a three-story house, Han dynasty (Kansas City, William Rockhill Nelson Gallery of Art).*

361. *Small ceramic model of a tower, Han dynasty (London, British Museum).*

conducted continual raids on Chinese soil, the Great Wall probably connected old lines of fortifications in pounded earth built for the same reason by the small Chou states. It consists at present of massive stone blocks that form a crenellated wall from 18 to 30 feet high, with watch- and garrison towers at frequent intervals. Though not architecture in the strict sense, the Great Wall, winding slowly along the undulating hills, imparts grace and majesty to the landscape, with which it merges (Plate 358). It thus becomes one of the best examples of the typically Chinese desire to achieve a harmony between the human (in this case, architectural) product and its natural setting.

Han Dynasty (206 or 202 B.C.–A.D. 220)

A dynasty divided into two periods, interrupted by the reign of a usurper, Wang Mang, was to emerge in opposition to revolutionary Ch'in innovations. Though bent on restoring Confucianism and traditional values, the Han dynasty—historically divided into Earlier, or Western, Han (206 or 202 B.C.–A.D. 9) and Later, or Eastern, Han (A.D. 25–220)—did not abandon all the achievements of the First August Emperor, particularly in the field of architecture. What is more, one might even say that Ch'in models, along with those of Shang and Chou, which in the Han period were from time to time patiently sought out in the ancient sources (as we have noted for the case of the Ming T'ang), now arrived at complete maturity. The great Han expansion on the Asian continent, despite occasional setbacks, reached from Korea to the Indochinese peninsula as well as into Central Asia; and led to the spread of Chinese architectural concepts in new territories, where the foundations were laid for continuous and fruitful artistic collaboration. It is precisely for this reason that evidence of Han architectural activity can be drawn not only from the remains existing on national soil, but also from the clues offered by works constructed in conquered areas. We find them in the small terra-cotta models of buildings (*ming-ch'i*) included among burial offerings, in stone reliefs, and particularly in the tombs in the Korean colony of Lo-lang. Numerous historical and poetical writings (for example, those characterized as *fu*, one of the genres of Han poetry) are rich in allusions to monumental buildings, and to the geomantic and sumptuary rules that regulated their construction.

Sufficient traces have been found to define the layout of the two principal capitals, whose sites were chosen for political and military reasons. We can conclude that the Earlier Han capital was located near Changan, and that of the Later Han near Loyang, though naturally the wooden buildings themselves have disappeared.

To whatever extent Changan was built by royal decree, the previous site, as well as the unevenness of the terrain, must have deter-

364. *Stone slab from a Han tomb with a relief depicting a building (New York, Metropolitan Museum of Art).*

365. *Outskirts of Pyongyang (North Korea), interior of the Tomb of Celestial Kings and Earth Spirits, Koguryo period (from Sickman-Soper, 1956).*

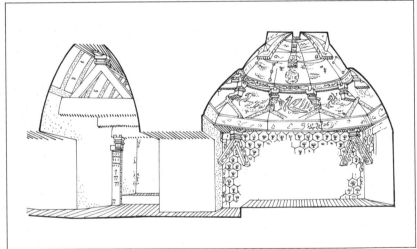

mined the shape of the city walls. They are about 12 miles in length, and do not form a perfect square, the northwest and southeast corners being irregular. And, though the principal new streets were laid out in a chessboard pattern according to the old Chou canon, the main axis, starting at the center gate of the southern side, was nevertheless abnormal in that it did not lead to any important palace complex. Actually, the two Han royal palaces, the Wei-yang and the Ch'ang-lo, occupied respectively two almost symmetrical areas to the southwest and southeast. The large sanctuaries and administrative buildings were also irregularly located. On the other hand, the layout of the Later Han capital was closer to the canonical quadrangular plan. According to the texts, the great south-to-north Processional Way rigidly followed the Chou canon and was flanked by government buildings.

The monumental, as the Chinese conceived it, was created by a large number of buildings of ample proportions, mutually related among themselves by arcades, loggias, terraces, staircases, and curtain walls, all in accordance with rules of axiality, symmetry, and rhythm that had already been formulated in the Ch'in period. This monumental effect was pursued as well by the Han rulers as a necessary axiom and manifestation of a stable, centralized government. At the same time, a certain sense of verticality was sought, with elevated structures that enlivened or acted to counterbalance the horizontal mass of the large halls. The texts, small terra-cotta models of buildings, and finally sepulchral reliefs all testify to the existence of structures with such isolated towers as represented by, for example, the ceramic tower in the British Museum (Plate 361). Some towers were placed to the sides of entrance gates; see the sepulchral tile with the representation of a monumental gateway (Plate 359), in the Hsi-ch'eng Museum, Cheng-tu, Szechwan, for an example of this practice.

Various types of these constructions are distinguished in the texts. The oldest, already documented in the Chou period, is the *t'ai*, rising on a high base of pounded earth. The *ch'iieh* (the two elements flanking gateways, and which vary in size from simple pillars to huge watchtowers) seem to belong to the Han period, as does the *lou* especially, an isolated wooden tower documented by numerous small models and perhaps the archetype of the Buddhist pagoda.

The Han remains found in Changan have shown that the extravagant dimensions reported by the texts for the great pavilions of the imperial palaces corresponded to reality. The audience hall of the Wei-yang, which according to the texts measured in plan more than 394 by 115 feet, has been identified on the spot with a platform of pounded earth over 300 feet long and about 49 feet high. Such buildings were often larger than those that came later, while porticoes and foreparts amplified the dimensions still more. Thus, the perimeter of the whole complex could even be measured in miles. Great technical innovations facilitated monumental construction. The corbel system, for example, for which it is impossible to establish a beginning date, seems to have been widely adopted for the first time in this period, and was apparently applied both to architecture in wood and to the translation of this into stone. Certainly the system makes it possible to build roofs with much wider and heavier tiles. Another great triumph of Han architecture is the devising of stone or brick structures with masterfully connected barrel or ogival vaults, rounded or pointed arches found in the imperial necropoli, and to which civilizations of the West may well have contributed.

Even the use of roofing tiles becomes perfectly defined, as is shown by the terra-cotta ming-ch'i in the William Rockhill Nelson Gallery of Art in Kansas City (Plate 360). On the other hand, the texts speak of coffered or actual cupola interiors, though they are not very clear on the disposition of the wooden elements. And, it is certain that the more important Han structures, whether palaces, temples, or monumental gateways, were replete with decorations: the sources describe the carvings and the incrustations of gold and jade, the wall paintings, the sculptures, and the plant and animal ornamental motifs that blended with the architecture itself.

We have a demonstration of this in some of the finest tombs (such as the one at Pei Chai Ts'un in Shantung), in which the entrance, the walls, and the pillars show a continuous decoration in very low or actually scratched relief, so dense as to create the sensation of a horror vacui, alien to the taste of classical China (Plate 364). In the tomb near Wangtu in Hopei, there remain traces of extensive wall paintings, representing dignitaries and historical personages, similar to those that, according to the texts, adorned Han palaces. Judging by the remains in our possession, this kind of ornamentation, though dense and sumptuous, did not lead to any disunity in the architectural mass; the flat—one might say, calligraphic—character of the design tended to emphasize and follow the structural elements without detracting from their rhythm.

Even in its tombs, the Han period expressed its inexhaustible fantasy, while remaining faithful to traditional Shang and Chou rules for orientation and symmetry, and adapting innovations proposed by the Ch'in. The introduction of the stone funerary chamber topped by a tumulus, which was adopted more widely under the Later Han (though we still see wooden structures applied in the tomb of General Ho Ch'ü-ping in Shensi), allowed for a more articulated modulation of the plan, with entrance spaces, corridors, and supplementary chambers, as in the two large princely Wangtu tombs in Hopei.

On the outside, the shên tao and funerary garden were enriched with pillars, portals, human and animal figures, and small sacrificial temples (tz'u) made of stone slabs, on which the masterful decorative skill of the Han was unfolded in all its elegance. The small sacrificial temple of Mount Hsiao-t'ang near Feicheng is the earliest example of such an open-air Chinese building that has come down to us, as are the four little temples of the Wu family necropolis near Kiasiang (Shantung), from Later Han times.

Though their structure is of stone, the interiors of these burial grounds have preserved enough elements to allow us to reconstruct Han wooden architecture as well. In fact, due to the predominantly wooden character of Chinese architecture, these perfect stone constructions very often utilize, with decorative value, typical elements of wooden architecture. Such is the case of the enormous boat-shaped bracket arms, a typically Han feature of the tomb at Pei Cha Ts'un near I-nan in Shantung. The same tomb, datable to the end of the Han period, has for the first time revealed a type of ceiling that German scholars have called Laternendecke (lantern ceiling), and which is constituted of diminishing squares, obliquely placed one within the other.

This ceiling was to find wide application in the later architecture of the Far East. Von Le Coq, and later Soper, examining this element of workmanship (in its constructed form but sometimes only as represented pictorially) in western and Central Asia, have advanced the hypothesis that it is derived from wooden roof coverings in Armenia and western Turkestan, whence through numerous intermediate stages to be found in the cave temples of Central Asia it would have reached the Far East. The considerably early date of the I-nan tomb, however, and the fact that the lantern ceiling is here already used as a decorative motif into which rosettes are inserted, suggests an opposite hypothesis. Moreover, the structure, obviously inspired by wooden prototypes, corresponds precisely to the clearest requirements of the Chinese aesthetic—specifically, the superimposition of similar elements—and only serves to confirm our conjecture that this type of ceiling is in reality an invention of the art of Chinese carpentry. There is no reason not to suppose a reverse direction for the diffusion of this type of ceiling, which, from the China of the Han dynasty, would have been carried to the West just as it also arrived in Korea, where it is found, for example, in the great mid-sixth-century Koguryo tomb near Pyongyang (Plate 365).

The architecture of the Han dynasty deserves credit, too, for having conceived the Chinese design for the Buddhist temple, though unfortunately we have only the texts here to rely on. Chapter CIII of the Hou Han shu (the chronicles of the Later Han) tells of a two-storied pavilion surmounted by nine rows of bronze disks, a building that would have been the ancestor of the pagoda. On the other hand, remains of non-Buddhist religious buildings have been found. The

Ming T'ang, for example, corresponds exactly to the textual descriptions, which emphasize the central plan, the sequence of circles and squares (symbolic references to heaven and earth), the relevant connections or intersections, the placing of openings at the four cardinal points, the foreparts and interior subdivisions, corresponding to the seasons, months, and days of the year. The foundations, discovered near Changan, of a monumental structure in the form of a Greek cross, superimposed on a square terrace and a broad circular platform, confirm this.

Eight other sanctuaries of this kind (square in shape, however) can be ascribed to the building activities of the usurper Wang Mang, who erected them in honor of his mythical ancestors. They have been uncovered in the capital and demonstrate the widespread acceptance of the centrally planned sanctuary, which will constitute the archetype of all future "altars" to heaven and earth from the T'ang dynasty to the Ch'ing.

Six Dynasties (A.D. 221–581)

We still know little about the layout of cities during this troubled period, but it can be supposed that in such major sites as Loyang, the Chin capital and later that of the Wei, the Han plan was preserved. A description of the city, primarily of its Buddhist sanctuaries, has come down to us in the *Memories of the Sangharāma of Loyang* by Yang Hsüanchi. It is substantially the account of a visit made in 547, and confirms this hypothesis.

Nanking, the capital of the southern dynasties, which more than the others kept alive the Han tradition, must also have been close to the traditional plan. Unfortunately, the major part of the monuments at Nanking have sunk into the ground. The necropolis has remained accessible, however. Though not excavated in depth, it shows its derivation from the Han in its tumuli, which are surrounded by an enclosure oriented according to canonical rules.

Since no specimens of wooden architecture remain on Chinese soil, we are obliged to use the sculptured images from tombs or Buddhist cave temples, or else the Korean and Japanese examples that give evidence of the spread of Chinese architecture throughout the Far East, in order to form an idea of the wooden buildings of this period (Plates 369–372).

The image of a quadrangular pavilion, very simple in design, with openings at the center of each side—to be found in Cave No. 6 at Yunkang in Shensi (second half of the fifth century)—shows how a third central arm was added to the boat-shaped Han brackets, as well as the evolution of the acroteria that topped the simple double-sloped roof, assuming the classical "owl-tail" form that was later to be adopted

on T'ang buildings. The three-armed brackets were then interpolated with wooden supports in the form of an inverted "V." This is a characteristic that we will find in certain seventh- and eighth-century buildings (Plate 382). It appears in the representation of a wooden pavilion on the architrave of the Ta-yen-t'a at Hsi-an-fu, and in the *kondō* as well as on the southern door of the Horyuji at Nara.

In these latter two examples the position of the support (under the balconies) is already of less importance, a sign of the progressive abandonment of the use of this motif, despite the fact that one still sees it represented in the Koguryo tombs at Pyongyang and in the sepulchral stone pagoda of Ching-ts'ang in the Hui-shan-ssu on Mount Sung (Honan), dating from the middle of the eighth century.

The adoption of curved roofs with concave slopes, which seems to have begun at this time, certainly as a contribution of the styles of the south, led to the search for solutions that would allow a greater lateral expansion of the slopes themselves, as can be seen in the Tamamushi shrine in Japan, probably of Korean ancestry.

Such innovations, widely employed by the T'ang, emphasize a body of technical knowledge—the science of building, we would call it—and on another level tend to augment an interest in mechanics and automatic devices. The texts mention a "rotating mechanism placed below the ceiling, embellished by a view of the sky, on which celestial bodies were painted,"[7] constructed for the Ming T'ang built by the northern Wei (A.D. 386–534). Other structural innovations were introduced by the so-called Western world. In fact, the "barbarian" states of the north were undoubtedly more open to influences from the West; they were much less subject to Confucian conservatism, and were driven by the new religion of Buddhism to adopt forms of Indian and Central Asian origin that had been created to fulfill the liturgical and doctrinal requirements of Buddhism itself.

In addition to the decorative motifs revealed in the sculptures and paintings from cave temples and tombs, and absolutely unknown to China in previous epochs (such as Classical acanthus leaves, Indian lotus blossoms, capitals with the heads of Persian animals), one might point out the use of entasis in wooden columns, this being perhaps a remote Classical reminiscence. Proof can be seen in the Japanese Horyuji temple complex at Nara (Plate 507), which by now almost all scholars would seem to agree is stylistically derived from the architecture of the Six Dynasties, even though it represents a later reconstruction.

The phenomenon that better than any other demonstrates the ability of the Chinese, or of the barbarians converted to their civilization, to adapt the traditional architectural style to foreign building models is the pagoda. Its genesis is difficult to reconstruct, primarily because the earliest prototypes are unknown. Undoubtedly inspired,

368. *Yunkang (Shensi), interior of Cave No. 39, central pillar sculptured in the form of a pagoda, period of the Six Dynasties.*

both in its sacred function and its structure, by the Indian stupa, it is of two principal types: one in stone or brick, and one in wood. And, if in the stone type the connection with the stupa is more obvious (one must remember that up to this point, with the exception of certain sacrificial chambers, fortifications, and terracings, no open-air stone building had appeared in Chinese architecture), in the wooden type a comparison with the towers of the Han period comes spontaneously to mind. In fact, in the earliest stone examples that have come down to us, the influence of various kinds of shrines elaborated by Indian and Central Asian architecture is evident.

The square pagoda of Shen-t'ung-ssu in Shantung, dating to A.D. 544 (Plate 366), is very close to the traditional stupa. It is essentially a cube, with arched openings at the four sides, and a molded entablature to which is added a pyramidal roof topped by the characteristic "owl-tailed" acroteria. Very close to Indian stupas of the Gupta period is the oldest example of a brick pagoda, belonging to the Sung-yüeh-ssu complex on Mount Sung in Honan, datable to the first decades of the sixth century (Plate 367). The characteristic spire shape with its curved line, its twelve-sided base, its second level with columns at the angles and representations of pagodas (similar to the Shen-t'ung-ssu) in the intervening spaces, its series of fifteen diminishing eaves, make it a totally new type of construction for the Far East. Only a single other contemporary example, hexagonal in shape, has been found, in the Wu Tai Shan temple of Fo-kuang-ssu in Shansi (Plates 375–378), but the later Liao pagodas (Plate 390) seem certainly to have been inspired by these early prototypes. More widespread and perhaps even older must have been the single-story type that we frequently find represented in reliefs, on stelae and the walls of caves, such as the one already mentioned in Cave No. 6 at Yunkang. The wooden type of pagoda is closer to Chinese architectural conceptions. The texts agree in describing the numerous installations carried out by the various dynasties, the progressive increase in the number of stories and thus in height, the richness and variety of the decoration and carving. The wooden pagoda, probably inspired by the famous Kanishka tower or stupa erected in the second century A.D. near modern Peshawar, employs this starting point to develop a type of structure directly related to the ancient Chou and Han towers, whose cultural connection with Taoism is likewise underlined by the texts. From the sculptural evidence that we have of these wooden pagodas, we can assume that they were towers square in plan, with roofs supported at every level by columns and corbels. Two striking examples of such representation are the three-storied pagoda shown in relief on the north wall of the Ku-yang cave at Lüng Men (Honan), from the beginning of the sixth century, and the five-storied one sculptured at the center of Cave No. 39 at Yunkang

◁ *370. Lüng Men (Honan), complex of cave temples.*

371. Lüng Men (Honan), complex of cave temples.
372. Lüng Men (Honan), complex of cave temples.
*373. Changan (Sian, Shensi), remains of the imperial Lin-te-tien pavilion,
T'ang dynasty.*

(Shensi), of the late sixth century.

The exceptional vitality of Chinese architecture ensured that even
so fundamentally foreign a structure as the stupa would acquire
traditional dress, while maintaining the strong tendency toward verticality already apparent in works of northwest India. On the other hand,
the other buildings inside the temple enclosure, such as the hall of the
Buddhas, the reading hall, and the entrance gates, were to be entirely
Chinese in taste. The shape of the temple complex was also to be
defined at this time, with the pagoda situated on the axis of the southern
entrance gate and followed by the Buddha pavilion and the reading
hall, in accordance with the traditional south-to-north orientation.
This is shown by the descriptions in such historical texts as the *Wei-shu*.
However, another type of layout was to be developed with the pagoda
at the center, flanked by the pavilion of the Buddhas and the reading
hall, on a line parallel to the side of the entrance. Proof of this has been
found in the remains of Korean Buddhist temples from the Koguryo
and Pakche reigns, the final result of which was the construction of the
Horyuji at Nara in Japan.

Except for stone pagodas, the works that more than any others
constituted an architectural novelty were the Buddhist cave temples,
built according to the plan of analogous Indian and Central Asian ones.

In the oldest caves, especially some of those in the Yunkang group,
the Indian vihara and chaitya are recognizable, with either a central
pilaster carved out of the rock in imitation of the central axis of the
stupa, or with an actual stupa; while the entrance with its horseshoe
arch (*kūdu*) and the use of Classical capitals and Western decorative
motifs brings this architecture still closer to its prototypes. In time the
typical structures of Chinese wooden constructions would be sculptured or painted on the walls. Corbels, columns, and tile roofs are all
reproduced on the rock or painted in the numerous cave temples dug
out of mountain cliffs or built in natural caves—at Tunhwang in
Kansu, at Lüng Men in Honan—while the entrances sometimes tend to
resemble those of Han tumuli. We must not forget that building in
caves was by no means alien to the Chinese, as we know from the
dwellings dug out of loess in Honan, Shansi, Shensi, and Kansu. There
is likewise the evidence of Han rock sepulchers, discovered in Honan
and Szechwan, which often display the carved architectural elements
of constructed tombs and are preceded by an ordinary vestibule that
takes the place of a sacrificial chamber.

Sui (A.D. 589–618) and T'ang (A.D. 618–907) Dynasties

With the reunification of the Chinese nation, it was only natural
that, in order to consolidate this unity, the brief Sui dynasty (A.D. 589–
618), and to an even greater extent the long-lived T'ang dynasty (A.D.

374. *Relief showing a wooden building in the Ta-yen pagoda at Changan (Sian, Shensi), T'ang dynasty.*

375. *Wu Tai Shan (Shansi), Fo-kuang-ssu, elevation, longitudinal section, and transverse section of the principal pavilion, T'ang dynasty (from Sickman-Soper, 1956).*

376. *Fo-kuang-ssu, detail of the sloping roof, T'ang dynasty (from Sickman-Soper, 1956).*

377. *Fo-kuang-ssu, detail of the interior, T'ang dynasty (from Sickman-Soper, 1956).*

378. *Fo-kuang-ssu, detail of the interior, T'ang dynasty (from Sickman-Soper, 1956).*

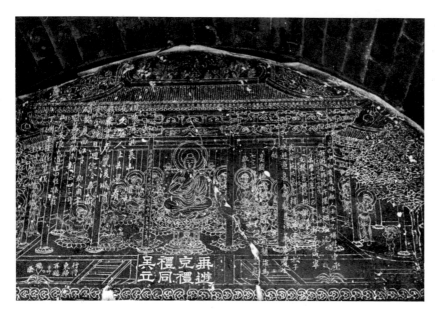

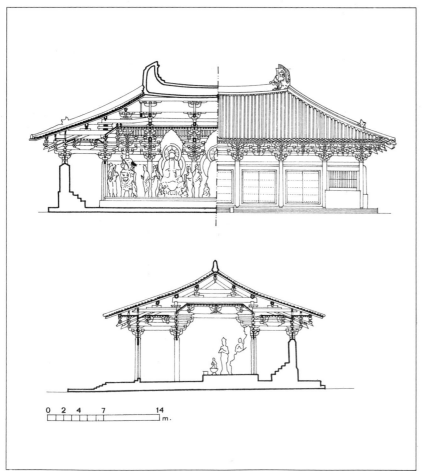

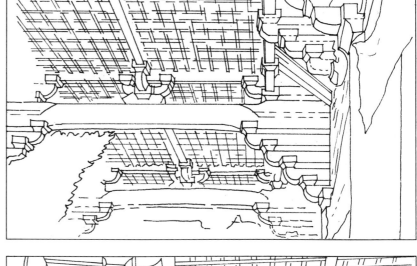

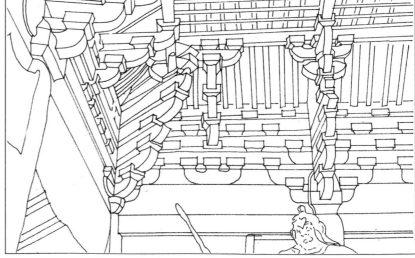

618–907), should look back to the Han period as the model in all economic, political, cultural, and artistic fields. Nevertheless, the period of the Six Dynasties, though undervalued because of its chaos and instability, had its importance in the development of T'ang architecture. It can even be said that many T'ang structures, particularly Buddhist ones, are a natural derivation from those of the Six Dynasties phase. Moreover, the great territorial expansion of China into Central Asia, Korea, and Indochina, and her relations with the ruling houses of India, Central Asia, and Persia—which also acted as intermediaries with Greco-Roman civilization and later with Islam—brought Chinese architecture, by a process of comparison, to a better knowledge of its own nature and to an improvement of its peculiar characteristics. On the other hand, the introduction and adaptation of new foreign elements, aided by the travels of Buddhist pilgrims, would produce important changes.

As early as the first century of the T'ang dynasty, the characteristics of its particular architectural style take on clear shape. Buildings have ample proportions and a monumental character, and there is an obvious love for clear, linear, and simple forms. In general, these structures, severely functional, are conceived in a spirit of rigorous logic, while in the building plans we witness the realization of the ancient traditional principles, but applied with a new and clear sense of symmetry, rhythm, and harmony. It is not impossible that this search for harmony, rhythm, and clarity was favorably influenced by the development of Chinese music, determined among other things by the success achieved by Central Asian musical groups in the T'ang period, with the greater compositional, rhythmic, and instrumental knowledge that was thereby produced.

Be that as it may, it was to these truly clear urban and architectural forms that the Great Silla Kingdom of Korea and the Japan of the Asuka and Nara periods were to look, thus achieving in their own territories works that were related among themselves and so obviously inspired by the China of the T'ang that it is not hazardous to speak, for this phase, of an "Eastern pan-Asian" style, with its center in the Chinese capital.

The Japanese city of Nara was built on the plan of the Changan of the T'ang (Plate 396), which was enclosed by a wall 18 by 15 *li* (the Chinese unit of distance equivalent to about one third of a mile), with the area of the royal palace and government buildings concentrated at the central part of the northern wall, to be approached along the great Processional Way. The rigid axiality of this main artery divided the city into two halves, western and eastern, each with its own central market. The two sections were further subdivided by a chessboard network of streets into rectangular districts, each of which might

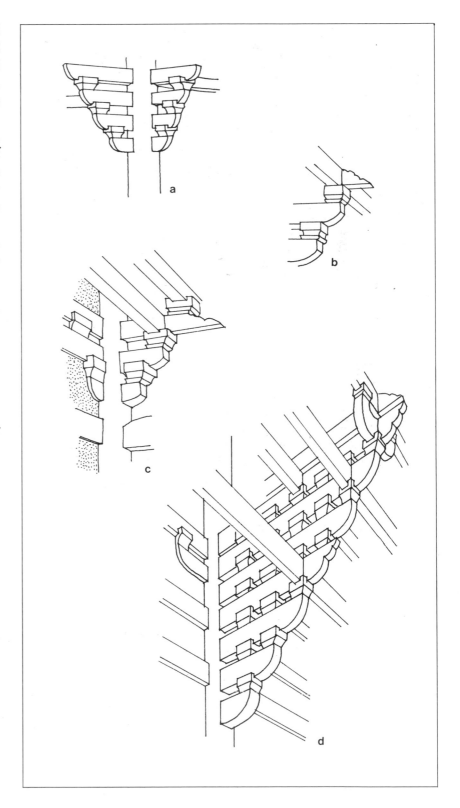

380. *Changan (Sian, Shensi), Ta-yen-t'a pagoda, T'ang dynasty.*

381. *Courtyard in front of the Ta-yen-t'a pagoda, T'ang dynasty.*

382. *Examples of the development of the bracket system: a) pavilion of Kuan-yin in the Tu-lo temple at Chi-hsien (Hopei); b)* kondō *of the Horyuji temple at Nara; c)* kondō *of the Tōshōdaiji (from Willetts, 1958).*

383. *Mount Fang (Hopei), small pagoda of Yün-chü-ssu, T'ang dynasty.*

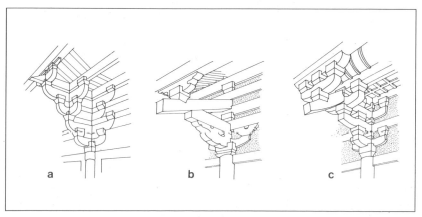

384. *Mount Sung (Honan), pagodas of the Hui-shan-ssu, T'ang dynasty.*
385. *Mount Sung (Honan), pagoda of the Hui-shan-ssu, T'ang dynasty.*

386. *Changan, pagoda-tomb of Hsüan-tsang, T'ang dynasty.*

consist of up to four lesser rectangles separated by narrower streets. Outside the walls to the northeast was another imperial residence—the so-called Ta-ming Palace, which has recently been scientifically excavated and was itself enclosed by ample rectangular walls. This residential complex was symmetrically constructed, as always, adhering to an axis laid out by its major pavilions along a south-to-north line. The monumental entrance to the entire complex was at the south. A less official complex, the Lin-te-tien, situated near the western wall of the Ta-ming-kung and much more varied in shape, is probably the prototype of the freer designs shown by the later "pleasure palaces."

Very few examples of wooden buildings have survived. Remains of the main pavilion of Fo-kuang-ssu on Wu Tai Shan, from the middle of the tenth century (Plate 375), and the Nan-ch'an-ssu in the same area, from 782, still stand, however. In addition, the descriptions provided by historical texts and such chronicles as those of the Japanese pilgrim Ennin, together with sculptured or painted representations (especially those in the Tunhwang caves), and, above all, such remains of the Buddhist complexes of Nara as the Golden Hall of the Tōshōdaiji, allow us to form an adequate picture of the architectural development. The corbel system increases in height, augmenting the number of orders but preserving a solid unity; the use of the *ang* bracket at the corners becomes aesthetically and structurally more coherent; columns slowly lose their entasis. In the Tōshōdaiji *kondō* (Plate 382), they still preserve a slight final swelling, while bases become increasingly elaborate, assuming lotus blossom forms in the middle and late T'ang. On the other hand, toward the roofs, for which the simplified type of slope is preferred, levels are very graduated, with only a slight curvature at the eaves.

An important innovation is shown in the interiors with the progressive adoption of chairs, which had already appeared in China under the Han but were now used more widely, perhaps also due to the influence of foreigners staying in Changan. Up to this time, Chinese interior furnishings had been very similar to the classical Japanese ones that are still in use, but now the elevation of the "working level" ensured the adoption of furniture that would raise the life and activity of the inhabitants from the floor level. Such furnishings, however, unlike in our Western dwellings, were always few in number, thus leaving the interiors free and uncluttered.

The technical skill of Sui and T'ang builders is further attested by the texts, which record, besides such truly original works as a "rotating pavilion" by Yü-wen K'ai,[8] and a pavilion cooled in the summer by artificial rains, a number of great public works. The Grand Canal, for example, is described as connecting the Yellow River with the Yangtze (A.D. 584 to the end of the eighth century); and the royal

palace of Loyang, the other great monumental city of the T'ang, was enhanced by a large artificial lake. An example of this skill and originality survives today in the large reduced arch, flanked by four auxiliary arches, of the Great Stone Bridge (whose span measures about 124 by 24 feet) near Chaohsien in Hopei, the work of the master builder Li Ch'un (sixth to seventh century).

The anti-Buddhist persecutions during the year 845 and during the tenth century, a natural reaction to the ostentation of the large monasteries, destroyed the splendid temples in Changan and Loyang. There still remain, however, as we have seen, a few peripheral temple halls and some brick and stone pagodas, which together with the cave temples of Tunhwang, T'ien-lung Shan, and Lüng Men, as well as the Korean and Japanese complexes, constitute what survives of the great Buddhist architecture of the T'ang period.

The plan of the temple complex increasingly takes the shape of the royal palace, in accordance with a natural development that keeps pace with the acclimatization of foreign elements. The prayer hall, which is seen as a substitute for the imperial audience hall, can now be found, especially in the later shrines, isolated on the axis of the entrance gate. The two pagodas, on the other hand, are placed to the sides of the façade, thus forfeiting their role as fulcrums of the sanctuary. This is the so-called twin-pagoda plan (Plate 395), which is imitated in the temples of the Silla Kingdom and in those at Nara and will be widely followed by the Sung. Lanterns in stone, a new type of two-story pavilion (the *ko*), other pavilions such as the reading hall, symmetrically placed and sometimes even octagonal in shape (the Yumedono in the Horyuji at Nara), completed the complex, which at times assumed the dimensions of a royal palace. The brick pagodas, direct descendants of types from the period of the Six Dynasties, become much more linear and harmonious. They may be cube-shaped, like the small pagoda of Yün-chü-ssu on Mount Fang, of the eighth century (Plate 383); or polygonal, like the Hui-shan-ssu pagodas on Mount Sung, also of the eighth century (Plates 384, 385); or square in plan and with the upper stories slightly diminishing in size, like the splendid seventh-century Ta-yen-t'a of Changan (Plates 380, 381). All of them develop slowly, adopting a type of architectural decoration that increasingly tends to imitate the wooden structures. This trend is evident in the Hsüan-tsang pagoda at Changan (Plate 386) and even more so in the octagonal Chung-hsing-ssu pagoda at Chou-hsien (Shantung), which dates to the beginning of the ninth century and is the prototype of later Liao and Sung pagodas.

We have direct testimony for wooden pagodas in the constructions at Nara, such as the Daigoji tower, built in the tenth century, and the older Yakushiji, which are extraordinarily similar to those represented at Tunhwang, square in shape and generally with five diminishing

390. *Mount Fang (Hopei), Pei-t'a (northern pagoda), Liao dynasty.*
391. *Chi Hsia, near Nanking, Buddhist monastery, view of the caves.*

392. *Kaifeng (Honan), Kuo-hsiang-ssu, Fan pagoda, Sung dynasty.* ▷

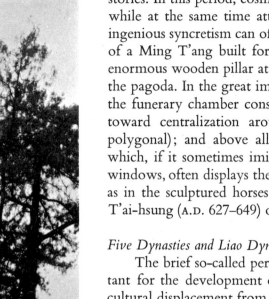

stories. In this period, cosmopolitan and open to contacts from abroad while at the same time attentive to traditional values, a particularly ingenious syncretism can often be observed in every field. We are told of a Ming T'ang built for the empress Wu (A.D. 684–704), with an enormous wooden pillar at the center, clearly derived from the axis of the pagoda. In the great imperial necropoli the traditional shape, with the funerary chamber constructed in brick, shows a strong tendency toward centralization around the main room (square, round, or polygonal); and above all a great wealth of sculptural decoration, which, if it sometimes imitates to perfection a wooden pavilion and windows, often displays the potent and realistic plasticity of the T'ang, as in the sculptured horses in the sacrificial chamber of the tomb of T'ai-hsung (A.D. 627–649) on Mount Chiu-tsun.

Five Dynasties and Liao Dynasty (A.D. 907–1125)

The brief so-called period of the Five Dynasties is highly important for the development of Chinese architecture: it marked a new cultural displacement from the north (invaded by the Khitan and Sha-t'o barbarians) toward the south, where the northern emigrants were to bring a fresh contribution of the already widespread T'ang culture. Here ambitious canal works were to improve agriculture and increase prosperity, and Arab, Indian, and Persian merchants would carry out a thriving sea commerce. The architecture that developed, while traditional, was at the same time rich in local influences, and would reach its full flowering in the period of the Southern Sung. In the northern regions wars and the succession of barbarian kingdoms that were only superficially assimilated to Chinese culture led to the almost total destruction of Changan and Loyang, while, in the beginning, the only new constructions were banal imitations of the T'ang style. The foreign dynasty that more than any other showed itself capable of originality in architecture and town planning—and this was facilitated by its longevity and a long process of acclimatization—was the Khitan dynasty of the Liao (907–1125). In its native Jehol in Mongolia and in its areas of expansion in Shansi and Hopei, we find many remains of Liao architecture, and in particular traces of the five great capitals. The archaeological evidence, together with the buildings attributed to this period by the sources, make it possible to single out these "barbaric" reinterpretations—sometimes highly successful—of the complicated geomantic and structural rules of the T'ang. Often the façades of the royal palaces are placed east instead of south (probably a reminiscence of the ancient cult of the sun); this innovation is also found in the Buddhist complex of Hua-yen-ssu at Tatung.

The octagonal shape was preferred for the typical Liao brick pagoda (Plate 403), generally seven or thirteen stories in height, permit-

393. *Cheng-ting-hsien (Hopei), Lung-hsing-ssu, exterior of the Mo-mi-tien,*
    Sung dynasty.

394. *Plan of the city of P'ing-chiang (Suchow), incised on stone (London, British Museum).*

395. *Suchow (Kiangsu), the "Twin Pagodas."*

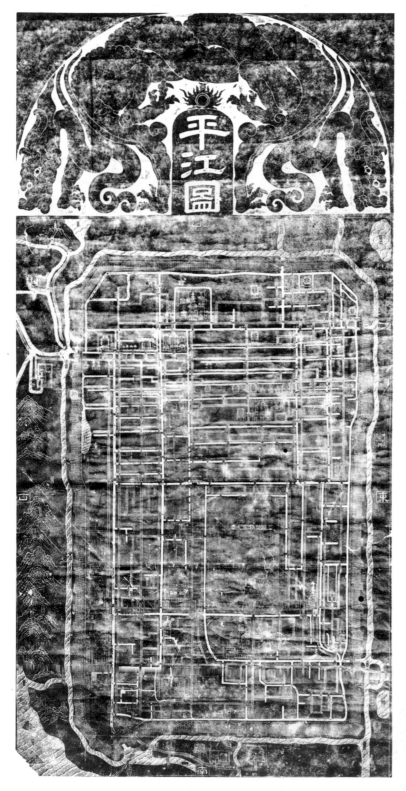

396. a) Plan of the city of Changan, T'ang dynasty; b) plan of a complex of Japanese private houses of the Heian period (from Willetts, 1958).

397. Yinghsien (Shansi), pagoda of Fo-kuang-ssu, Liao dynasty.
398. Chin-tz'u, near Yangku (Shansi), Shen-mu tien (Pavilion of the Holy Mother), detail, Sung dynasty. ▷

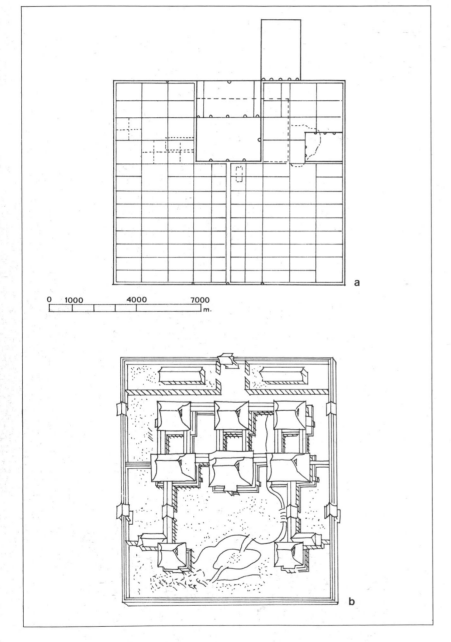

a

0 1000   4000   7000
                    m.

b

ting a greater modulation of the surfaces by pillars, corbels, niches, and often by reliefs. These reliefs, of animals and divinities, in a tireless search for variety, succeed in transforming at least a few of the numerous pagodas that have come down to us into sculptural treasures, such as the eastern pagoda of Pehchen at Chinhsien (Manchuria), from the middle of the eleventh century. Pagodas closer to the southern borders of the kingdom seem to be less baroque, and thus more susceptible to the linear clarity of the Northern Sung, like that of Yün-chü-ssu on Mount Fang near Peking, which dates back to 1117. Its external walls display only harmonious doors and windows. The first wooden buildings appear to be more traditional. The Kuan-yin-ko of Tu-lo-ssu at Chihsien, in Hopei, from the end of the tenth century (Plate 405),

399. *Kaifeng (Honan), "Color of Iron Pagoda," Sung dynasty.*

400. *Vertical section of a pavilion (note the excessive bracket system). Diagram of a wooden structure in the so-called Imperial style. From the* Ying-tsao fa-shih *construction manual, written in the twelfth century by the functionary Li Chieh.*

401. The Return of Lady Wen-chi to China, *by an unknown artist of the Sung dynasty (Boston, Museum of Fine Arts).*

402. *Nan-K'ou (Hopei), Chu-yung gate, Yüan period.*

403. *Peking, T'ien-ning temple, octagonal pagoda, Liao dynasty.* ▷

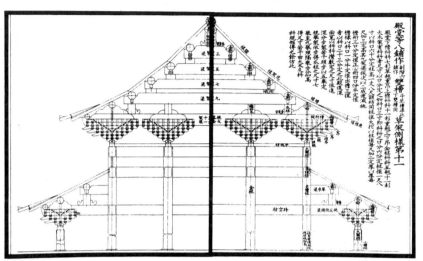

404. *Schematic perspective and plan of the Sheng-ku-miao at An-p'ing-hsien (Hopei), Yüan period (from Sickman–Soper, 1956).*

405. *Kuan-yin-ko pavilion of the Tu-lo-ssu at Chihsien (Hopei), Liao dynasty (from Sickman–Soper, 1956).*

406. *Tatung (Shansi), upper temple of the Hua-yen-ssu, plan of the main building, Liao dynasty (from Sickman–Soper, 1956).*

407. *Tatung (Shansi), Shan-hua-ssu, plan of the main building (from Sickman–Soper, 1956).*

408. *Sūtra cupboards in the library of the lower temple of Hua-yen-ssu, Tatung (Shansi) (from Sickman–Soper, 1956).*

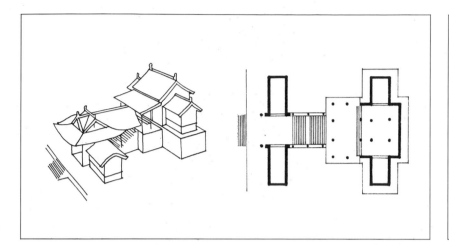

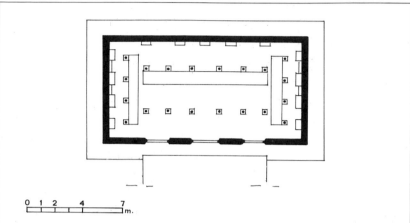

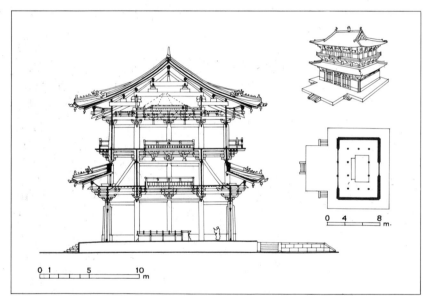

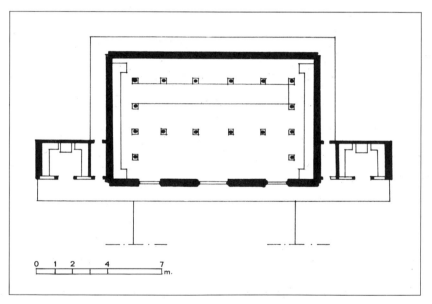

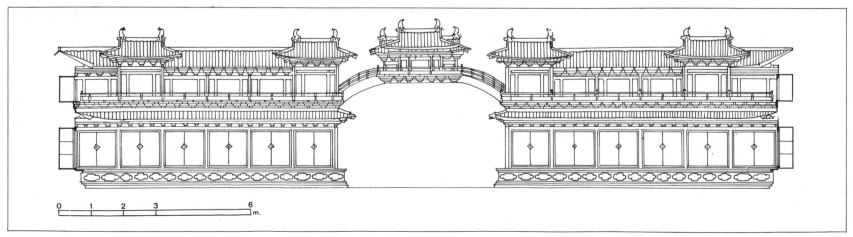

seems to be an imitation of a T'ang prototype, while the five-story wooden pagoda of Fo-kuang-ssu at Yinghsien, in Shansi, from 1058 (Plate 397), has strongly projecting roof slopes, demonstrating a development parallel to the one that occurred with the Sung in the transition from the large isolated brackets of the T'ang to a system of smaller and densely repeated ones, in which the use of the *ang* bracket is frequent.

The relationship of dependence that surely existed between at least some wooden structures of the Liao dynasty and those of the contemporary Sung is clearly shown—in a rather unique way—by the *sūtra* cupboards in the library of the lower Hua-yen-ssu at Tatung, which imitate buildings (Plate 408). Here the ideal delicacy of the bracket system—much varied and with multiple elements, together with the harmonious union of different building types, the graceful curvature of the roofs, with chamfers and gable—would suggest that these cabinets were constructed by Liao craftsmen intent on reproducing in this particular type of wooden architecture the peculiar characteristics of the Sung. One might also say that Liao builders found masonry a more congenial means of construction, precisely because it was less linked to an age-old tradition that almost had the power to paralyze them, just as it was to restrict their successors, the Jurchen dynasty of the Chin, to a mere repetitive admiration of the ancient styles.

Nevertheless, in their tombs, the Liao gave proof of extraordinary ability and strong originality by covering the funerary chambers with perfectly constructed cupolas, perhaps in imitation of their old nomadic tents.

Sung Dynasty (A.D. 960–1280)

In its efforts at unification, the Northern Sung dynasty (A.D 960–1127) looked back to the vanished T'ang dynasty as its ideal. The imposing monumental constructions of the T'ang inspired it to develop, from the middle of the eleventh century on, a happy combination of visual unity and structural agility, and the results were buildings with slender and harmonious lines, elegant and functional at the same time. Only in a later period, especially during the reign of the Southern Sung (1127–1280), did the architectural style tend toward greater elaboration. Columns then became excessively thin, and the increasingly smaller brackets were superimposed one over another to impart to the buildings pronounced contrasts of volume and chiaroscuro, accentuated by the coloristic effects produced by the use of brightly glazed tiles and by the shadows generated by the bold curves of the roof corners. These are typical characteristics of the architecture of the southern regions, to which the Chinese had been driven back by

the advance of the Jurchen. One should not forget, however, that Yü Hao, the famous architect who helped to plan the first Northern Sung capital of Pien-ching, the present Kaifeng, was a southerner. This means that from the beginning of their architectural development, the Sung welcomed and manifested a considerable contribution from the south (Plate 399).

We can get an accurate idea of the suburbs of the Kaifeng of the Sung through the famous scroll painting in the Palace Museum in Peking, the work of Chang Tse-tuan (1085–1145), and can reconstruct the magnificence of its monumental buildings from the enthusiastic descriptions of the Japanese pilgrim Jojin.[9] Multistoried buildings, pagodas, gateways, and ornamental towers attest the Sung preference

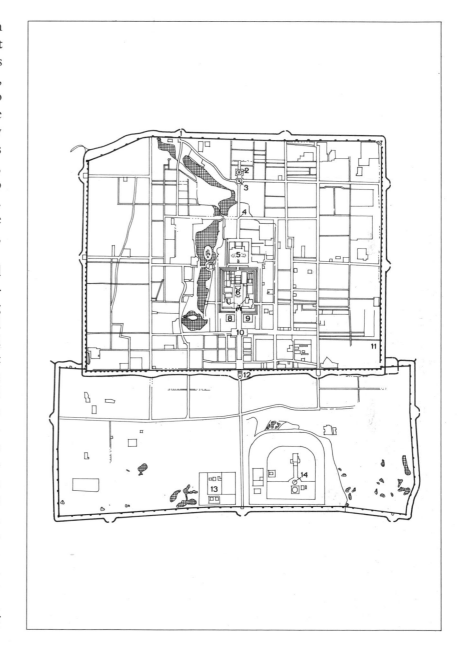

for vertical structures, while the need to enlarge the city inherited from the T'ang produced irregular alterations in the city walls and street network, though an effort was made to follow the canonical rules as much as possible. Even more irregular was the layout of Hangchow, capital of the Southern Sung and the Kinsai of Marco Polo, who visited it in 1280 and left a description so minute that the plan of the period can be reconstructed.[10] Laced by canals and crisscrossed by bridges that permitted the effective coexistence of a network of streets and one of waterways (a Grand Canal ran parallel to the main artery), Hangchow's royal palace area was placed in an irregular position (to the south), as a concession to the particular conditions of the terrain. The natural variety of the landscape with its lakes and islands, and the way in which the architectural structures were related to the setting, made this Chinese Venice even more fascinating.

Irregularity of plan, in contrast with traditional rules, is also found during this period in temple complexes. The Lung-hsing-ssu, at Cheng-ting-hsien in Hopei, is long and narrow in shape: two pavilions facing each other on the axis are followed by the Mo-mi-tien or Pearl Hall (Plate 393), by another main pavilion (with two bell towers to east and west), and by the drum tower. This is a new disposition, and one that we will find later in the Ming and Ch'ing periods. As for wooden structures, the *Ying-tsao-fa-shih*—the technical construction manual written in 1100 by the functionary Li Chieh (which we have in its entirety; that compiled a century earlier by Yü Hao has been lost)—allows us to reconstruct their development, and to integrate the evidence supplied by surviving Chinese, Korean, and Japanese buildings. The bracket system, highly diversified but rigorously coherent in its structural values, with the brackets well spaced and the *ang* arms more oblique and elegantly exposed, enlivened the whole (Plate 400); the architrave, in section, assumed the shape of a "T," as in the double-storied twin pavilions of Lung-hsing-ssu at Cheng-ting-hsien (Hopei), of the eleventh century. In some cases, the striving for ornamentation is accentuated, especially in such small wooden examples as the *sūtra* cupboard in the same temple. These touches break up the functionalism of the bracket structure—which is reduced to the simple exercise of craftsmanship—and create a new type of bracket, crushed and flat, designed to compensate for the exaggerated slenderness of the columns. Later, we will find widespread use of this bracket in Ming and Ching architecture.

As for the Southern Sung, on the other hand, only a few wooden examples survive. But the buildings respectively called *Karayō* (Chinese style) and *Tenjikuyō* (Indian style) in Japan, and *Tap'o* and *Chusimp'o* in Korea, testify to the presence of two currents formed in this period. The first is defined as "imperial," and carries to the extreme the

accretion of brackets by useless additions lacking in static value, and imparting graceful curves to the roof slopes, under which the brackets are thickly clustered. We can observe these innovations in embryo in the San-ch'ing-tien of the twelfth-century Taoist sanctuary of Yüan-miao-kuan at Suchow, and more clearly in the Founder's Hall (or *Kaisandō*) of Eihoji near Nagoya in Japan (1352), extraordinary in its composition.

There remain no examples in China of the second, or "Indian," style, called *Tenjikuyō* in Japanese. It perhaps arose in the southerly regions as a reaction to the excessive delicacy of the official style, and may relate to former T'ang prototypes. But the twin pagodas of Ch'üan-chou (Fukien), from the first half of the thirteenth century, repeat in granite the simple, powerful transverse bracket arms embedded above a tall trunk column that is typical of this style, and which we will find in the Keuk-nak Chon of the Pong-chong-sa, at An-dong-kun in Korea (twelfth to thirteenth centuries), and even more emphatically in the great southern gate of the Tōdaiji at Nara, of the late twelfth century (Plate 379). Given the Sung preference for slender, multistoried structures, it is natural that pagodas in brick should have flourished up to the twelfth century; beginning in the thirteenth century, however, the predominance of the Ch'an sect would limit their construction. Sung pagodas were covered with sculptures and enamel tiles, with imitations of wooden sculpture, and, in the later types, with actual wooden beams and brackets. Nevertheless, the Sung were able to preserve in their pagodas—the "Color of Iron Pagoda" of Kaifeng (Plate 399), from the middle of the eleventh century, is one such striking example—an elegance of line with a compactness and solidity that was not undermined by this excessive ornamentation.

Yüan Dynasty (A.D. 1280–1368)

The "barbarian" spirit that appeared in the Liao period—with its love for ornamentation and for contrasts in volume and chiaroscuro—achieved under the great Mongol dynasty of the Yüan (heirs to the pan-Asianism of Genghis Khan) one of its most complete manifestations. For this very reason, we may consider Yüan architecture a Baroque phase of Chinese architecture. Of course, the term Baroque here signifies a taste for lively surfaces and for effects of light and shadow, a taste so deeply rooted in the human spirit that it reappears whenever the natural environment allows. It is fortunate that Marco Polo has left us in his *Travels* precise descriptions of the monumentality and richness of Mongol Peking, for few vestiges of its greatness remain.

It is certain that the nomadic Mongol warriors, once they had occupied the city of Peking, imitated the Liao and Sung architectural masterpieces, carrying to maturity an almost fatal evolution toward

414. *Peking (outskirts), necropolis of the Ming emperors, stela atop a sculptured turtle, part of the tomb of Yung-ling.*

415. *Peking, Forbidden City, marble* hua-piao *in front of the T'ien-an men.*

Baroque forms, but also welcoming numerous foreign elements related to their traditional taste. The regularly shaped pavilion gave way to the composite form, with porticoes, annexes, and galleries to connect the individual parts. The composite aspect of Yüan buildings is accentuated by the different types of roofs used simultaneously, apparent in the Sheng-ku-miao at An-p'ing-hsien in Hopei, from 1309 (Plate 404), and in Li Jung-chin's painting of a Yüan "pleasure palace." We also have evidence of circular or irregular pavilions, perhaps the work of Arab master builders who had arrived at the court of the Mongol emperors.

The Tibetan architectural style, so remote in its heaviness from the Chinese, also appears as a result of the protection accorded by the

416. *Peking (outskirts), necropolis of the Ming emperors, monumental entrance portal.*
417. *Hangchow (Chekiang), Lin Ho pagoda.*

418. *Peking (outskirts), Temple of the Five Pagodas (Wu-t'a-ssu), detail of sculptured reliefs, Ming dynasty.*
419. *Peking (outskirts), Temple of the Five Pagodas (Wu-t'a-ssu), detail of sculptured reliefs, Ming dynasty.*
420. *Peking (outskirts), Temple of the Five Pagodas (Wu-t'a-ssu), Ming dynasty.* ▷

421. *Peking, "Pagoda of Glazed Ceramic," Ming dynasty.*
422. *Canton, so-called Ming dynasty tower.*

423. *Ch'u-chou (Ahnwei), "bath" of Emperor Hung-wu, Ming dynasty.*
424. *Peking, Altar of Heaven, general view, Ming period.*
425. *Peking, Altar of Heaven, p'ai-lous of the entrance road.*

426. *Peking, Altar of Heaven, Pavilion of Annual Prayers (Chi-nien tien).*

427. *Peking (outskirts), necropolis of the Ming emperors, funerary complex of Yung Lo, stairway.*
428. *Peking, Forbidden City, T'ai-miao, Ming dynasty.*
429. *Peking, Forbidden City, T'ai-miao, Ming dynasty.*

430. *Peking, Wu men, monumental entrance gate to the Forbidden City.*
431. *Peking, Wu men gate as seen from the north (from inside the Forbidden City).*
432. *Peking, Forbidden City, detail of a building.*

Yüan to Lamaistic Buddhism. Among the most typical examples of this style, we find the Miao-ying-ssu pagoda in Peking (1271), bottle-shaped, and showing a massive round drum devoid of decoration, on which rests a conical roof (Plate 409). Traditional pagodas, on the other hand, are often excessively animated in contour and varied in shape by symmetrical foreparts on the lower stories, like the Kyong-ch'on-sa pagoda at Seoul in Korea, clearly inspired by the Yüan. In this pagoda the movement of the numerous and diversified roof slopes at every level, and the chiaroscuro of the projecting and receding masses well justify the name "Baroque" commonly used to describe it.

Ming Dynasty (A.D. 1368–1644)

Many modern Western scholars, from Fontein[11] to Soper, have seen in Ming and Ch'ing architecture "a prolonged decadence of the art and science of fine building."[12] Paradoxically, the judgment of Western scholars on the late works of Chinese architecture seems to coincide, with certain exceptions, with that expressed by nineteenth-century European "classicists" with regard to our own Baroque and Rococo. Actually, such evaluations cannot be accepted. Ming constructions, far as they are from the strength of the T'ang and the delicate elegance of the Sung that they would seem to claim as their inspiration, nevertheless have a value of their own. Basically linear, Ming buildings reject excessively curved roofs and regular plans. Rigidly symmetrical in layout, they also achieve a highly pleasing blend of several strong elements—simplicity of shape, the monumentality of structural complexes inherited from the T'ang style (to which the Ming looked back with particular interest), and the richness and chiaroscuro typical of the architectural decoration practiced by the Sung, the Liao, and even the Yüan.

The capital, Peking, was formed by the merging of the Yüan or Tatar city with a vast suburb to the south, the Chinese city. In 1564 it was encircled by a wall and then was subsequently divided by the traditional Processional Way, which, running from south to north, arrived at the imperial palaces—the "Forbidden City." Its major buildings were aligned on this central axis (Plate 412), which crossed through various masonry walls under monumental gates (Plate 430) that opened onto vast expanses with terraces and stairways, striking the visitor with an almost scenographic impression of grandiose majesty. The imperial necropoli (Plates 414, 416, 427) evoked a similar sense of august power. Here, through magnificent wooden and stone portals, the Road of the Spirits, flanked by large marble figures, led to a succession of courtyards and pavilions that imitated the form of the royal palace. This layout consisted of sacrificial halls, of "soul towers"—that is, monumental towers with eschatological meanings (Plate 422)—and

finally the sepulchral tumulus, the pivot of the complex, where the funerary chamber with its numerous annexes was located. In Peking, the refined construction technique of the period is clearly shown in its large craftsmanship productions as well as in the Ming preference for masonry structures.

Ming military architecture is demonstrated by its large walls and fortifications (Plates 437, 439); it is to the Ming that we owe the reconstruction of the Great Wall and of many city walls that still survive today. The typical monumental gateways of the period and even the watchtowers often consist of a wooden pavilion of several stories built on a massive platform base of brick masonry, pierced by a wide barrel-vaulted gate and with staircases and balustrades. The so-called Bell Tower of Hsi-an-fu, one such structure, achieves a surprising harmony in the contrast between its closed and imposing lower part and the light and airy upper structure.

Within the framework of this interest (both technical and aesthetic) in brick constructions, we may include such imitations of the Tibetan stupa, *the chorten*—which had first appeared under the Yüan—as the Sarire-stupa of Ching-ming-ssu near Yangku (formerly Taiyüan), dating from 1385, and the arbitrary replica of the very famous Indian temple of Mahabodhi at Buddh Gaya, carried out in the Wu-t'a-ssu near Peking, a massive parallelepiped in masonry surmounted by five pyramidal pagodas, one at the center and the other four at the corners—an obvious reference to cosmological theories (Plates 418–420).

Traditional pagodas, however, were often miniature in size, becoming small monuments no higher than the sculptured lanterns placed in the courtyards of Buddhist temples. Perhaps an indirect Western influence of European missionaries is discernible in the appearance of two temples constructed of brick and covered by barrel vaults in the Shung-t'a-ssu at Yangku and at Suchow. Both date from the end of the sixteenth century.

As we know, it was at this time that buildings of a European type were erected in China—the Catholic churches built by Father Matteo Ricci and the colonial establishments of Macao and Canton. But aside from the two brick temple structures described—which may also have been the result of contacts with the Indian or Arab world—no important traces of Western influence have been found in the architecture of the period.

Still, much earlier, in the middle of the Yüan period, Giovanni di Montecorvino had at least two Catholic cathedrals constructed in a Gothic style, using, however, Chinese materials and wall coverings of glazed tiles.

Apart from the two archaeological remains, and the steady recognition on the part of the Chinese of their technical interest in the lessons

of Western builders, there is no sign of any vaster or deeper influences. Chinese architecture is separated from the West by taste, a different sense of space, by completely different sociological implications—and even by a divergent appreciation of the visual effect produced by architectural structures, which must, of course, be appropriately placed in their natural surroundings. For these reasons, foreign influences that were not sustained by religion evoked little interest among the Chinese and were very limited in scope. They were, basically, lessons in technique that produced no echoes in the taste or standards of a compact civilization so substantially proud of itself as that of the Chinese.

Returning to the traditional line of development, wooden architecture showed a new symmetrical and rhythmic equilibrium, owing to spatial modifications (width of the intercolumniation in the central part of the construction). Lesser importance was given to the factor of traditional bracketing in the structural economy of the building as regards the lower architrave (which was richly decorated) and the two flat brackets embedded at the sides of the column, which we have already seen appear under the Sung. The bracketing, however, preserves the "grape cluster" form, achieved by the superimposition of secondary brackets—multiplying the number of supporting arms—on the lower central one, on which the main support was concentrated.

These innovations are to be seen in the three ceremonial halls of the Forbidden City in Peking. Aligned on a south-to-north axis, along a gigantic courtyard of about 200 square yards, these halls rise on high and majestic terracings with several enclosed levels, with delicate balustrades of white marble and enlivened by many staircases, which also serve as a symbolic reference to the inaccessible charisma of the imperial power. Reconstructed in 1700, the three halls recapture perfectly the style of Ming buildings of a century before (1627).

Ch'ing Dynasty (A.D. 1644–1912)

However much the Manchu dynasty of the Ch'ing had affirmed since the first years of its rule its clear and absolute wish not to allow itself to be assimilated to Chinese culture, but indeed to impose its own customs on the Chinese, it was inevitable that in the field of architecture no real break occurred. Since the Manchus had no real tradition of their own, there took place simply a development of the Ming style toward less monumental forms, which were also to be more vividly colored and copiously decorated with paintings (of flowers and birds), with carving and sculpture both in wood and stone, and with enamel tiles.

As had happened in past periods of domination by foreign "barbarians," the Manchus proved to be open to new architectural forms originating in the most diverse countries. The Tibetan style of architecture, though not new in China, had never been so widespread as at

446. *Peking, Forbidden City, throne room of the T'ai-ho tien, Ch'ing dynasty.*

447. *Peking, Forbidden City, detail of a building, Ch'ing dynasty.*

448. *Peking, Forbidden City, detail of a building, Ch'ing dynasty.*

449. *Peking, Forbidden City, detail of an acroterion, Ch'ing dynasty.*

450. *Peking, Forbidden City, detail of an acroterion, Ch'ing dynasty.*

451. *Peking, Forbidden City, Chung-ho tien, Ch'ing dynasty.*
452. *Peking, wooden street* p'ai-lous.

this time, and was related primarily to the trend of Lamaistic Buddhism. It is amply demonstrated by the building complexes of Jehol, the northern capital (Plates 462, 463), and the bottle-shaped pagodas scattered through the gardens of Peking (Plate 457)—which were often covered with enamel tiles, like the Pai-t'a of the Pei-Hai, dating from 1651 (Plate 456), and including characteristic masonry structures with small trapezoidal windows on the Wan-shou-shan near Peking. Owing to the lack of a true Manchu tradition, Western influences were more easily absorbed. This is especially apparent in the Yüan-ming-yüan (Plate 458), the complex of pavilions and park built by Ch'ien Lung, Ch'ing emperor from 1736 to 1796. It is a singular transplantation, the work of two Europeans (the Jesuits Giuseppe Castiglione and Jean-Denis Attiret), commissioned by the emperor to "build in the European fashion." Elements of Western Rococo are grafted onto such traditional Chinese architectural forms as terracings and curved roofs.

This unusual experiment, corresponding in the reverse sense to the Western taste for chinoiserie, gave rise to works endowed with a certain exotic charm, whether from the standpoint of a Western critic observing the effect of the Chinese component, or that of a Chinese evaluating the effect of the Western.

The great imperial "pleasure palaces" were, however, the preferred field for architectural experiments by the Manchus, and in specific cases a particular exoticism was sought. But even elsewhere—in the vast gardens thronged by structures of the most varied forms, with round, polygonal, and multilinear pavilions, with galleries and bridges, and with the insistent use of round, polygonal, lobate, or ogival apertures in the various walls—the will to experiment is obvious. Sometimes Manchu creations can be defined as true caprices—for example, the marble boat with tall shafts raised on a masonry hull and moored in a pool of water in the new nineteenth-century Summer Palace (Plate 461).

The numerous pagodas scattered throughout the royal parks (more as elegant decorations than as places of worship) are often covered with enamel tiles. They resume the niche motif and the polygonal shape used by the Sung, but now the sides of the polygon are of unequal measure, the wider faces alternating with narrower ones, creating a broken rhythm (which we also find in wooden colonnades). This is to be seen especially in the Pao-liu-li-t'a pagoda of the Summer Palace in Peking—a true jewel, finely chiseled and surmounted by a finial that, while not conflicting with the whole, is similar to the finials of the Tibetan chorten. Here it exists in a Chinese copy that is another interesting demonstration of the exotic taste and wish for variety typical of the Ch'ing. Inside the capital of Peking, however, the tendency toward axiality and the symmetrical structures typical of the Ming were

453. *Peking, Temple of the Ten Thousand Buddhas, Ch'ing dynasty.*

preserved. The classic example is that of the complex centered on the Altar of Heaven, culminating in a circular building with obvious cosmological references in its structure, and which, while preserving the characteristics of the original construction (in 1421, under the emperor Yung Lo), owes its present appearance to the radical restoration carried out by the emperor Ch'ien Lung in 1754. In the sequence of round and square courtyards, terraces, and staircases reappear the age-old, rigidly traditional geomantic and ritual rules, which the Ming (Plates 424–426) had made concrete and Ch'ien Lung here rendered with still greater clarity. In wooden buildings, for which we have an exhaustive treatise in the *Kung-ch'eng-tso-fa* (Plate 466), compiled by a Ch'ing minister of public works, there is a complete loss of the structural value of the bracket system; it is now reduced to a continuous cornice of wooden ribs, at times actually covered by a long carved plank with a "cloud" motif that hides them like a valance. It is exemplified in the eighteenth-century Wan-fu-ko of the Yung-ho-kung in Peking.

The exaggerated slenderness of the columns, often reduced to thin pilasters quadrangular in section, required the constant use of the type of bracket with a flattened capital, such as we first noticed under the Sung, elegantly decorated with scrolls and painted.

Such tasteful slenderness in wooden constructions and the consequent small scale of the buildings were a direct result of the extensive deforestation carried out under the Ming. For the Pavilion of Annual Prayers (Plate 426) of the Altar of Heaven in Peking, built at the end of the nineteenth century, it was necessary to send to the United States (to the state of Oregon) for timber large enough for the construction of columns of the traditional size. The lack or grave scarcity of suitable lumber was by now an insurmountable obstacle for an architecture that for three millennia had expressed itself primarily in the harmony of its wooden structures.

Modern Period (1912–   )

The Chinese encounter with the modern Western technological world was rendered more violent by the long centuries of proud isolation that had preceded it. At first, beginning in the middle of the nineteenth century, recognition by the Chinese of their own scientific and technical inferiority was so profound that in their new works, inspired by European and American constructions, there was no suggestion of the ancient architecture of China.

This anxiety to adopt wholesale a Western way of life, which is apparent in the first reformers led by K'ang Yu-wei (1858–1927), also had repercussions in the field of architecture. The results were structures in an eclectic style, derived strictly from buildings in the foreign

457. *Peking, Pei-Hai, kiosks and gardens, Ch'ing dynasty.*

458. *Peking, Yüan-ming-yüan (Garden of Perpetual Light), Western-style building, Ch'ing dynasty.*

459. *Peking, Summer Palace, bridge with seventeen arches, Ch'ing dynasty.*

460. *Peking, Summer Palace, garden pavilion, Ch'ing dynasty.* ▷

461. *Peking, Summer Palace, marble boat, Ch'ing dynasty.*

462. *Jehol (Mongolia), Hsu-mi Fu-shou, detail of a roof, Ch'ing dynasty.*

463. *Jehol (Mongolia), Hsu-mi Fu-shou, detail of an acroterion, Ch'ing dynasty.*

464. *Suchow (Kiangsu), Cho-cheng-yuan garden, wall with "moon opening."*

465. *Suchow (Kiangsu), Cho-cheng-yuan garden.*

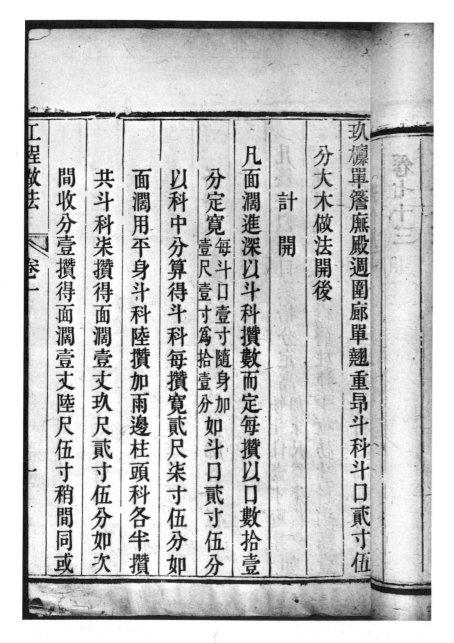

colonial concessions, which offered no better examples than the absurd Neo-Gothic Town Hall of the British concession at Tientsin.

Only in 1920, coinciding with the social and political turning point characterized by the spread of nationalism that followed the first struggles of the Kuomintang, did a new style appear that tended toward the reassessment of traditional values. This was the so-called Chinese Revival. However, except for a few valid examples, such as the Chung Shan Hospital in Shanghai (1937), a true merging of Western building methods and techniques with typically Chinese traditional structures was not achieved. Liang-Ssu-ch'eng[13] has rightly observed that there were only to be foreign buildings covered by Chinese roofs.

This movement nevertheless deserves credit for having led Chinese architects toward a historical perspective of their own. In fact, immediately after the chaos of World War II, the search for a national style in architecture seemed to emerge, while naturally not excluding the presence of the major contemporary trend—the so-called International Style—and, to a lesser degree, that of Soviet classicism.

For the moment, it would seem that the more interesting experiments have been conducted in the sphere of the International trend. Buildings have been constructed that recall only by their love for symmetry and by the repetition induced by single structural standards the ancient artistic and traditional forms. This is obviously a poor result. In other cases, Western structures have been blended with suggestions offered—one might say, accidentally—by particular pre-existing masonry buildings already instilled with the Chinese tradition. It is a question of the exploitation of an outlying heritage little known for architectural forms, which draws on Hakka dwellings, on those of the Anhui region, or tries to renew the so-called Tibetan style.

One recalls, however, that the most tenacious characteristics of traditional Chinese architecture are, at least in certain respects, extremely close to the most modern theories of building and city planning. For a long time, there have existed in China a flexibility in the town plan, a tendency toward decentralization, urban expansion by the aggregation of fixed units, the mobility and prefabrication of buildings (given their wooden structure), and the use of a precise standard—the *chien*, the basic unit of construction derived from the width of the central beam. It is thus perfectly possible that from this point of departure, from these realized objectives, a true and profound "Chinese Revival" may emerge in the future.

Paola Mortari Vergara Caffarelli

467. *Puyo, stone pagoda erected by the Chinese general Su Ting-fang, Pakche Kingdom.*

Unfortunately, only a very few ancient examples survive of the architecture of the Korean peninsula. The materials of which many of its buildings were constructed have long since deteriorated, and continual devastating wars, invasions, and destruction have wracked the whole territory of Korea in the course of centuries.

A threefold relationship of borrowing, assimilation, and exchange with the two great neighboring architectural traditions—the Japanese, and above all, the Chinese—characterizes the architecture of Korea. The conception of architecture not as an art but as a craft—that is, an expression not of the desire to create aesthetically valid forms, but rather of a response to practical, functional, and also traditional needs—is common to the whole Far East. This is not to deny that love for structural equilibrium, concern for detail and decoration, and for harmonious placing of the architectural work in its natural surroundings have ensured that from the modern point of view Far Eastern constructions not only have a specific artistic value of their own, but actually anticipate by centuries some of our present architectural and city-planning concepts.

The cities—with their tendency toward a chessboard pattern of streets, flexibility of plan (owing to the deliberate presence of empty areas inside the city walls), decentralization (every quarter with a marketplace and administrative and religious buildings of its own), expansion by the aggregation of small fixed units (the classical family dwelling), and even the mobility of their buildings (given the notable facility by which wooden structures can be assembled and dismantled)—offer infinite points of contact with the most modern urban complexes.

In its more purely structural and aesthetic conceptions, Far Eastern architecture reveals a surprising modernity. For proof of this we need only examine our interest in traditional Japanese architecture and the manifold influence of, and the acclaim received by, modern Japanese masters in Europe and America. The application of a basic standard or measure, derived from the space between supporting columns (which in Korean is called *kan* and corresponds to 10.83 by 10.83 feet), and the use of similar construction elements superimposed or juxtaposed over one another in accordance with precise proportions and relationships, have both been taken up by various modern architects from Frank Lloyd Wright to Helmut Hentrich.

Despite such correspondences with modern architectural thought, it is clear that the architecture of the whole Far East has always had independent characteristics, to be distinguished according to successive periods and different national entities, and sometimes opposed to those of the West.

The architecture of Korea, while closely linked to the Chinese, from which since earliest times and for the entire course of its history it

468. Kyongju, pagoda of Punhwang-sa, Old Silla Kingdom.
469. Kyongju, pagoda of Punhwang-sa, detail of a door sculpture.
470. Kyongju, tomb of King Muryol, Old Silla Kingdom.
471. Kyongju, tombstone with turtle from the tomb of King Muryol.

accepted methods and examples of construction, nevertheless developed in an independent manner; these foreign models were transformed according to Korean requirements of taste, tradition, and climate. Thus, the open arcades with wooden columns that surround the most common Chinese type of building, the *tien* (the rectangular pavilion on a high base, topped by a conspicuous roof), in Korea preserve their primitive structural lines but are almost always closed by a continuous, thin masonry wall, or one of light wooden planks, in order to meet the needs of the more severe climate.

Ancient elements of aboriginal cultures also appear. Often they are utilitarian, like the type of heating called *ondol* ("hot pavement") that utilizes pipes for steam and heat placed under the floor, and which already existed in the protohistorical period. At times these elements are simply traditional, such as the reminiscences of primitive log huts; or, finally, of a religious nature. The habit of orienting dwellings with the entrance to the south, for example, has been observed in prehistoric underground houses.

But it is primarily in the refined way in which buildings are adapted to nature, common to the whole Far East but outstanding in Korea, that the essence of Korean architectural concepts is expressed. It is apparent in the plan of the cities, which, though constructed on the model of the Chinese, do not acquire the fixed rigidity of imperial prototypes; rather they follow the contours of the terrain with greater freedom, both in the line of the city walls and in the layout of the streets. The ornamentation of buildings never attains the overloaded heaviness or exaggerated chromatic vivacity of late Chinese architecture, maintaining instead a smooth and free surface in accordance with a taste for archaic simplicity. The use of natural—that is to say, uncolored—materials for construction (wood, tile, stone) and the restricted chromatic scale they offer contribute to a greater sense of blending with the colors and forms of the natural surroundings.

Prehistory

The scarcity of archaeological evidence on prehistoric structures in Korea—even the ethnic composition of its early inhabitants is in doubt, since it would seem that the Tungusic population was overlaid by migrations from Southeast Asia—makes it necessary to resort to the uncertain data reported in ancient Chinese texts. Above all, we must examine attentively those constructions of an ethnological type that are still in use. All that archaeological excavations have brought to light in the northeast are pit dwellings, circular spaces 13 to 16 feet in diameter with a hearth at the center. In the more western areas a preference for the square plan has been noted, as well as the existence of well-defined street connections, suggesting a high degree of village activity. Such

finds are in accord with the descriptions in the Chinese annals. They mention, besides the type of dwelling consisting of log huts (still used today in mountain forests), houses dug in the subsoil with a tumulus roof (of which examples remain even in the outskirts of Seoul); and the characteristic habitations of coastal fishermen, constructed always in the form of pits and covered with heaps of conch shells. These, too, are to be found in more northern areas and are related to the prehistoric cultures at the ethnological level of the whole coastal strip and the islands of the Far East. In the religious sphere there are remains of dolmens, attesting probably to the existence of a special form of shamanism together with a cult of the spirits, the so-called Kwisin (demons and gods), which still exists today and takes the form of the *shang-sung*: large tree trunks carved with terrifying faces, very similar to the totem poles of North America; and the *sodo*, posts surmounted by a crudely sculptured bird.

Lo-lang Colony (108 B.C.–A.D. 313)

Though ancient legends state that in 1122 B.C. Ki Tse (Ki Ja in Korean), a member of the royal house of the Shang, established his rule in Korea after fleeing from China with five thousand followers, no trace has been found of this first Chinese settlement. On the other hand, the presence of Chinese colonies during the Han dynasty in the northwest areas of Korea is well documented—in the provinces of Lo-lang (Nang-nang in Korean), Hsiian-tu, Chen-fen, and Lin t'un, which, according to Chinese texts, were founded around 108 B.C.

This first significant entry of Chinese architectural elements occurs precisely in the Han period at a time when the old Shang and Chou building and city-planning standards had arrived at complete maturity.

Actually, an urban complex of the Chinese has been discovered at the Lo-lang site near Pyongyang. Its form is a little irregular, with a high platform in pounded earth to support the ceremonial hall, with the foundations of other structures, and in particular a necropolis whose plan, structural elements, and even architectural decoration all indicate a direct contact with the mother country. It thus represents a phase in which foreign models were simply accepted and executed by immigrant specialists, with probably only a few Korean craftsmen involved. Nevertheless, even this phase has its importance in the development of Korean architecture, since it constitutes the matrix from which Chinese architectural concepts were diffused all over the territory of the peninsula. The influence was not restricted to just the neighboring Koguryo Kingdom, which was later to absorb the Chinese colonies; it reached even the tribal states of the south, Ma-han, Sin-han, and Pyon-han, that were to take shape in the historical period of the Pakche and Silla kingdoms.

479. *Kyongju, "ice house," Li dynasty.*
480. *Kyongju, tomb of King Wousang.*
481. *Kyongju, tomb of King Wousang, entrance avenue.* ▷

482. *Yongju Kun, Pu-sok-sa monastery, exterior of the main building, Koryo period.*

483. *Seoul, Kyong-bok palace,* pudo *of the monk Hong-pob, Koryo period.*

484. *Yongju Kun, Pu-sok-sa monastery, interior of the main building, Koryo period.* ▷

Three Kingdoms Period (57 B.C.–A.D. 668)

This is the span of time during which Korean civilization, as a result of its encounter with the Chinese, slowly acquired an awareness of its own values. This does not diminish the fact that in the architectural sphere skilled Korean craftsmen of the three kingdoms into which the peninsula was divided—Koguryo in the north, Pakche in the southwest, and Silla in the southeast—were limited in the beginning to a mere effort at assimilation. Actually, the task that the Koreans had to accomplish was a very arduous one. One thinks of the differences in building types and the symbolic implications of Buddhism, of the complicated sumptuary and structural rules required by Confucianism, and, to a lesser extent, the geomantic and magical conceptions of Taoism. The Koguryo Kingdom, which even extended into vast areas of Manchuria, was more prepared for this assimilation, also because of the presence of Chinese colonists on its soil. The wall decorations discovered in the necropoli of the two capitals—one situated in the T'ung-kou district of Manchuria, the other at Pyongyang—represent pavilions, monumental complexes, religious and reception halls; they imitate all the structural and characteristic elements of contemporary Chinese architecture, especially of the northern Wei period (A.D. 386–534). Inside the burial chambers, dug in the soil and topped by a tumulus of earth or squared stones, we find the representation of such false supporting elements of wooden buildings as columns, architraves, and corbels. These are features that, together with "lantern" ceilings—as in the famous and splendidly decorated "Tomb of the Two Columns" in Pyongyang—show a clear derivation from Chinese prototypes. The foundations of an octagonal pagoda and of three other rectangular buildings (religious and reading halls, etc.) surrounding it, discovered in 1937 near Pyongyang, show how Buddhist temples had already reached a typical monumental scale; similar traces have been found in Puyo, the capital of the Pakche Kingdom (Plate 467). But it is in Japan, in the Horyuji complex near Nara, that we still find intact despite successive fires what the Japanese call the Kudara plan (from the name given in Japan to the kingdom of Pakche). The layout of the Korean temples of this period introduced by Pakche builders into Japan is classic: the pagoda and main hall are situated on the same axis and oriented orthogonally with respect to the entrance. The so-called Tamamushi shrine, also in the Horyuji, seems likewise to have had the same Korean origin; the decoration with iridescent beetle wings is typical of southern Korea. In any case, it repeats, on a reduced scale, the harmonious lines and measured sense of proportion of contemporary buildings.

It was in fact by being filtered through and re-elaborated in Korea that Chinese art, culture, and civilization reached Japan in this early

485. *Seoul, Nan-dai Mun (south gate), Li dynasty.*
487. *Seoul, Ch'ang-dok palace, main building, Li dynasty.*
486. *Pyongyang, gate of the city.*
488. *Punguae-myon, eight-story pagoda of Silluk-sa.*

period, just as more Western art and culture, the Indian and Central Asian, had arrived in Korea by way of China.

On the other hand, we have some examples of stone architecture, primarily in granite, from the Pakche and Silla kingdoms. The two seventh-century pagodas in the complexes of Miruk-sa at Iksankun and of Chong-nim-sa at Puyo in the Pakche Kingdom are the oldest examples that have come down to us, and repeat in stone the shape and supporting structures of similar Chinese and Korean wooden buildings. They are square in plan and rise in diminishing levels, with false pillars, architraves, and roofs whose corners are slightly curved. Meanwhile the Punhwang-sa pagoda at Kyongju, capital of the Old Silla Kingdom, takes as its model the brick pagodas of the T'ang dynasty (Plates 468, 469). Built of stones cut in the form of bricks, it shows a majestic simplicity and harmony in its overall purity of line and geometric unity, a prelude to later religious structures.

Great Silla Kingdom (A.D. 668–935)

The Silla government played a unifying role and promoted a great artistic flowering, which also owed much to the adoption of Buddhism as the state religion. This was the classical period of Korean architecture, which, while belonging to the style that Japanese scholars call "pan-East Asian" that initially emerged in the China of the T'ang dynasty, succeeded in acquiring autonomy. It became so through certain definitions of type and structure in its various buildings, through certain peculiarities of shape, and primarily by a harmonious and measured sense of proportion among its different structures. In stone pagodas (*t'ap*), beginning in the second half of the sixth century, a happy and highly original compromise was achieved between the two previous kinds that they were intended, respectively, to imitate: those in wood and those in brick. Thus the so-called Silla type of pagoda emerged (Plates 474, 475), square in plan, generally with three diminishing stories on a pedestal of two levels and topped by a high finial, of which numerous examples remain, such as the twin pagodas of Kamcun-sa at Wol-ssong Kun. And even though, beginning in the eighth century, the pedestals and stories were to be decorated with figures of divinities (Plate 472), while the whole acquired a greater vertical thrust (Plates 476, 477), this did not alter the linear harmony of the building. The structure constituted a model for constructions of the next period, like the other two more widespread types of stone structures, the *pudo* and the lantern. The first of these is a funerary monument for Buddhist monks, inspired by the stupa and consisting of a base, a pedestal, a central structure, and a roof with a high finial. The so-called lantern, which often assumes considerable proportions and is connected in front to a pagoda or to a principal religious hall, is similarly structured,

491. *Seoul, Seonjeonjeon palace.*
492. *Seoul, secret garden of the Ch'ang-dok palace, Li dynasty.*

despite infinite variations owing to the prevalence of one or another construction element—by a base, a pedestal in the form of a more or less slender pilaster, a central body, and a roof topped bȳ a finial with several umbrellas.

As for the sumptuous civic and religious buildings in wood, almost nothing remains. The splendid Kyongju capital—square in plan, with high city walls pierced by twenty large gates, with its wide rectilinear streets laid out in a chessboard pattern, with fortress towers at each angle of the walls, and situated in a fertile valley—contained almost a million inhabitants. Its wooden buildings, together with its numerous religious complexes and palaces, were completely destroyed during the Japanese invasion of 1592–98. Nevertheless, the foundations of some buildings have come down to us, along with a number of tombs with tumuli in which precious funeral offerings have been found (Plate 470); the stone monuments that surrounded the royal tombs, graced by imposing figures of men and animals (Plate 481); the pagodas; the *pudo*; the lanterns of the religious complexes (often constructed in accordance with the twin-pagoda plan—two pagodas placed to the sides of the façade of the main hall); and above all, the two temples of Pulguk-sa (Plate 473) and Sokkulam (Plate 472), which confirm the level of maturity achieved by builders of the Silla Kingdom. Tradition tells us that both temples were ordered by the prime minister Kim Taisung, but while only the entrance stairs of the first complex remain, the balustrades, a few stone pagodas and lanterns—sufficient to indicate the scope of the grand style of the period—the cave temple of Sokkulam has survived almost intact. It is a singular example of its kind, first constructed with large square stones to create an artificial domed structure and then covered with earth. Its plan is a typical one that might be called an apse plan, consisting of a rotunda preceded by a rectangular access antechamber. As such, it is related on the one hand to primitive Indian plans for Buddhist rock constructions, and on the other to tombs of the Three Kingdoms period, especially by the two imposing octagonal pillars placed at the entrance to the rotunda. A colossal statue of Buddha at the center of the circular shrine, around which the faithful can perform the rite of *pradakshinā*, takes the place of the stupa of the Indian prototypes, while statues and reliefs of Buddhas and Bodhisattvas are harmoniously placed in niches or as panels along the walls of the two rooms.

Both at Pulguk-sa and Sokkulam, the imitation in stone of wooden structural elements is accomplished by preserving all the massive bulk of the material, without falling into the minute study of details that is found in some stone works of the Chinese T'ang dynasty. Since we so sorely lack evidence, we have no way of knowing whether or not there existed a typically Korean style in wooden architecture. But it would

493. *Seoul, Kyong-bok palace, throne room, exterior, Li dynasty.*

seem that such Japanese examples as the main hall of the Tōshōdaiji and the Hokkakudo of the Eizanji may in a certain way—in their simplicity of line and also in the essential nature of their structures—reflect the skill of Silla carpenters.

Koryo Kingdom (A.D. 918–1392)

It is said that the Koryo period represents the medieval phase of Korean civilization and that, at least until the twelfth century, what was taking place in the artistic field represented a late and provincial repetition of T'ang examples. It seems more readily demonstrable that what took place in architecture was a coherent development from classical prototypes of the Silla period toward a greater decorative sensibility and a search for more fanciful forms, though these are always measured and contained. It is undeniable that the successive invasions of the Khitan (Liao dynasty), the Jurchen (Chin dynasty), and finally the Mongols (Yüan dynasty), together with the close ties between Korea and the Sung court, contributed to the formulation of new structural and stylistic conceptions and of new types of buildings. The octagonal pagoda of the Khitan and Jurchen was taken up, for example, in the nine-story pagoda of Wol-chong-sa at P'yong-ch'ang Kun (eleventh century). The Indian style of wooden buildings, called in Korea *Chusimp'o*, is inspired by T'ien-chu, the so-called Indian style of southern China, especially in the forms it assumes in Fukien. It is probable that Mongol craftsmen had worked on the ten-story pagoda of Kyong-ch'on-sa in Seoul (A.D. 1348), a jewel of architectural and decorative forms. Unfortunately, only a very few examples of wooden architecture have come down to us. The splendid capital of Song-do (Kaesong), with its ample staircases, gardens, and palaces—which while respecting the requirements of the mountainous terrain, preserved an integrally balanced harmony of its own—has been totally destroyed by the continuous invasions. One might, however, observe that in the Indian style—that is, in *Chusimp'o* works—the outlines of similar Chinese models are maintained, with the column assuming by itself the weight of the architrave and with brackets jutting perpendicularly to the façades that support the strong projection of the roof. In Korean works, however, the bracket system is never transformed into a complicated tangle of projecting members, as occurs in some Japanese buildings. Here structural tension is counterbalanced by bracket arms placed in the traditional position (parallel to the façade) and by the lesser height of the pillars.

In the oldest examples—the twelfth-thirteenth century Keung-nak Chon of the Pong-chong-sa at An-dong Kun, which for certain architectural details may be considered the archetype, and the slightly later Mu-ryang-su Chon of the Pu-sok-sa (Plates 482, 484)—the brackets and columns, set off against lighter walls, are placed at intervals with measured potency; in the interiors, the usual coffered ceiling is replaced by beams of different dimensions and height supported by a system of brackets. The traditional style, called *Tap'o* or multibracket style, in which brackets are placed in an intermediate position between the columns, comes to be applied at this time with less frequency, however much constructions of the *Chusimp'o* kind, especially of the later period (the Tai-ung Chon of the Su-dok-sa at Yesan Kun, for example) have an increased number of bracket arms placed in the traditional position. Among stone constructions, pagodas of the Silla type (Plates 474–477) become smaller, but accentuate their verticality through a greater number of stories and the changed proportion between the base and the body of the building.

The dimensions of the stone blocks with which they are constructed increase enormously, until each story comes to be constituted by a single monolith. Even the traditional shape is often modified, leading to pagodas that are polygonal in plan, or circular, like those of the so-called Hill of the Many Pagodas (Tat'ap Pong), which go back to the thirteenth century. The *pudo* and the "lanterns," in addition to their greater vertical thrust, also show considerable variety of form and shape; they may be cylindrical, bell-shaped, or polygonal. Often, they are covered with delicate ornamentation, like the lantern of the Silluk-sa at Yonju Kun (second half of the fourteenth century), or the *pudo* of the monk Hong-pob (1017) in the Kyong-bok at Seoul (Plate 483); with its spherical body and covering in the form of a mushroom, it is one of the most valid examples of the fantasy and creative power of Koryo architecture.

Li Dynasty (A.D. 1392–1910)

A particular phenomenon that in reality forms part of the tradition of Far Eastern architecture, but that is highly accentuated in this period, is the imitation of the antique, shared by the China of both the Ming and the Ch'ing. This is partly due to the importance given by the Li dynasty to a rigid application of Confucian doctrine, and thus to the cult of the past, in a vast area extending from political and social organization to art and culture. This, despite the fact that in an early period—that is, up until the Japanese invasion of 1592–98, which represents a historical gap not only politically but also artistically, because of the destruction of works of art and the disordering of the social fabric—palaces, temples, and fortifications preserve intact their great strength and majesty of line. Beginning in the late sixteenth century, these characteristics undergo a decline, and buildings show an exaggerated grandeur and an excessive elaboration of decoration, with lotus blossoms, peonies, geometric motifs, and densely intertwined vine tendrils,

494. *Seoul, Kyong-bok palace, banquet hall, exterior, Li dynasty.*

495. *Seoul, gardens of the Kyong-bok palace, Li dynasty.*

especially in the interiors. Another peculiar characteristic of the period, due in part to the diminished importance of Buddhism, is the gradual disappearance of ceremonial constructions in stone. In the fifteenth century, stone pagodas inspired by Koryo examples were still being built, like the ten-story pagoda of Won-gak-sa in Seoul (1468), which imitates the Kyong-ch'on-sa, or the more traditional one of Nak-san-sa at Yang-yang-kun (late fifteenth century). Except for a few other rare instances, we no longer witness that repetition of votive monuments that, since the period of the Three Kingdoms, had constituted the characteristic element of religious complexes. What is preserved, on the other hand, are the traditional forms and structures of dynastic necropoli; the skill of Korean craftsmen in the use of stone is attested by numerous bridges with one or more finely worked spans, and by the massive vaults of "ice houses" (Plate 479), used to preserve ice during the summer months. This period saw the flourishing of civic architectural structures in many materials—brick, stone blocks, wood. The colossal brick or stone fortifications surrounding the principal cities, which were often surmounted by wooden pavilions or roofs, definitely show close ties with similar Ming and Ch'ing constructions, but also demonstrate a sense of measure and rhythm that is typically Korean (Plates 486, 490).

The city walls and gates of Suwon (1794–96), for whose construction tools introduced from Europe by way of China were used, are a typical example, as is the Nan-dai Mun, the principal gateway of Seoul, the southern one of 1448 (Plate 485), and the much later eastern one of 1869. Both are remains of the monumental walls that surrounded the capital. Wooden architecture undergoes a new flowering of the *Chusimp'o* style up until the fifteenth century, as demonstrated by the classical proportions and measured harmony of the Hai-t'al Mun, the To-kab-sa at Yong-am Kun (middle of the fifteenth century), and of the Hall of Paradise (Keuk-nak Chon) of the Mu-wi-sa at Kang-jin-kun, which belongs to the same period. By the beginning of the sixteenth century, we find a revival of the traditional local style, the *Tap'o*, which in the seventeenth century will completely supplant the *Chusimp'o* style. An example from the period of transition between the two styles is the Myong-jong Mun of the Ch'ang-kyong: on the outside it shows a bracket system placed integrally with respect to the supporting columns, typical of the *Tap'o* style, and on the inside has an uncoffered ceiling, with the framework of roof and beams exposed in accordance with the *Chusimp'o*. After the Japanese invasion, the *Tap'o* style was to evolve toward greater decoration, such as can also be found in Chinese architecture of the time. The increased use of the *Shoi-so* (literally "ox tongue," so called for its elongated form) is proof of this tendency.

From their initial inconspicuous position as ornaments situated at each corner of the building (for example, in the Nan-dai Mun in Seoul), the *Shoi-so* become a recurrent decorative motif. They take the form of long curved hooks placed on the bracket arms, making the linear structure heavier and more complicated, as in the Tai-ung Chon (1765) of the old and renowned complex of Pulguk-sa. The development of the bracket structure toward a purely decorative form is even more obvious. In the so-called *Ik-kong*—a bracket system in which, with every supporting function lost, the brackets are reduced to a single richly decorated block—the search for ornamentation goes beyond all bounds, as in the Pang-hwa Su-ryu Chong at Suwon (1796). At the same time, both the shape and form of roofs become more complicated. To "T" and "L" shapes are added round and polygonal ones, while the roofs acquire more ridges and are adorned with acroteria in bronze, wood, or ceramic. Façades and interiors are decorated with luminous colors in a hitherto unknown search for chromatic effects. Such great complexes as the Kyong-bok (Plates 493–495) and Ch'ang-dok (Plate 487), residential palaces in Seoul, whose splendid gardens are filled with pavilions of the most varied forms, are an example. Here the buildings blend marvelously with nature, and the intervention of man in the sphere of nature itself tends to be limited to the minimum necessary to preserve its genuine beauty. The two complexes are the most valid example of the remarkable aesthetic value inherent even in some of the latest works of Li architecture.

Modern Period (1910–   )

Korea was opened to modern Western technology under political pressure by Japan, which by the terms of the Treaty of Kang-kwa (February 27, 1876) forced the Li dynasty to open certain ports to foreign trade. In the long period of Japanese rule, from 1910 to 1945, not only were Western building types, forms, and techniques introduced, but systematic archaeological research and the scientific study of ancient traditional architecture were also begun, resulting in numerous excavation expeditions and the widespread restoration of monuments.

At the same time, however, the weight of Japanese rule suppressed, at least in part, any independent development in a modern direction and obstructed the emergence of a new national architecture. Attempts to exploit the past ignored its most vital aspects. Buildings were thus erected that were often the fruit of a Japanese (and not Korean) interpretation of Western trends. As such, the value of such structures is limited, and in any case they were the expression of a foreign taste. The broad urbanization policy that enlarged the principal cities was carried out in some cases in a disorganized and artificial manner.

Even during the later postwar period, political events made it impossible to achieve an organic formulation of a modern Korean architecture, despite the Koreans' enthusiasm for their regained independence and their re-evaluation of traditional values.

Only at present is the attempt being made (in a different manner in each of the two republics into which the peninsula is divided) to examine international techniques and adapt them to the traditional needs of the country. Some interesting results have been obtained, especially for the interiors and rooms of buildings. These may constitute a point of departure for future developments.

Paola Mortari Vergara Caffarelli

Chapter Seven JAPAN

Prehistory and Protohistory

The most recent archaeological discoveries date the presence of man in the Japanese islands from the Old Stone Age. The Paleolithic Japanese—in the course of an uninterrupted cultural evolution that lasted for several hundred thousand years, specifically until the Neolithic cultures emerged in the last millennia before the Christian Era—never lived as troglodytes in caves or rock shelters, but dwelt in the open on the slopes of mountains or on river banks. We have no evidence to assist us in a reconstruction of their primitive types of dwellings; we can, however, assume that they must have been hidden in forests and thickets and covered with branches or animal skins. An ancient Ainu legend speaks of a population in the archipelago known as *koropok-guru*, a word signifying the inhabitants of underground dwellings. We do not know precisely to which people the name refers, but it is nevertheless significant that the earliest huts of which we have archaeological evidence appear to have been sunk in the ground, with the floor dug to a depth that varies between 16 and 40 inches. This type of pit dwelling remains characteristic for a great part of the Neolithic period, and is connected with a widespread prehistoric tradition of hut architecture for cold climates in many northern regions of the Eurasian continent. Such huts, square or circular in plan, usually measured some 13 to 20 feet in width (Plate 496). Elevation was obtained by a wooden framework consisting of a number of poles driven into the ground and crossing at the top (Plate 497). In those huts with a square plan, a horizontal beam was employed for the whole length of the hut and served to secure the crossed poles along the roof line. The structure was covered with the branches and bark of trees, and was essentially a shed, since the walls of the hut were to all intents and purposes constituted by the sides of the pit.

In later Neolithic settlements—that is, until the middle of the first millennium B.C.—types of huts appeared in which the floor was at ground level. This innovation is surely due, at least in some regions, to milder climatic conditions and may indicate a process of adaptation to the environment. In any case, it marks the beginning of a true architectural development; it was no longer a matter of extracting shelter from the earth, but of constructing a building whose elevation was required not only to support the roof but also to define the interior space or spaces by walls, even though these were still covered by vegetable materials.

The next stage in this process is marked by the appearance, in the final pre-Christian centuries, of new types of huts with floors raised on posts—that is, with platforms elevated above ground level. This kind of architecture, essentially of lake dwellers, was perhaps introduced into the Japanese islands from southeastern Asia, along with agriculture and

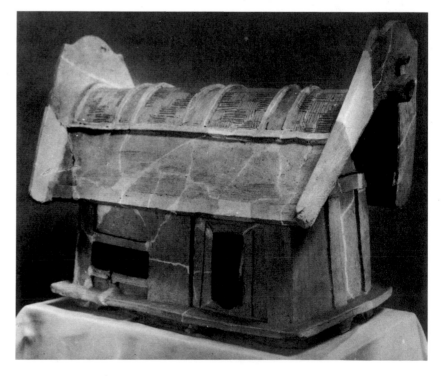

500. *Small model of a house of the Kofun period, originally from the Prefecture of Gunma (Tokyo, National Museum).*

501. *Small model of a house of the Kofun period, originally from the Prefecture of Gunma (Tokyo, National Museum).*

in particular the cultivation of rice by irrigation. But not all of the old construction methods were abandoned. That the use of a scissors crossing for the poles and a horizontal beam for the roof was preserved can be deduced, for example, from the long survival of these elements in Japanese architecture of the historical era, still to be seen in modern replicas of such ancient Shinto shrines as Ise and Izumo. We must nevertheless keep in mind that such elements are very common in wooden architecture, and it is difficult to determine whether they are firmly connected with the architectural tradition already established in the islands in Neolithic times or with some other influence of foreign origin. In any case, the possibility of frequent encounters with the architecture of southern China, of Indochina, Indonesia, and in general with the island areas of the South Pacific exists. Such encounters are easy to explain when we remember that during the Bronze Age the growth of a settled agricultural civilization, under the preponderant influence of the Chinese, provided these regions with common economic and social foundations.

The fact that, as a result of an entirely new cultural influx, Japan should have adopted a typically southern architecture in the first centuries of the Christian Era—which was not relinquished despite many disadvantages owing to the environmental and climatic conditions of much of the archipelago—reveals the importance and scope of the new cultural inheritance of the Bronze Age. Various factors favored the choice and spread of light and open building structures in preference to the more solid and enclosed ones suitable to a continental climate. The first is that a tradition of southern life established itself from the beginning in the subtropical area of the southern Japanese islands and from there was gradually carried toward the central ones. A second factor is that the northern part of the archipelago had scant influence on the development of Japan's culture and long remained an area for colonization, prone to submit to external pressures rather than offer alternatives even in the sphere of architecture. Only certain types of fortification structures may reveal a northern inspiration. Japanese architecture has invariably remained, for all of its history, a southern architecture; whatever technical and structural improvements have been accepted in the course of centuries—even as regards the positioning and adaptation of the building structure—have done nothing to alter this basic characteristic. The predominant use of wood was encouraged by ample forests, and this contributed to the development and perfection of techniques for utilizing its natural qualities (for absorbing humidity from the air and restoring it to dryness). Such observations on the part of the Japanese discouraged the use of paints or varnishes, or the covering of wooden surfaces with waterproof materials. This led to the habit of leaving every structural element exposed, and of main-

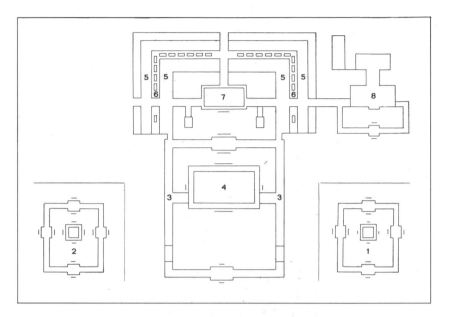

taining a raw appearance, the most natural one possible, for the architectural work (Plates 499–501).

Asuka Period (A.D. 552–645)

The Chinese influence in the historical era, penetrating Japan first by way of Korea, brought the introduction of new architectural structures and techniques, new ways of arranging building areas, and principles for urban planning. Buddhism introduced new types of religious architecture of a monumental kind that had already been known to China for at least three centuries. There also appeared a new residential type of architecture, which must have been sponsored and built by a good number of the more than one hundred thousand immigrants from Korea and Manchuria who at this time were settling in the Japanese islands.

Unfortunately, there is little remaining evidence of such works. Recent archaeological discoveries have brought to light the foundations of the city that after the fourth century A.D. served as the capital of the first Japanese state body. Official historical tradition speaks of the palaces built by the sovereigns Ōjin and Nintoku from the fourth to fifth centuries A.D. in Naniwa, on the outskirts of present-day Osaka. Later, some imperial residences were erected in the area of Asuka and Fujiwara, in the vicinity of modern Nara. An age-old custom of Japanese political life allowed each sovereign on his accession to the throne to establish in a chosen place the seat of his own residence, where a palace was built that could later be moved to, or reconstructed in, other localities in the event that particular circumstances required it. The custom hardly indicates an attitude of permanence, and may perhaps be related to the Japanese nation's unification and political organization by a class of warrior knights with nomadic traditions who came from the outlying steppes of Central Asia and established themselves in the archipelago about the fourth century A.D. A seminomadic tradition, or at least one not rigidly sedentary, has moreover remained characteristic of the whole of Japanese history. The house, which is not at all conceived to last for centuries, and its scant furnishings are almost symbolic of an atavistic reminiscence of life in a tent, where one is subject to all the shifts and changes of the natural condition. To this may be added the characteristics of the Japanese islands—the frequent earthquakes, hurricanes, and fires, all of which have combined to increase a sense of precariousness and instability.

At least a partial consequence of the frequent transfer of the imperial residence was the lack of any notable urban development, or in any case until the remodeling of government institutions along the lines of imperial China required the construction of a permanent capital. Nevertheless, Asuka had already been laid out between the

504. *Nara, Tōdaiji, hall of the Great Buddha, exterior.*
505. *Nara, Tōdaiji, hall of the Great Buddha, interior, detail of crossbeams.*

sixth and eighth centuries, and with its numerous public and residential buildings, Shinto shrines, and Buddhist temples, had the appearance of a capital.

The support of Buddhism granted by Shōtoku as emperor (A.D. 593–621) had made it possible to construct the first temples at the expense of the treasury. The oldest monumental complex for which we have the best documentation is the Hōryūji in the vicinity of Nara (Plate 507); its original nucleus goes back to the seventh century. The monastery consists of a large quadrangular cloister, with its principal entrance gate to the south, enclosing a broad open area within which rises a five-story pagoda and a low pavilion. The latter (Plate 508) contained the chief iconostasis of the cult; a building for the reading of sacred texts is situated behind it, flanked by lesser structures for the library and the temple bell. The cloister has a projecting roof and four intercolumniar spaces on its façade—the two center ones for passage, and those to the sides to hold statues of the "protector kings." The Golden Hall, rectangular in plan, rises on a stone platform with twenty-eight pilasters that support the upper part of the structure with its curved eaves and form four spans on one side and five on the other. The columns show a slight entasis remotely derived from the West, to which even the low stone stylobates are related. The function of the capitals, on the other hand, is replaced by a system of bracket arms connected by horizontal beams. The pagoda—which is the symbolic equivalent of the stupa, or Buddhist shrine generically inspired by the funerary tumulus—is developed on a square plan, with a central pilaster that ends at the top in a series of bronze rings symbolizing the parasols of Indian stupas. The stories are of decreasing size, the four lower ones with three trusses on each side, the fifth with two trusses; the roofing has curved eaves, as in the other buildings. The pagoda is certainly the most characteristic and most successful structure in Buddhist architecture, and the one to achieve the greatest vertical elevation and number of stories. Intended in its capacity as a shrine to be a closed structure, it remained exempt from any need to articulate its interior spaces, and thus its organic composition is wholly external. In Japanese architecture, it is perhaps only the pagoda that obeys standards of monumentality wherein the aesthetic is divorced from the functional. But in so doing it also represented the limit, and an obstacle to the stylistic development of this type of building, which rarely departed from the traditional pattern of construction.

Nara Period (A.D. 645–784)

Heijōkyō, modern-day Nara, was founded in 710 as the first permanent capital of the state. Its rectangular plan, the chessboard layout of the streets, the removal of the imperial court and government

506. *Nara, Tōdaiji, nandaimon (southern portal).*
507. *Nara (outskirts), Hōryūji, plan of the central complex: a) original disposition of the buildings; b) present disposition; c) transverse section of the* kondō. *1.* chūmon / *2.* horō / *3.* tō / *4.* kondō / *5.* kōdō / *6.* kyōzō / *7.* shōrō *(from Ritti, 1963).*
508. *Nara (outskirts), Hōryūji,* kondō, *exterior.*

buildings to the north-central sector of the city were all elements modeled after Changan, the Chinese capital of the Sui and T'ang dynasties. The architecture, too, follows the plans and forms of Chinese buildings, and the T'ang palace was the prototype of the new courtly residences. A complex of buildings was distributed symmetrically at the cardinal points around a central area designated as a garden. The main building, which housed the head of the family, was oriented to the south and connected to the lesser buildings by covered verandas.

Within a few years, the new metropolis had become an important Buddhist center; many monasteries were transferred there and other new ones built. Between 755 and 770 construction was begun on the Tōshōdaiji, founded by Chien-chên (Ganjin, 688–763), who had been summoned to Japan from China to re-establish the rules for correct monastic discipline. The temple offers a synthesis of Chinese and Japanese structural and stylistic elements, and also represents a free translation of continental models from stone into wood. Structures were more simple and proportioned, but nevertheless still tended toward a grandeur produced by rather rigid and heavy forms (Plate 503). The original buildings of the Tōshōdaiji were perhaps the reading hall and the Golden Hall. The first, we are told, had been built as a pavilion of the imperial palace of Heijōkyō and was later turned over to the temple. The tradition is suggestive of the ties between religious and residential architecture. The Golden Hall, which unfolds on a plan of seven intercolumniations by four, likewise perpetuates in all probability the example of Chinese T'ang palaces.

The most grandiose architectural achievement of the Nara period was the Tōdaiji, the "Great Eastern Temple," the first Buddhist religious center built wholly at the expense of the treasury (Plate 502), by the wish of the emperor Shōmu (A.D. 701–756), who in 741 also decreed that a monastery for men and a convent for women be erected in every province of the country at state expense. In the construction of the Tōdaiji, it was ensured that each building of the cult should constitute a complex in itself and be built within a cloister.

Heian Period (A.D. 784–1185)

The network of temples officially built for the protection of the country provided an impetus for the development of architecture, the arts, and culture in general. At the same time, however, they signaled a pervasive penetration by Buddhism into every sector of Japan's public and political life that ended with a massive interference by the clergy in affairs of state. To escape from the influence of Buddhism, the emperor Kwammu, who ruled from 782 to 805, decided in 784 to transfer his residence to Nagaoka, where the work of building a new capital was immediately begun. When a series of calamities and unlucky cir-

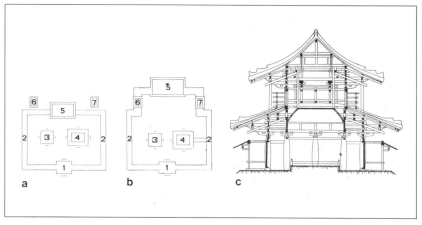

509. *Nara, Yakushiji, plan. 1.* nandaimon / *2.* chūmon / *3.* horō / *4.* kondō / *5.* kyōzō / *6.* shōrō *(from Ritti, 1963).*

510. *Nara, Yakushiji, eastern pagoda.*

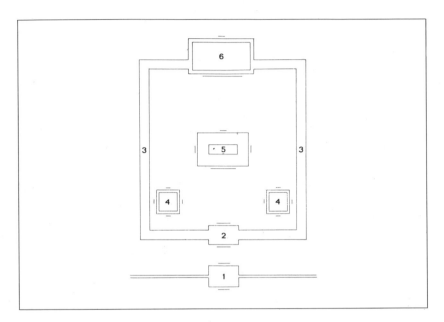

cumstances in 793 discouraged progress on this selected site, a new location was chosen in the region of Yamashiro. There, in the following year, the first foundations of Heian-kyo were laid, the city that was later to be known by the name of Miyako or Kyoto and which remained the imperial residence until 1869.

Kyoto was situated in the center of the country, a better geographical position than that of Nara, which was surrounded by mountains and rather isolated and difficult to reach. Furthermore, Kyoto was linked to the coast by the Kamo River, which emptied into the Yodo and thus constituted a line of communication with Osaka, already the chief commercial port of the Japanese archipelago. The layout of the city did not differ from that of Nara, or in the final analysis from that of Changan. A rectangular area of about 3.1 by 2.8 miles, with the lesser sides to the north and south, was crisscrossed by wide parallel and perpendicular streets. A wall with a double moat enclosed the perimeter of the urban center, on whose northern side rose the imperial palace with a complex of residences and offices occupying in all an area of about 1,800 square yards (Plate 516). In addition to its greater dimensions, the new capital differed from Nara in the character of its architecture; Kyoto's palaces, temples, and private dwellings employed the first truly original Japanese results. The buildings, while still inspired by Chinese models, were marked by local taste and by suggestions of the already operative admixtures of Buddhist architecture. Materials, structures, and construction methods increasingly recalled the ancient traditions of the Japanese islands. The use of wooden and brick roofing tiles was combined with coverings of tree bark and rice thatch; wall elements in mortar, stone, and clay were abandoned for exclusively wooden structures. The buildings of the imperial palace, for example, were planned in a pure Japanese style, and constructed in simple wood with plank floors and partitions; and the roofs were covered with the bark of the *hinoki*, a variety of cypress.

The notable dimensions of the buildings involved a series of technical solutions definitely stemming from Japanese architecture. Pilasters were established as the main supporting structures, and thus the walls were conceived merely as curtains extending among the various supports to allow for the articulation of interior spaces. The basic unit of measurement was the *ken*, which indicated the distance between two pilasters and might vary from approximately 10 feet to 6. Some buildings of the imperial palace, for example the Shishinden, set forth the lines of what was later to become the typical aristocratic residence (*shinden-zukuri*). According to this style, which had already appeared under Chinese influence during the previous Nara period, buildings were placed symmetrically on two arms that defined a broad inner area as a garden. In the garden, there was usually a lake, from whose waters emerged rocks that symbolized islands, connected to each other and to the shore by small stone or wooden bridges (Plate 518). The *Sakuteiki*, a thirteenth-century manual on the art of gardening, describes this style of garden in minute detail. Its miniaturist criteria were intended to harmonize the architecture with the landscape, blending in a single expression the work of nature and that of man through a combination of two distinct orders of compositional elements—one vegetable (flowers, small trees, shrubs), the other tectonic (hills, rocks, ponds, streams). By a careful attention to proportions, the spatial effects of nature were to be kept intact.

Among the few surviving examples of Heian residential architecture, albeit from the end of the period, we may note the Byōdōin, whose *Hōōdō*, or "phoenix hall" (from the gilded bronze phoenix that surmounts one of its structures), is the only original complex and one of the most elegant and refined works in all of Japanese architecture. The pavilion, built in the eleventh century, is formed by a series of structures with halls and side galleries that on different levels face the shores of a lake. The interior spaces are richly decorated with polychrome lacquer, inlays of mother-of-pearl, applications of gilded copper, and painted coffering. A lavish taste for ornament is also displayed in the decoration of the internal structural elements of Buddhist temples. Brackets and beams are lacquered or covered by thin metal sheets, and the ends decorated with openwork, as in the Golden Hall of the Chūsonji temple, from the first half of the twelfth century, and also the Jingoji in Kyoto.

The esoteric Buddhist doctrines of Tendai and Shingon, transplanted at this time to the Japanese islands, revived the fervor of the primitive Buddhist communities, cultivating ideals of mysticism and the hermit's life that in turn encouraged the construction of monasteries in the solitude of the mountains. The abandonment of level urban areas for the rocky slopes of mountains brought numerous innovations to Buddhist architecture. Strict standards of symmetry in the disposition of buildings were given up, and structures were lightened and reduced in size. This general structural and stylistic reconsideration led to the search for a more organic adaptation of the architectural work to the surrounding landscape. Kongōbuji and Enryakuji were the two most important mountain monasteries of the period and served as models for later ones. Their buildings, scattered through the forest, literally merged with nature, while borrowing a traditional simplicity from Shinto architecture (Plate 520).

This was the moment of return for an influence that hitherto had been exercised in only one direction—by Buddhist on Shinto architecture. Shinto-Buddhist religious syncretism now encouraged a mixture of architectural forms and elements, for the most part decorative ones, like the metal trimmings that had been completely unknown to more ancient Shinto structures. On the whole, however, the original characteristics of the architecture of the islands were not lost—the austere simplicity of form and essentially linear conception of each level of the building, with scant structural differences even in their stylistic variations. Diverse styles were distinguished more than anything by the disposition of colonnades, the incline and projection of roofs, and the removal of entrance structures to the shorter or longer sides of the building, parallel or orthogonal in relation to the roof line. The wood, originally left in its unfinished state, was now customarily painted, in red or cinnabar, as in Buddhist temples; the roof beams and hips were curved; and the eaves, supported by brackets, became increasingly complex and elaborate.

The brackets, placed between pillars and architraves to diminish the opening of the latter and ensure an effective system of support, constituted perhaps the most notable structural element introduced from the architecture of the continent, allowing an equilibrium of forces between horizontal planes and vertical structures, as well as a greater load capacity on the pillars. Various types were employed, in accordance with numerous systems, and combined in a more or less composite fashion—projecting, hanging, etc.—but the usual bracket was boat-shaped (called *funa-hijiki* in Japanese), and connected to the pillars by means of intermediate structures that took the place of capitals and normally consisted of square blocks. In more complex forms, the use of brackets was extended not only longitudinally and sideways but also vertically, and gave way to an increased number of orders corresponding to the various levels that served to support intermediate reinforcing beams. First used in Buddhist architecture, they were later adopted in residential buildings, and finally in Shinto shrines at the time when a number of technical innovations were being introduced in the latter during the Heian period.

The Hachiman sanctuary at Tsurugaoka, which goes back to the twelfth century, is one of the most characteristic examples of architectural commingling, with its high canopy roofs and playfully curved structures that form the central entablatures of certain buildings. It represents, moreover, one of the more standardized types of late Shinto architecture, and together with *nagare*, *kasuga*, and *hie* models, figures among the principal styles followed by later shrines, which rarely carried out new stylistic experiments. The Hachiman shrine was composed of two groups of buildings joined by a structure in the middle. A double entrance was placed on the sides parallel to the roof line. Even in their general composition, the structure of new Shinto sanctuaries, as compared to the more ancient places of worship, was modified. The number of auxiliary buildings was increased, as well as

their size, while even Buddhist pagodas and pavilions were erected within the same enclosures.

Kamakura Period (A.D. 1185–1333)

The establishment of the Kamakura shogunate, which transferred the powers of the state from the hands of the imperial court to those of a military class, had profound effects on the arts and culture of Japan. A general sobriety asserted itself in architecture, leading to a preference for simple, unadorned structures. New residences heralded the "warrior style" (*buke-zukuri*), in which buildings were surrounded by narrow moats or stockades. Buildings were no longer distributed around a garden but preferably grouped in a single body under the same roof, or a group of adjoining roofs, so as to ensure better defense. The old gardens were replaced by training grounds.

Even Buddhist religious architecture underwent numerous modifications. Two new styles were imported from the continent: the Indian style (*Tenjikuyō*)—introduced, however, from southern China; and the Chinese style (*Karayō*), so called to distinguish it from the *Wayo*, which by now had become the national style in the Japanese islands. Many temples were destroyed during the civil wars that broke out at the close of the Heian period; they were now rebuilt in the *Tenjikuyō* style. This was the case of Tōdaiji, for whose reconstruction absolutely new structures were employed, such as the *nandaimon*, or southern portal (Plate 506), which sums up the technical characteristics of the *Tenjikuyō* style by the use of large beams placed for the most part in a rigidly orthogonal manner (Plate 505). A greater vertical development of buildings was obtained by an increased number of bracket orders, which were often of only two arms, placed perpendicular and parallel to the walls, and these were inserted directly into the trunk of the pillar with no intermediate block. Roofs were frequently of a double order, in typical pavilion form and covered with tiles (Plate 504).

Some characteristics of *Tenjikuyō* architecture were common to *Karayō*, such as the structural elements of the brackets, roof tiles, and roofs, which in this unifying sense represented the result of a Chinese architectural tradition. The *Karayō* style was nevertheless distinguished by the layout of the monasteries, which were going back to the old rectangular plan with its symmetrical disposition of the major buildings, placed chiefly along the central axis. Applied to Chinese Ch'an (Zen) temples of the Southern Sung dynasty, the new style was introduced into Japan by the monk Eisai (1141–1215), and was first used in 1202 in the construction of the Kenninji monastery in Kyoto. It was later employed for the five great Zen monasteries of Kamakura. Engakuji, dating from the thirteenth century, is considered one of the purest examples of the *Karayō* style. The *Shariden*, or hall of relics, is the main building of the temple. The portico displays the typical yoke arch; the wood, left in its natural color, bears some sculptural decoration, which softens the solidity and linearity of the architectural structure. Moreover, the building represents a new interpretation of the reliquary shrine, hitherto constituted by the pagoda. The pagoda now begins to decline in importance, and while it does not actually disappear, it is erected outside the main enclosure. The meditative and contemplative doctrine of Zen gave precedence to other structures within the central enclosure. These might be the meditation hall, or even the garden, conceived so as to dissolve the architectural work in the landscape, in a setting that helps to coordinate the lines and proportions of the buildings in accordance with standards of sobriety that annul any monumental effect.

Muromachi Period (A.D. 1333–1573)

The warrior spirit and the austere ideals of Zen encouraged a simplicity of life and customs that spread widely throughout the provinces of the archipelago, and architecture conformed to this orientation. But things soon began to change in the surroundings of the capitals of Kyoto and Kamakura. Along with Zen, the new art of the Yüan and Ming dynasties had been imported from China, producing a decided tendency toward decoration and a taste for ostentation and luxury. When the old shogun seat of Kamakura was abandoned and the new Ashikaga shogunate was established in the Muromachi quarter of Kyoto, the distances between the military aristocracy and the court nobility were once again reduced. Rivalry and exhibitionism at the upper levels of society led to a profuse indulgence, as a show of wealth, in gold and bright color for the interiors of sumptuous dwellings, in their furnishings, wall paintings, and screens. Residential architecture particularly abounded in sculptural ornamentation and gilt decoration, while new stylistic solutions were sought in order to adapt the rigid *buke-zukuri* to the *shinden* style of ancient aristocratic houses.

One of the best works of the period is the Kinkakuji, a three-story building from the end of the fourteenth century. Its wide verandas are decorated in a lacquer and gold-leaf pattern that makes a striking contrast with the slender simplicity of the structures, and with the austere bark covering of the broad roofs of the second and top stories (Plate 521). Another example of such architecture, of an overall refinement in composition despite the sumptuousness of the decorative materials, is the Ginkakuji, or silver pavilion, built in the first half of the fifteenth century for a sophisticated circle of artists and monks.

The tea ceremony (*cha-no-yu*), introduced by the Zen masters, pointed the way for the planning of new buildings and acted to mitigate the tendency toward ostentation. The *cha-seki* and *cha-shitsu* (respectively, the tea hall and tea pavilion) were structures that contributed to the formulation of a new conception of residential architecture. Their unadorned simplicity and modest dimensions suggested lighter and more intimate types of buildings, with slender rafters and pillars and with broad open surfaces on the outer walls achieved by means of sliding structures (*shōji*). Similarly, a more organic dispersal of buildings in the landscape was sought, and this also had a profound effect on the art of the garden. The classical elements of the *shinden* garden—its lakes, islands, and bridges—were no longer distributed so as to create a static scene, but rather a panorama that could be viewed from different observation points, as from pavilions scattered along the shores of lakes. Moreover, gardens adopted the symbolism characteristic of Zen, replacing, for example, water with sand to create the "dry garden," an area of terrain covered with white sand or with gravel, in which a succession of flagstones might symbolize a ford, or rocks stand for islands emerging from water. A typical example of this style is the Ryōanji garden in Kyoto, dating from the second half of the fifteenth century.

Momoyama Period (A.D. 1573–1614)

The first Europeans landed in the Japanese islands in 1542, and in no time the influence of the West was apparent, even in architecture. The warlike atmosphere of previous periods had already produced a fortress architecture in Japan. The introduction of firearms imposed new conceptions of defense, and in various localities castles and forts were built that were inspired as well by elements of the corresponding architecture of Europe. Fortresses, which had hitherto preferably been built in elevated positions, were now constructed on level ground and took on greater dimensions, with thicker walls, deeper moats, and high towers. Groups of buildings with an increased number of stories and diminishing roof orders were erected in wood, and reinforced by masonry on massive stone foundations in the form of a truncated pyramid. Among the more spectacular examples are the castles of Matsumoto (plate 522), Kumamoto, and the "White Heron" of Himeji, with its four towers joined by narrow passages with turrets. The work, in stone and masonry, is also striking for certain minor innovations, such as the windows of the gratings, with small columns with or without capitals, and the open wall embrasures whose forms reflect the corresponding structures of Western castles.

Almost immediately, however, these architectural hybrids were to undergo—owing to the lack not only of a local architectural tradition but also of any tradition of castle life—a realignment with classical

512. *Kyoto, Nishi Honganji, the Hyunkaku, exterior.*
513. *Nikko, Tōshōgū, Yōmei-mon (Portal of Sunlight).*
514. *Himeji, view of the castle.*

515. *Himeji, interior of the castle, detail.* ▷

palace architecture. The most eloquent example of this process is seen in the Nijō castle (Plate 519), built in Kyoto in 1602 and remodeled in 1626. In slightly more than twenty years the original construction was radically altered. The three wall and moat enclosures designating the three fortresses, one inside the other, were kept. The feudal lord's residence—a complex of buildings grouped around a high central tower—was habitually erected in the inner enclosure (*honmaru*). But the castle lost its original compact appearance, and its buildings were separated and distributed over a vast area, part of which was assigned to gardens. The functionalism of fortified structures was replaced by a monumentality that was still in the Chinese taste, and the sense of solidity was expressed only symbolically by the heavy entablatures and roof gables, elaborately decorated with wooden and metal arabesques, openwork, and carving.

The merging of castle and classical palace architecture found its practical fulfillment in such cities as Kyoto, where the whole architectural tradition pointed in this direction. Elsewhere, in more provincial or peripheral areas, castles represented an isolated phenomenon, almost devoid of consequences. Nevertheless, their importance remained decisive, not for a renewal of architecture but for the urban development that they brought to the country, since it was around them that cities emerged and grew.

Yedo (Tokugawa) Period (A.D. 1615–1867)

The most imposing fort in the country was the castle of Yedo, which became the seat of the Tokugawa shogunate. The feudal lords, or daimyos, summoned to collaborate with the government built their residences within its moats and broad bastions. Around this grandiose complex a city grew up, part of modern Tokyo; in a century it became the largest in the country. Not only did it represent the center of the state administration, but the actual heart of the nation, from which a network of roads and canals ensured communication with the most remote castle-cities of the daimyos. The exceptional growth experienced by urban centers at this time—one might say that hitherto Japan had known only capital cities and commercial ports—promoted building activity in all areas of the country. When we remember that Yedo alone reached a total of more than one million inhabitants in 1700, it is not hard to imagine the innovations introduced, especially in residential architecture. First of all, the scarcity of building sites required an ever more frequent elevation of two stories. Houses were habitually erected on raised stone platforms, 28 to 40 inches in height, on which rested the wooden flooring and pilasters that together with the horizontal beams formed the framework of the structure. Outer walls were now constructed with increasing frequency in

516. *Kyoto, aerial view of the old imperial palace.*

517. *Osaka, Shitennōji, plan. 1.* nandaimon / *2.* chūmon / *3.* horō / *4.* tō / *5.* kondō / *6.* kōdō / *7.* kyōzō / *8.* shōrō / *9.* ponds / *10. secondary hall (from Ritti, 1963).*

518. *Kyoto, Ryōanji, detail of the stone and sand garden.*

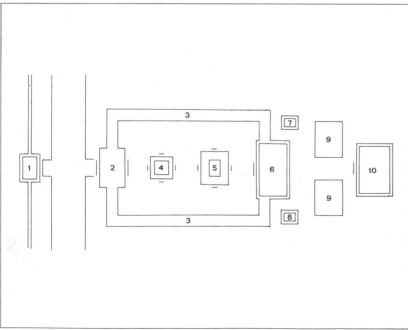

519. *Kyoto, Nijō castle, exterior detail of a pavilion.*

520. *Types of Shinto shrines. Left to right: façades, side views, and ground plans.* 1. shinmei *(shrine of Ise)* / 2. taisha *(shrine of Izumo)* / 3. nagare *(shrine of Kamo in Kyoto)* / 4. kasuga *(Kasuga shrine in Nara)* / 5. hachiman *(Usa–Hachiman shrine in Oita)* / 6. hie *(Hie shrine in Shiga) (from Ota, 1966).*

521. *Kyoto, Kinkakuji (Temple of the Golden Pavilion).*

522. *Matsumoto, view of the castle.*

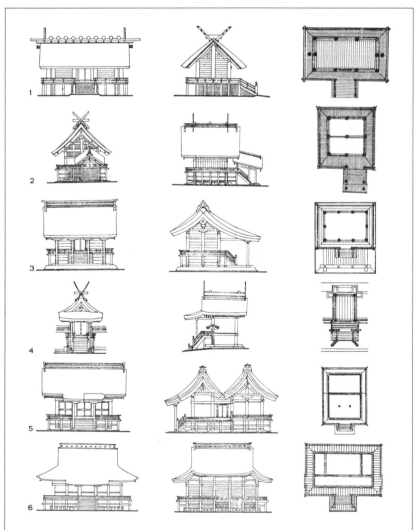

masonry and plaster, at least on two sides; on the others, mobile partitions (*shōji*) were applied, or ample windows opening on verandas (*shoin*). The roof, always reinforced by wooden beams, was now commonly covered with tiles. The interior was divided into several rooms by means of sliding walls (*fusuma*) and screens (*byōbu*), thus providing maximum flexibility of living quarters.

The increasingly widespread use of floor mats (*tatami*), whose dimensions were fixed at 32.94 by 72.32 inches, required new measurement units for the placing of pilasters; these could not be calculated as formerly on the basis of the distance between the centers of the pilasters, but in terms of the real space between one pilaster and another, taking into consideration the variations in their diameter. Greater freedom in planning, primarily for the distribution of rooms, was obtained by removing the supporting structures to the more external points of the building, especially to the corners, in such a way as to leave the interior spaces as free and uncluttered as possible. This resulted in a more complex scaffolding for roofs, so as to make up for the lack of supporting structures at the central points. In addition to the frequency of earthquakes and fires, this was one more reason why a limit was imposed to vertical elevation, which had recently been fixed at 101.7 feet for monumental buildings, as opposed to the approximately 312 feet once reached by the Tōdaiji pagoda.

The essential lines of Yedo civil architecture produced the so-called *sukiya* style, with which the development of Japanese residential architecture reaches its peak, establishing the type of dwelling to which the everyday house in the traditional style has remained firmly attached. The architectural masterpieces of the period, the Shūgakuin and Katsura villas—built in isolated settings in the environs of Kyoto during the first half of the seventeenth century—foreshadowed the transition from the *shoin* style to the *sukiya* by their deliberate search for suggestive spatial effects, their sense of measure and proportion, their position in a surrounding garden, and their simplicity of line and decor, as shown also by their use of wood left in its natural state. As for the monumental architecture of the period—omitting from our discussion the temples, which are generally modest and unadorned—it is best displayed in such mausoleum shrines as the renowned Tōshōgū at Nikko (Plate 513). Built in accordance with hybrid Shinto-Buddhist forms, these new complexes welcomed numerous Chinese influences, especially in the structure of their masonry arcades, and perhaps European ones as well in their internal twin vaults and columns with convex fluting. Ultimately, however, they constitute a phase of degeneration in Japanese architecture, perpetuating for a time a monumental conception that was a direct continuation of the castles and palaces of the Nijō type.

Modern Period (1868–   )

The Meiji restoration that began in 1868 transformed Japan politically and economically into a modern nation that more and more looked toward the West for inspiration. Among the many new programs undertaken, those relating to urban building and development were given a certain precedence. Traditional systems of wood construction were abandoned, since—especially for public utility works—they no longer corresponded to current needs. Attention was directed to techniques of Western architecture and building systems of the colonial type, which meanwhile had been developed and were spreading in the maritime cities of the archipelago as a result of the establishment of the first European and American settlements. Many of the new constructions consisted at first of buildings in a Westernizing style, whose wooden frameworks and structures were externally covered in stone or stucco. Among the first local architects to specialize in these new building techniques were Tadahiro Hayashi and Kisuke Shimizu II, both of whom were initiated into Western architectural methods through construction work at the foreign settlement of Yokohama. One of Shimizu's works was the famous Tsukiji Hotel in Tokyo, built in 1867–68 in a style that, though derived from the West, nevertheless preserves some traditional elements of native architecture.

Beginning in 1870, many European and American architects arrived in the principal cities of Japan. Together with other exponents of Western culture and on the invitation of the Japanese Government, they set in motion a program of modernization to which they themselves contributed greatly, by their own work and also by teaching in the universities that were founded during the same years. They included the Englishmen T. J. Waters and Josiah Conder, the American R. P. Bridgens, the Frenchman C. de Boinville, the Italian C.V. Cappelletti, and the German H. Ende. Under their guidance, numerous public buildings were planned and executed in the varying historical styles of nineteenth-century Western architecture: Renaissance and Neoclassical, Romanesque and Gothic. Celebrated works of this period are the Mint in Osaka, built by Waters; the Shinbashi railway station, designed by Bridgens; the Historical Museum of Tokyo by Cappelletti; and the Nicholai Cathedral by Conder. These were for the most part imposing two- or three-story constructions, massive in form, which in their meeting and mingling of different styles reflected the late nineteenth-century atmosphere of ferment in European architecture.

It was in this climate and with this formal eclecticism that the first Japanese architects trained by their Western counterparts (through courses in architecture and civil engineering inaugurated in 1875 at the College of Technology of the Imperial University in Tokyo) began to produce works. Among the first were Kingo Tatsuno, Tōyū Katayama, Yoriki Tsumaki, Yuzuru Watanabe, and Tamisuke Yokogawa. The considerable achievements of some of these architects—in Tokyo alone—included the stone and brick Bank of Japan building, built by Kingo Tatsuno in 1890–96; the Akasaka Palace, finished in 1909 after designs by Tōyū Katayama; the National Museum, built in 1908 by the same architect; the Central Station, of steel and brick, built in 1914 by Kingo Tatsuno; and the Imperial Theater of 1911 by Tamisuke Yokogawa. From the work of these first Japanese architects, building activity passed gradually into the hands of local designers and skilled workers, and a slow process of re-examining the values of traditional architecture began. The introduction in 1887 of a course in the history of architecture at the Imperial University must surely have helped to call attention to the values of the tradition, and to disseminate the first theories whereby the old might be fused with the new and the classical forms of Japanese architecture adapted to modern construction techniques.

The early decades of the twentieth century saw the appearance in Tokyo and other cities of the first constructions in reinforced concrete; their number was to grow following the disastrous earthquake of 1923. As a result of the construction materials employed for protection against earthquakes, buildings took on a certain heaviness of form and a massive solidity of structure. Nevertheless, new construction methods were soon adopted, in which there was a tendency to reduce wall structures as much as possible by the use of reinforced concrete pillars and wide glass windows.

Meanwhile, there was a notable influx of ideas from the new rationalistic European theories—to which Shinichirō Okada and Riki Sano were among the first to adhere—which championed an architectural dynamic to be achieved on the formal level by the geometric placing of volumes. The International Style, which thus seemed capable of development, was overwhelmed, however, upon the emergence of the Bunriha Kenchiku group, which, inspired by the Viennese Secession of the early twentieth century, welcomed to its ranks a large number of architects—among them Kikuji Ishimoto, Sutemi Horiguchi, and Mayumi Takizawa—who proposed the birth of a "new architecture." Their activities, which bore results in the 1920s, received support and corroboration from the work of Frank Lloyd Wright; the latter, with his naturalistic theories, had the opportunity to indicate during his stay in Japan for the construction of the Imperial Hotel in Tokyo the direction in which the new architecture should proceed. On the other hand, close contact with such famous architects as Le Corbusier, Walter Gropius, and Ludwig Mies van der Rohe

facilitated an evaluation of the functional and artistic needs to which the architectural work ought to respond. The failure of the rationalistic approach was due to the inevitable lack of spiritual and psychological sympathy for imported forms, and a solution was then sought in the reacquisition of the fundamental principles of traditional Japanese architecture: the articulation of space, harmony and rhythm of composition, fluency of volumes, luminosity and color. The German architect Bruno Taut and the Japanese Sutemi Horiguchi were important figures in this new orientation toward classical and traditional values. Interesting results were obtained by the readoption of classical stylistic models, as adapted to constructions that were very modern technically, and in which formerly wooden structures were replaced by metal. The principal buildings constructed in Tokyo during this period were the Kabuki Theater by Okada in 1922, the Imperial University's Institute of Technology by Uchida in 1923, and the University Library in 1925, designed by the same architect.

Meanwhile, a clear separation had emerged between the theoretical formulations of avant-garde architecture and the practical results achieved. Except for a very few works built in accordance with the new criteria, construction for the most part followed strictly functional forms, since the progressive extension of urban centers had produced a growing need for houses and public buildings. Domestic architecture, however, continued in its traditional ways, with small wooden constructions, usually of a single story. The question was raised as to whether the new principles of modern architecture might not be applied on a wider scale, and the work of Horiguchi, Hideto Kishida, Kunio Maekawa (Plates 523, 524), and other architects led to the formation of the Nihon Kōsaku Bunka Remmei movement; among its chief objectives was the concrete realization of the new theories.

The major works of the 1930s include the central post offices in Tokyo and Osaka, designed by Tetsuo Yoshida; the large Sōgo department store in Osaka, designed by T. Murano; and the hospital for postal-telegraph workers built in Tokyo by Mamoru Yamada. They were for the most part constructed of reinforced concrete, with large windows, and broad verandas or projecting penthouses at the sides that at times resolved their heaviness of structure in dynamic perspective. These and other architectural works marked a definite orientation toward the new tendencies of modern architecture. The political atmosphere, however, soon made such a program unfeasible. Official architecture, under the banner of the now prevailing nationalism, turned back to a massive solidity of form and a static juxtaposition of structures that expressed the rigid, martial exterior imposed by the new artistic directives of the government. A classic example of this kind of architecture is the solemn and imposing Army Palace in Tokyo.

With the end of World War II, and as a result of the almost total destruction of many cities, the problem of rebuilding came urgently to the fore. But since the work of reconstruction had first to confront the more impelling needs, whole quarters of cities—largely composed of traditional wooden buildings or small masonry houses—were rebuilt without any preconceived plans. The difficulties of an organic and radical urban plan turned out to be insurmountable. A compromise solution was attempted by laying out new peripheral neighborhoods, built according to modern urban conceptions of

autonomous centers and satellite cities. Official as well as residential architecture definitely adopted the new construction techniques and materials of reinforced concrete, as well as an ample employment of metal and glass. A clear rapprochement with rationalist criteria took place under the guise of a re-established tie with the ancient architectural tradition of the country. Among the first and more important works are the Reader's Digest complex, the Shinjō (temple), and the Nippon Gakki building, all three in Tokyo. A rationalist approach to structure was also tried in residential and domestic architecture.

On the whole, an architecture has emerged that is free of orthogonal rigidity and tends toward curvilinear or angular surfaces, divorced as much as possible from a concern for volume. The use of new materials has moreover permitted surfaces to be arranged in unforeseen perspectives, with combinations of discontinuous levels balanced on pillars. These new tendencies are also exemplified in the monumental complex of buildings at Hiroshima, the Ehime Convention Hall, and other structures designed by Kenzo Tange, one of the major exponents of modern Japanese architecture (Plates 525–527). But here we are dealing with an architecture of the summit, a display of showpieces that have little in common with the average building activity that determines the face of a city. It is a question of an avant-garde architecture, not only Japanese but worldwide, in search of aesthetic solutions (in recent years more plastic than linear, whence the substitution of glass-and-concrete for glass-and-metal). It is an architecture that, despite the growing resources of prefabrication, has few possibilities for application on a broad scale and tends to transform the architectural project into an industrial *design*.

The existing rupture between an elite architecture and the building trade is accentuated by the fact that Japan is surely one of the industrial countries that has invested least in public housing, which explains the lack of any true direction in the sphere of everyday architecture. This failure is also reflected in the area of city planning, where residential neighborhoods have ended by bearing no relation to the city as a whole. In addition, Japanese architects have been more concerned with areas of collective rather than individual life. They have turned their attention to stadiums and recreation centers, to university campuses, and above all have indulged in ideal city-planning projects in pursuit of a spectacular avant-garde vision that not infrequently confounds the future with utopia. This is true despite the fact that in recent decades a few organic approaches have been studied and in part carried out, especially for the unification of lesser urban centers, as in the case of Kita-Kyushu, formed by the merging of five cities, and the urban project to achieve a single great Osaka-Kobe metropolis. Tokyo itself is the prime example of such projects for the enlargement of the great

525. *Totsuka, Golf Club, by Kenzo Tange.*
526. *Matsuyama, Ehime Convention Hall, by Kenzo Tange.*
527. *Tokyo, Catholic Center of St. Mary's Cathedral, by Kenzo Tange.*

528. Kamakura, Museum of Modern Art, by Junzō Sakakura.

metropolises: one of the plans presented foresees the city as constituting the geographic center of the plain of Kwanto in the near future, with the construction of a certain number of satellite cities in order to decentralize industry and other economic activities. A rapid transport system would link the satellite towns to each other and with Tokyo. The whole complex would constitute a Greater Tokyo, or the "metropolitan circle" of Japan. Another project, first offered in 1958 by Hisarō Kano, predicts a future development of the city as the capital of the nation and as an industrial, commercial, and maritime center for the whole Far East as well as for Japan. With this objective in mind, a radical exploitation of Tokyo Bay has been recommended, in order to reclaim an area of some 600 to 650 million square yards. Other plans have been developed to exploit Tokyo Bay, not through drainage and refill operations, but by constructing elevated or sealevel platforms supported on pillars or other structures set into the sea floor.

The plan offered by Kenzo Tange falls within the context of these studies. His overall scheme provides for a gradual reconstruction of the existing city and its progressive expansion into the bay area. The restructuring of the city would be carried out along an axis connected to various cyclical units constituting a complex of administrative centers. The civic axis would begin at the present metropolitan center and extend toward the bay. Constructions would be erected either on artificial platforms or on reclaimed land. The first, because of the greater guarantee of solidity and stability, would allow these areas to be developed vertically through multilevel structures; the second would call for a horizontal distribution of various building complexes. With the subway laid out along the civic axis, transportation could be easily dispatched from stations along a single line through a cyclical transport system on three levels, from the present center of the city to all points on the bay. The criterion substantially unfolded by the project is that of the necessity for the transition from a centripetal radial system to one of urban development in the linear sense. It promotes the combination in an organic unity of both the elements of urban planning and the architectural structures of the city, including the communications and transportation system. Finally, it aims at the realization of a new urban spatial order, one reflecting the organization and mobility of present society, of which present-day Tokyo is one of the most dramatic expressions, not only in Japan but in the entire world.

Adolfo Tamburello

NOTES/SYNOPTIC TABLES/SELECTED BIBLIOGRAPHY
INDEX/LIST OF PLATES/LIST OF PHOTOGRAPHIC CREDITS

NOTES

INTRODUCTION

1 Kautilya in the *Arthaśastra*, the principal text of political theory in India, warns that one of the most serious dangers a sovereign can incur is that of allowing the *śrenī* to flourish. If these guilds are too powerful, an eventual clash with them may lead to the collapse of the system and the fall of the sovereign.

2 Cf. J. Gernet, "Notes sur les villes chinoises au moment de l'apogée islamique," *The Islamic City*, edited by A. H. Houtrani and S. M. Stern, Oxford, 1970, pp. 77 ff.

3 Jean Chesneaux, "Le Mode de production asiatique: une nouvelle étape de la discussion," *Eirene*, III, 1964, and "Récents Travaux marxistes sur le mode de production asiatique," *La Pensée*, 114, 1964.

4 Asia was the first to use nickel for coins (the Indo-Grecian and Greco-Bactrian kingdoms) and paper money (used in China), and later would even use clay *fiches* for coins of scant value (as did Thailand in the eighteenth and nineteenth centuries).

Chapter One

INDIA AND CEYLON

1 Cf. J. Auboyer, *Introduction à l'étude de l'art de l'Inde*, Rome, Is.M.E.O., 1965, pp. 59 ff.

2 Indeed, there seem to be traces of conduits (unfinished) designed for this purpose. On the other hand, it was thought at first—as Father Heras also pointed out—that the trench was meant to be eroded away, widened, and open at least on the side facing the valley.

3 Cf. M. Bussagli and C. Sivaramamurti, *5000 Years of the Art of India*, New York, 1971.

4 Note that bricks change dimensions and consistency according to the period, as can be seen in the following tabulation: the average dimensions of a brick in the Maurya period—height or thickness 2 inches, length 19 5/8 inches, width 12 1/4 inches; at Sanchi (Stupa 1, second century B.C.)—height 3 inches, length 16 inches, width 10 inches; at Mathura (second century A.D.)—height 3 inches (also maintained elsewhere until the eighth century and beyond), length 13 5/8 inches (but also 10 7/8), width 10 1/4 or 8 1/2 inches. In later temples, especially those of Orissa, the dimensions are less (height 3 inches, length 13 inches, width 10 1/4 inches).

5 Cf. C. Sivaramamurti, *Sanskrit Literature and Art, Mirrors of Indian Culture*, M.A.S.I., No. 73, Calcutta, 1955, which mentions in this regard the verses of the *Rāmāyana* (V. 2.23; repeated 3.32) in which a temple is compared to the crests of the Kailasa grazing the sky; the same image recurs in a commemorative inscription. Similarly, the comparison with Mount Meru, the cosmic mountain, recurs both in the *Rāmāyana* and in commemorative inscriptions in the south. In other cases, however, the reference is to gigantic beings (such as elephants), clouds, and cosmic changes. All this has nothing to do with the technical texts. The *Mānasāra*, the *Purānas*, and the *Śilpas* are followed by a great many other such works that indicate rules, measures, and techniques—all directed to obtaining aesthetically valid, and in their way functional, forms. They do not, however, dwell on the effect of *rāsa* that the work may arouse in the beholder.

6 The *samgha*, or Buddhist community, is, along with Buddha and the Law he preaches, one of the Three Jewels—that is, one of the essential pillars on which this religion is founded.

7 E. Lamotte, *Histoire du Bouddhisme indien des origines à l'ère Saka*, Louvain, 1958, pp. 365–66.

8 Cf. A. Volwahsen, *Living Architecture: Indian*, New York, 1969, pp. 144 ff.

9 Cf. J. Auboyer, *op. cit.*, p.84.

10 Cf. *Epigraphia Indica*, I, p. 159. The inscription in copper is reproduced in Plates 104 and 105.

11 S. Kramrisch, *The Art of India*, London, 1954.

Chapter Two

INDONESIA AND INDOCHINA

1 M. Bussagli, "India Esteriore," *Enciclopedia Universale dell'Arte*, VII, Rome-Venice, 1958, col. 318.

2 *Ibid.*, col. 326.

3 C. Holt, *Art in Indonesia*, New York, 1967, p. 5.

4 *Ibid.*, p. 39.

5 J. G. de Casparis, *Prasasti Indonesia*, I, Bandung, 1950, pp. 160–92.

6 M. Hallade, *L'Asie du Sud est*, Paris, 1954, p. 5.

7 B. P. Groslier, *Indocina*, Milan, 1961, pp. 56–57.

8 *Ibid.*, p. 105.

9 *Ibid.*, p. 147.

10 G. Coedès, "Birmania, centri e tradizioni," *Enciclopedia Universale dell'Arte*, II, col. 605.

11 *Ibid.*, col. 607.

12 Groslier, *op. cit.*, p. 230.

13 G. Coedès, "Arte dell'Indonesia," *Civiltà dell'Oriente*, IV, Rome, 1962, p. 943.

14 H. Parmentier, *L'Art du Laos*, Paris, 1954, pp. 3–4.

15 Groslier, *op. cit.*, pp. 40–42.

16 *Ibid.*, pp. 252–54.

17 *Ibid.*, p. 254.

Chapter Five

CHINA

1 Laurence Sickman and Alexander Soper, *The Art and Architecture of China*, Baltimore, 1956, p. 285.

2 E. Biot, *Le Tcheou-li*, II, Paris, 1851, pp. 555–56.

3 Arthur Waley, *The Book of Songs*, London, 1937, p. 33.

4 Sickman and Soper, *op. cit.*, p. 207.

5 *Ibid.*, p. 216.

6 *Shih Chi*, VI, translated by E. Chavannes, "Les Mémoires historiques de Se-ma Ts'ien," Paris, 1895–1905.

7 Imperial Ch'ing Encyclopedia: T'u Shu Chi Ch'eng, quoted in *Shui Ching Chu*.

8 Sui Shu, Chap. LXVIII.

9 San Tendai Godaisan Ki.

10 A. C. Moule, *Quinsai, with Other Notes on Marco Polo*, Cambridge, 1957.

11 J. Fontein, "Cina storica," *Enciclopedia Universale dell'Arte*, VIII, Rome-Venice, 1958, col. 638.

12 Sickman and Soper, *op. cit.*, p. 283.

13 "China's Architectural Heritage and Tasks of Today," in *People's China*, I, 21, November 1952.

SYNOPTIC TABLES

Pre-Christian Era/1st century A.D.

INDIA AND CEYLON	INDONESIA AND INDOCHINA	HIMALAYAN REGION AND CENTRAL ASIA
INDUS CIVILIZATION (mid-third millennium–1500 B.C.)		
Kot Diji (to 1st half of third millennium B.C.)		
Mohenjo-Daro		
Harappa		
Lothal (port built later)		
VEDIC PERIOD (1500–c. sixth century B.C.)		
Rajagriha (Rajgir): bastions in masonry		
Malabar: rock tombs		
	Dong-Son culture (2nd half of first millennium B.C.)	
PRE-MAURYA PERIOD (sixth–third century B.C.)		
MAURYA (322–185 B.C.) AND SUNGA (185–72 B.C.) DYNASTIES		Patan (Nepal): chaitya of Asoka (third century B.C.)
Pataliputra (Patna): palace of Chandragupta (fourth–third century B.C.)		
Sitamarhi, Lomas Rishi (Barabar), Nagarjuni (Bihar): rock temples of Asoka's time (264–226 B.C.)		
Bairat (Rajputana): temple (c. 250 B.C.)		
Sanchi, Bharhut, Buddh Gaya, Kumrahar: stupas (second–first century B.C.)		
Bhaja, Ajanta, Pitalkhora, Kondane: rock sanctuaries (end of first century B.C.)		
		Wangath: Jyestharudra (second–first century B.C.)
		Vijapur: Vijayesvara (second–first century B.C.)
		Ushkur, Harvan (Kashmir): ruins (second century B.C.–first century A.D.)

CHINA

Pan-po-ts'un: Neolithic settlement, Yangshao culture (fourth millennium B.C.)

Ch'eng-tzu-yai: Neolithic settlement, Lungshan culture

SHANG DYNASTY (1766–1122 B.C.)

Chengchow (Ao): founded c. 1500 B.C.

Hsiao-t'un (Anyang): founded c. 1300 B.C.

Hsi-pei Kang (Anyang): royal necropolis

CHOU DYNASTY (1122–255 B.C.)

P'u Tu Ts'un (Changan): tomb (tenth century B.C.)

Loyang: royal necropolis (tenth–ninth century B.C.)

Tombs at Tangshan, Tung-sun-pa, Changsha

Hsia Tu (I-hsien): city of the Yen kings

Han Tan (Hopei): city of the Chao kings

CH'IN DYNASTY (255–206 B.C.)

Hsien-Yang (outskirts): tomb of Emperor Shih Huang Ti

Portion of the Great Wall (rebuilt in Ming period)

HAN DYNASTY (206 or 202 B.C.–A.D. 220)

Changan: Wei-yang and Ch'ang-lo royal palaces

Loyang (outskirts): capital of the Later Han

Feicheng (outskirts): small sacrificial temple of Mount Hsiao-t'ang (129 B.C.?)

Hsing-p'ing: tomb of General Ho Ch'ü-ping (117 B.C.)

Kiasiang (outskirts): necropolis of the Wu family

Pei Chai Ts'un (Shantung): tomb

Wangtu (outskirts): tomb

KOREA

NEOLITHIC PERIOD (third–first millennium B.C.)

Western coastal settlements of the comb-marked pottery people (third–second millennium B.C.)

Inland settlements of the undecorated pottery people: dolmens (first millennium B.C.)

AGE OF METALS (2nd half of first millennium B.C.)

Pyongyang: Tungusic kingdom

Wei-man (Chaohsien) (198 B.C.)

JAPAN

Settlements of the Jōmon period (sixth–first millennium B.C.)

Settlements of the Yayoi period (third century B.C.–third century A.D.)

INDIA AND CEYLON	INDONESIA AND INDOCHINA	HIMALAYAN REGION AND CENTRAL ASIA
MATHURA STYLE (first–third century A.D.) Architecture documented only by bas-reliefs (Devakula of Mat) Pitalkhora: rock sanctuaries (first–second century; additions fifth–sixth century) Karli: rock sanctuaries (from 120) Nasik: vihara (second century) Kanheri: chaitya (second–third century)	Chen-la	Ajaz-kala: fortress (second–third century) Miran (third century)
AMARAVATI STYLE (first–fifth century) Amaravati: Great Stupa (second century) Ghantasala Nagarjunakonda: Buddhist establishments (third century)	Funan (Indochina) (second–sixth century)	Ravaq: monastery (third–fourth century) Harvan: Buddhist monastery (third–fourth century)
GANDHARA STYLE (first–fifth century) Surkh Kotal (Afghanistan): Temple of Fire Takht-i-Bahi: stupa Taxila: palace of Sirkap; temple of Jandial (second century) Shah-ji-ki-Dheri (near Peshawar): stupa of Kanishka Mohra Moradu: stupa (third century) Haibak: stupa and monastery (fourth or fifth century) Jaulian: stupa Khair-Kanek: Temple of the Sun (fifth century)	Lin-yi	Toprak-kala (third–fifth century) Kizil: caves (fourth–eighth century) Patan: shrine of Siva Pasupatinath and Vishnu Gangu-Narayama (mid-fifth century) Patan: palace of Managriha and Manavihara (late fifth century)

CHINA	KOREA	JAPAN
	Pyongyang (outskirts): settlement and necropolis of Lo-lang (108 B.C.–A.D. 313)	
	THREE KINGDOMS PERIOD (57 B.C.–A.D. 668)	
	Chi-an: tombs at Koguryo (first–second century A.D.)	
I-nan: tomb (early third century)		
SIX DYNASTIES (A.D. 221–581)		Necropoli of the Kofun period (third–fourth century)
Loyang		
Nanking: necropolis		
Sung-yüeh-ssu (Mount Sung): brick pagoda (early sixth century)		
Shen-t'ung-ssu: square pagoda (544)	Pyongyang: "Tomb of the Two Columns" (sixth century)	
Chu-yung hsien: tomb of Hsiao Chi (sixth century)	Kyongju: Punhwang-sa, pagoda (634)	
Yunkang, Tunhwang, Lüng Men, Ma-chi: caves	Kyongju: tomb of King Muryol (662)	
	Puyo: Chong-nim-sa, pagoda (seventh century)	
	Iksankun: Miruk-sa, stone pagoda (seventh century)	

INDIA AND CEYLON

GUPTA AND POST-GUPTA PERIODS (fifth–tenth century)

Badami: caves and temples

Deogarh: temple of Siva (early sixth century)

Aihole: temple of Lad Khan (sixth century); temple of Durga

Sarnath: stupa of Dhamek

Ajanta: establishment of caves (sixth–seventh century)

Bhumara: temple (sixth–seventh century)

Nalanda: monastic center (seventh century)

Mamallapuram: Pallava temples (seventh century)

Pattadakal: Papanatha (c. 680)

Sirpur: temple of Laksmana (seventh–eighth century)

Ellora: rock sanctuaries (seventh–eighth century)

Kanchipuram: temples of Narasimhavarman (630–668); Kailasanath (eighth century); temples of Vaikunthaperumal, Mallikarjuna, Galagnatha (mid-eighth century)

Martand: Temple of the Sun (eighth century)

Ellora: Kailasanath (mid-eighth century)

Rajputana: temples of Osia, temple of Mahavira (late eighth–ninth century)

Bhuvanesvar: temples of Parasuramesvara, Uttaresvara (eighth–tenth century); temple of Vaital Deul (ninth–tenth century)

Khajuraho: temples of Caunsat Yogini, Lalguan Mahadeva, Brahma (ninth century)

Konarak: Temple of the Sun

INDONESIA AND INDOCHINA

Sambor Prei Kuk (Cambodia) (1st half of seventh century)

Prei Kmeng and Kompong Prah (Cambodia) (seventh century)

Kedu (Java): Candi Pawon, Candi Mendut (seventh–ninth century)

Nagara Pathama (Siam): Wat P'ra Men, Wat P'ra Pathama (from the seventh century)

Hmawza, ancient Prome (Burma): stupas of Bawbawgyi, Payagyi, Payama; temples of Bebegyi, Lemyethna, Payatan (from the seventh century)

Tower of Mi-son A 1 (Champa) (eighth century)

Hoa-lai, Panduranga (Champa) (mid-eighth century)

Dieng (Java): Hindu shrines (from the eighth century)

Borobudur (Java) (eighth–ninth century)

Prambanam (Java): Candi Kalasan, Sari, Sewu, Plaosan, Lumbung; Loro Jongrang (eighth–ninth century)

Tower of Hoa-lai (Champa) (eighth–ninth century)

Phnom Kulen (Cambodia) (1st half of ninth century)

Prapeang Phong (Cambodia): Prasat Kok Po (2nd half of ninth century)

Ak Yom, Prasat Andet, Phum Prasat (Cambodia) (ninth century)

Duong Dong (Champa): Laksmindra Lokesvara (ninth century)

Roluos (Cambodia): Prah Ko (879), Bakong (881), Lolei (893)

HIMALAYAN REGION AND CENTRAL ASIA

Berkut-kala, Tesik-kala (from the fifth century)

Dandan Uiliq: sanctuaries (from the fifth century)

Tumshuq (fifth–seventh century)

Duldur-aqur (fifth–seventh century)

Takht-i-Sulayman: temple fo Sankaracarya (fifth–eighth century)

Qumtura (fifth–ninth century)

Subasi (sixth century)

Qarasahr (Shorchuq) (from the sixth century)

Lhasa: bSam-yas (seventh century)

Pjandzikent (seventh–eighth century)

Patan: palace of Kailasakuta (eighth century)

Ludov: temple (eighth century)

Norwa: temple (eighth century)

Parihasapura: Raj Vihara (eighth century)

Ushkur: stupa and monastery of Kuviska, restoration (mid-eighth century)

Vantipur: temples of Avantisvami and Avantisvara (ninth century)

Tholing (mT'o-glin) (from the ninth century)

Patan: temples of Sankaragaurisvara and Sugandhesa (late ninth–early tenth century)

CHINA

SUI (A.D. 589–618) AND T'ANG (A.D. 618–907)
DYNASTIES

Changan

Loyang: royal palace

Tunhwang, T'ien-lung, Shan, and Lüng Men:
caves

Chaohsien (outskirts): Great Stone Bridge
(sixth–seventh century)

Changan: Ta-yen-t'a (seventh century)

Mount Chiu-tsun: T'ai-hsung tomb (627–649)

Changan: Hsüan-tsang pagoda (669 or 828)

Wu Tai Shan: Nan-ch'an-ssu (782)

Yün-chü-ssu (Mount Fang): small pagoda (eighth
century)

Hui-shan-ssu (Mount Sung): pagoda (eighth
century)

Wu Tai Shan: Fo-kuang-ssu, main pavilion (mid-
ninth century)

Li-cheng-hsien: Shen-t'ung-ssu, Liang-tzu pagoda
(ninth–tenth century)

Chengtu: tomb of Wang Chien (847–918)

Chou-hsien: Chung-hsing-ssu, octagonal pagoda
(early tenth century)

KOREA

GREAT SILLA KINGDOM (A.D. 668–935)

Wol-ssong Kun: Kam-cun-sa, twin pagodas

Kyongju: Observatory (seventh century)

Kyongju: temples of Sokkulam and Pulguk-sa
(eighth century)

Ui-song: T'ap-ni (eighth century)

An-dong Kun: seven-story brick pagoda (eighth
century)

JAPAN

ASUKA PERIOD (A.D. 552–645)

Naniwa: palace (fourth–fifth century)

Asuka (outskirts): palace

Nara (outskirts): Hōryūji temple complex
(seventh century)

NARA PERIOD (A.D. 645–784)

Nara: founded 710

Nara: Tōshōdaiji (construction begun between
755 and 770)

Nara: Tōdaiji (1st half of eighth century)

HEIAN PERIOD (A.D. 784–1185)

Kyoto (Heian-Kyo): founded 794

Kyoto: Byōdōin

Kyoto: Jingoji

Tsurugaoka: Hachiman sanctuary (twelfth century)

Mount Kōya: Kongōbuji monastery

Hieizan: Enryakuji monastery

INDIA AND CEYLON	INDONESIA AND INDOCHINA	HIMALAYAN REGION AND CENTRAL ASIA
	Prasat Kravan (Cambodia) (921)	
	Pre Rup (Cambodia) (961)	
	Banteay Srei (Cambodia) (967)	
	Phnom Bakheng, Phnom Krom, Phnom Bok (Cambodia) (tenth century)	
	Hoa-lu' (Vietnam): tomb of Dinh Tien Hoang (tenth century)	
	Candi Gumung Gansir (Java) (mid-tenth century)	
	Jalatunda (Java): royal pool (2nd half of tenth century)	
	Ta Keo (Cambodia): pyramid (c. 1000)	
Rajputana: Pipala Devi (late tenth century)	Prasat Khleang (Cambodia) (tenth–eleventh century)	
Sunak: temple of Nilakantha (late tenth century)	Pagan (Burma): monuments (tenth–thirteenth century)	Ladakh (tenth–seventeenth century)
Bhuvanesvar: temples of Muktesvara (c. 975), Lingaraja (c. 1000), Brahmesvara and Ramesvara (eleventh century)	Tampak Siring (Bali) (eleventh century)	
	Nhatrang (Champa): tower (eleventh century)	
Khajuraho: temples of Kandariya Mahadeo, Visvanatha, Caturbhuja, Parsvanatha (c. 1000); temples of Devi Jagadambi, Surya (eleventh century)	Belahan (East Java): "bath" of King Airlangga (2nd half of eleventh century)	
	Angkor Thom (Cambodia): pyramid of Baphuon (2nd half of eleventh century)	
Tanjore: temple of Rajrajesvara (early eleventh century)	Wat Khna Seu Keo (Cambodia) (2nd half of eleventh century)	
Rajputana, Mount Abu: temple of Vimala (eleventh century)	Binh-lam, Thu-thien (Champa) (eleventh–thirteenth century)	
Karadu: temples (eleventh century)	Muara Jambi, Muara Takus (Sumatra) (eleventh–thirteenth century)	
Modhera: temple of Surya (eleventh century)	Thuy-Khe (Vietnam): Thien-phuc (altar, 1132)	
Somnathpur: Somnatha (twelfth century)	Angkor Wat, Beng Mealea (Cambodia) (1st half of twelfth century)	
Konarak: temple of Surya (twelfth century)		
Mysore: temples (twelfth–thirteenth century)	Binh Son (Vietnam): stupa (c. twelfth century)	Pandrenthan: temple of Siva Rilhanesvara (twelfth century)
Rajputana, Mount Abu: temple of Tejpal (c. 1230)	Lop Buri (Siam): Brah Prang Sam Yot, Wat Mahadhatu (twelfth–thirteenth century)	
	Angkor Thom (Cambodia): Bayon (twelfth–thirteenth century)	
	Lamphun (Siam): Wat Kukut (completed 1218)	
	Candi Kidal, Jago, Saventar (Java) (thirteenth century)	
	Candi Singhasari (Java) (thirteenth–fourteenth century)	
	Padang Lawas (Sumatra) (thirteenth–fourteenth century)	

CHINA

FIVE DYNASTIES AND LIAO DYNASTY (A.D. 907–1125)

Tatung: Hua-yen-ssu

Chihsien: Tu-lo-ssu, Kuan-yin-ko (late tenth century)

Ch'ing-chou: imperial Liao tombs (eleventh century)

Chinhsien: Pehchen, east pagoda (mid-eleventh century)

Yinghsien: Fo-kuang-ssu, five-story pagoda (1058)

Ch'ing-chou: Pai t'a (eleventh–twelfth century)

Yün-chü-ssu (Mount Fang): pagoda (1117)

SUNG DYNASTY (A.D. 960–1280)

Pien-ching (Kaifeng)

Hangchow

Kaifeng: Fan-t'a of Kuo-hsiang-ssu (c. 977)

Chin-tz'u: Shen-mu tien (1023–31)

Cheng-ting-hsien: Lung-hsing-ssu (eleventh century)

Kaifeng: "Color of Iron Pagoda" (mid-eleventh century)

Suchow: Yüan-miao-kuan, main pavilion (twelfth century)

Yu-yao: Pao-Kuo-ssu, main pavilion (twelfth–thirteenth century)

Lungshan: Taoist cave temple

Ch'üan-chou: twin pagodas (1st half of thirteenth century)

KOREA

KORYO KINGDOM (A.D. 918–1392)

Seoul: Kyong-bok, stupa of Hong-pob (1017)

P'yong-ch'ang Kun: Wol-chong-sa, nine-story pagoda (eleventh century)

An-dong Kun: Pong-chong-sa, Keung-nak Chon (twelfth–thirteenth century)

Yong-ju Kun: Pu-sok-sa, Mu-ryang-su Chon (twelfth–thirteenth century)

Yesan Kun: Su-dok-sa, Tai-ung Chon

Tat'ap Pong: pagoda (thirteenth century)

JAPAN

Hiraizumi: Chūsonji, Golden Hall (1st half of twelfth century)

KAMAKURA PERIOD (A.D. 1185–1333)

Nara: reconstruction of Tōdaiji

Kyoto: Kenninji monastery (1202)

Kamakura: Engakuji monastery (thirteenth century)

INDIA AND CEYLON	INDONESIA AND INDOCHINA	HIMALAYAN REGION AND CENTRAL ASIA
	Sukhodaya (Siam): Wat Mahadhatu (fourteenth century)	
	Po Klaung Garai (Champa) (fourteenth century)	
	Candi Tikus and Jabung (Java) (fourteenth century)	
	Tu'-mac (Vietnam): stupa (1310)	
	Panataram (Java) (fourteenth–fifteenth century)	lCags-pori (thirteenth century)
	But-thap (Vietnam): Ninh-phuc pagoda (fourteenth century; restored seventeenth–eighteenth century)	Rwa-sgren (fifteenth century?)
		rGyans at Bum-moc'e: chorten (fifteenth century)
	Ayuthia (Siam): Wat Rajapurana (1424)	Kantipur: temple of Matsyendranath (sixteenth century)
	Lan Nan (Siam): Mahabodharama and Wat Chet Yot (from 1455)	Kantipur: temple of Tulaij Devi (1549)
	Lam-so'n (Vietnam): royal tombs (fifteenth–sixteenth century)	Patan: temple of Mahabuddha (1570–c. 1580)
	Tran-ninh (Laos): Buddhist temples, Wat Ban P'ong (after the fifteenth century)	Patan: royal palace (from c. 1580)
		Gam-rtse (sixteenth–seventeenth century?)
	Luangprabang (Laos): Wat Visin (built 1503, destroyed 1887); Wat Ch'ieng T'ong (reconstructed 1561); Th'at Luang (1565–80)	Bhadgaon: royal palace (sixteenth–eighteenth century)
		Leh: castle (seventeenth century)
		Patan: temple of Radha Krishna (1637)
		Lhasa: Potala (begun 1645)
	Vieng Chan (Laos): Th'at Luang (founded 1586)	Kantipur: royal palace (2nd half of seventeenth century)
	Bac-ninh (Vietnam): tomb of Nguyen Dien (1769)	Katmandu: temple (eighteenth century)
	Nagara Pathama (Siam): Brah Pathama (nineteenth century)	
	Hué (Vietnam): royal palace (nineteenth century)	
	Hué (outskirts): Nguyen tombs (nineteenth century)	

CHINA

YÜAN DYNASTY (A.D. 1280–1368)

Peking: Miao-ying-ssu pagoda (1271)

Mount Sung: Shao-lin-ssu, bell tower (1302)

An-p'ing-hsien: Sheng-ku-miao (1309)

Chao Chen-hsien: Kuang Shen-ssu, pavilion (1325)

MING DYNASTY (A.D. 1368–1644)

Taiyüan (Yangku): Ching-ming-ssu, sarira stupa (1385)

Peking: walls (1564) and urban layout

Hsi-an-fu: bell tower

Peking (outskirts): Wu-t'ai-ssu

Taiyüan: Shung-t'a-ssu (late sixteenth century)

Peking: Forbidden City, three ceremonial halls (1627)

Peking: Ming necropolis

CH'ING DYNASTY (A.D. 1644–1912)

Peking: Pei Hai, Pai-t'a (1651)

Peking: Yüan-ming-yüan, pavilions and park (1736–96)

Peking: Temple of the Ten Thousand Buddhas

Peking: Altar of Heaven (1754); Yung-ho-kung, Wan-fu-ko (eighteenth century)

Peking: Summer Palace (nineteenth century)

Suchow: gardens

Jehol: Lamaistic temples

MODERN PERIOD (A.D. 1912–   )

Nanking: tomb of Sun Yat-sen

Nanking: Ministry of Communications

Peking: Light Athletics Building, Institute for Physical Education (1955)

Peking: Palace of Cultures and Nationalities (1959)

KOREA

Seoul: Kyong-ch'on-sa: ten-story pagoda (1348)

Yonju Kun: Silluk-sa (mid-fourteenth century)

Song-do (Kaesong): Koryo royal necropolis

LI DYNASTY (A.D. 1392–1910)

Seoul: Nan-dai Mun, or south gate (1448)

Seoul: Won-gak-sa, ten-story pagoda (1468)

Yong-am Kun: To-kab-sa (mid-fifteenth century)

Kang-jin-kum: Mu-wi-sa, Hall of Paradise (mid-fifteenth century)

Yang-yang-kun: Nak-san-sa, pagoda (late fifteenth century)

Seoul: Ch'ang-kyong, Myong-jong Mun

Kyongju: Pulguk-sa, Tai-ung Chon (1765)

Suwon: city walls and gates (1794–96)

Suwon: Pang-hwa Su-ryu Chong (1796)

Seoul: Kyong-bok, Throne Room (1865)

Seoul: east gate (1869)

Seoul: Li royal necropolis

MODERN PERIOD (A.D. 1910–   )

Seoul: Cho-son Hotel

Seoul: National Medical Center

JAPAN

MUROMACHI PERIOD (A.D. 1333–1573)

Kyoto: Kinkakuji (late fourteenth century)

Kyoto: Ginkakuji (1st half of fifteenth century)

Kyoto: Ryōanji, garden (2nd half of fifteenth century)

MOMOYAMA PERIOD (A.D. 1573–1614)

Kyoto: Nijō castle (1602; remodeled 1626)

Castles of Matsumoto, Kumamoto, and the "White Heron" of Himeji

YEDO OR TOKUGAWA PERIOD (A.D. 1615–1867)

Kyoto (outskirts): Katsura and Shūgakuin villas (1st half of seventeenth century)

Yedo (Tokyo): castle and urban development

Nikkō: Tōshōgū shrine

MODERN PERIOD (A.D. 1868–   )

Tokyo: Tsukiji Hotel (1867–68; Kisuke Shimizu II, architect)

Tokyo: Bank of Japan (1890–96; Kingo Tatsuno, architect)

Tokyo: National Museum (1908; Tōyū Katayama, architect)

Tokyo: Akasaka Palace (completed 1909; Tōyū Katayama, architect)

Tokyo: Central Station (1914; Kingo Tatsuno, architect)

Tokyo: Kabuki Theater (1922; Shinichiro Okada, architect)

SELECTED BIBLIOGRAPHY

(The abbreviations *E.U.A.* and *B.E.F.E.O.* stand for *Enciclopedia Universale dell'Arte* and *Bulletin de l'Ecole Française de l'Extrême-Orient*, respectively.)

INDIA

ACHARYA, P. K. *Indian Architecture According to Māna-sāra-Śilpaśāstra*, 3 vols. London, 1927–46.

AUBOYER, J. *Introduction à l'étude de l'art de l'Inde*. Rome, 1965.

——, and ZANNAS, E. *Khajuraho*. The Hague, 1960.

BATLEY, C. *The Design Development of Indian Architecture*, 2nd ed. London, 1948.

BEHARI DUTT, B. *Town Planning in Ancient India*. Calcutta, 1925.

BOSE, N. H. *Canons of Orissan Architecture*. Calcutta, 1932.

BROWN, P. *Indian Architecture*. Vol. I: *Buddhist and Hindu Periods*, 3rd ed. Bombay, 1961.

BUSSAGLI, M., and SIVARAMAMURTI, C. *5000 Years of Indian Art*. New York, 1971.

COOMARASWAMY, A. K. *A History of Indian and Indonesian Art*. London–New York, 1927.

——. "Indian Architectural Terms," *The American Oriental Society Journal*, 48, 1928, pp. 250–75.

COUSENS, H. *Somanatha and Other Medieval Temples of Kathiawād*. Calcutta, 1931.

FERGUSSON, J. *A History of Indian and Eastern Architecture*. London, 1876.

——, and BURGESS, J. *Cave Temples of India*. London, 1880.

FOUCHER, A. *L'Art gréco-bouddhique du Gandhāra*, 4 vols. Paris, 1905–51.

GRAVELY, F. H. *An Outline of Indian Temple Architecture*. Bombay, 1954.

HAVELL, E. B. *The Ancient and Medieval Architecture of India: A Study of Indo-Aryan Civilisation*. London, 1915.

JOUVEAU-DUBREUIL, G. *L'Archéologie du sud de l'Inde*, 2 vols. Paris, 1914.

KAK, R. C. *Ancient Monuments of Kashmir*. London, 1933.

KRAMRISCH, S. *The Hindu Temple*, 2 vols. Calcutta, 1946.

LONGHURST, A. H. *Pallava Architecture*, 3 vols. Calcutta, 1924–30.

MARCHAL, H. *L'Architecture comparée dans l'Inde et l'Extrême-Orient*. Paris, 1944.

MARSHALL, J., and FOUCHER, A. *The Monuments of Sāñchī*, 3 vols. New Delhi, 1939.

RAMACHANDRAN, T. N. "Tiruparuttikunram and Its Temples," *Bulletin of Madras Government Museum*, New Series, General Section, III, 1934.

RANGACHARI, K. "Town-planning and House-building in Ancient India According to Śilpaśāstra," *Indian Historical Quarterly*, December 1927 and March 1928.

RENON, L. "La Maison vedique," *Journal Asiatique*, CCXXI, 1939, pp. 481 ff.

ROWLAND, B. *The Art and Architecture of India*, 2nd ed. Baltimore, 1956.

SARABHAJ, N. *Jain Tirthas and Their Architecture*. Ahmedabad, 1944.

SASTRI, K. A. "The Economy of a South Indian Temple (Tanjore) in the Cola Period," *Malaviya Commemorative Volume*, Madras, 1932, pp. 302 ff.

SIVARAMAMURTI, C. "Sanskrit Literature and Art: Mirrors of Indian Culture," *Memoirs of the Archaeological Survey of India*, Vol. 73, Calcutta-New Delhi, 1955.

SMITH, V. A. *A History of Fine Art in India and Ceylon*, 2nd ed. (revised by K. de B. Codrington). Oxford, 1930.

VOLWAHSEN, A. *Living Architecture: Indian*. New York, 1969.

ZIMMER, H. *The Art of Indian Asia*, 2 vols. New York, 1955.

CEYLON

"Mahavamsa," or the Great Chronicle of Ceylon. Translation by Wilhelm Geiger. Published under the auspices of the Ceylon Government Information Department. Colombo, 1950.

PARANAVITANA, S. *Art and Architecture of Ceylon: Polonnaruva Period*. Colombo (?), 1954.

——. "Ceylon, correnti e tradizioni," *E.U.A.*, III, Rome-Venice, 1958, cols. 420–28.

——. *Encyclopedia of Buddhism (Volume of Specimen Articles): Architecture (Ceylon)*. Published under the auspices of the Department of Cultural Affairs, Government of Ceylon. Colombo, 1957.

——. *The Stupa in Ceylon*. Colombo, 1946.

SMITHER, J. G. *Architectural Remains of Anuradhapura*. Colombo, 1877.

INDONESIA AND INDOCHINA

General Works

BUSSAGLI, M. "India Esteriore," *E.U.A.*, VII, Rome-Venice, 1958, cols. 318–37.

COEDÈS, G. "Arte dell'Indonesia," *Civiltà dell'Oriente*, Vol. IV, Rome, 1962.

——. *Les Etats hindouisés d'Indochine et d'Indonésie*. Paris, 1948.

GROSLIER, B. P. *Indocina*. Milan, 1961.

HALLADE, M. *L'Asie du Sud est*. Paris, 1954.

MARCHAL, H. *L'Architecture comparée dans l'Inde et l'Extrême-Orient*. Paris, 1944.

MASPERO, P. *Un Empire colonial français: l'Indochine*, 2 vols. Paris, 1929–30.

PARMENTIER, H. *L'Art architectural hindou dans l'Inde et l'Extrême-Orient*. Paris, 1948.

Indonesia

BERNET KEMPERS, A. J. *Ancient Indonesian Art*. Cambridge, Mass., 1959.

HEINE-GELDERN, R. VON, and HALLADE, M. "Indonesia, culture e tradizioni," *E.U.A.*, VII, Rome-Venice, 1958, cols. 453–502.

HOLT, C. *Art in Indonesia*. New York, 1967.

LOHUIZEN-DE LEEUW, J. E. VAN, and TADDEI, M. "Arte dell'Indonesia," *Civiltà dell'Oriente*, Vol. IV, Rome, 1962.

MUS, P. "Esquisse d'une histoire du bouddhisme fondée sur la critique archéologique des textes," *B.E.F.E.O.*, XXXII, 1932, pp. 269–439; XXXIII, 1933, pp. 577–980; XXXIV, 1934, pp. 175–400.

SARKAR, H. B. *Some Contributions of India to the Ancient Civilization of Indonesia and Malaysia*. Calcutta, 1970.

SIVARAMAMURTI, C. *Le Stupa de Barabudur*. Paris, 1960.

WAGNER, F. A. *Indonesia: The Art of an Island Group*. New York, 1959.

Cambodia (the Khmers) and Champa

BÉNISTI, M. *Rapports entre le premier art Khmer e l'art Indien*, 2 vols. Paris, 1970.

BOISSELIER, J. *Le Cambodge, Manuel d'archéologie d'Extrême-Orient, Asie du Sud est*, Vol. I. Paris, 1966.

BOSCH, F. D. "Le Temple d'Angkor Vat," *B.E.F.E.O.*, XXXII, 1923, pp. 7–21.

COEDÈS, G. "Cambogia," *E.U.A.*, III, Rome-Venice, 1958, cols. 69–79.

——. "Cham, scuola," *E.U.A.*, III, Rome-Venice, 1958, cols. 446–51.

——. "Etudes cambodgiennes XXIII: La date du temple de Bantay Srei," *B.E.F.E.O.*, XXIX, 1929, pp. 289–96.

——. "Khmer, centri e tradizioni," *E.U.A.*, VIII, Rome-Venice, 1958, cols. 454–71.

CORAL-RÉMUSAT, G. DE. *L'Art Khmèr, les grandes étapes de son évolution*. Paris, 1940.

DUFOUR, H., and CARPEAUX, C. *Le Bayon d'Angkor Thom*. Paris, 1910.

DUMARÇAIS, J. *Le Bayon: Histoire architecturale du temple*. Paris, 1967.

FILLIOZAT, J. "Le Symbolisme du monument du Phnom Bakheng," *B.E.F.E.O.*, XLIV, 1954, pp. 527–54.

FINOT, L., GOLOUBEW, V., and COEDÈS, G. *Le Temple d'Angkor Vat*, 7 vols. Paris, 1929–32.

GROSLIER, B. P., and ARTHAUD, J. *The Arts and Civilization of Angkor*, rev. ed. New York, 1966.

LEUBA, J. *Les Chams et leur art*. Paris-Brussels, 1923.

MASPERO, P. *Le Royaume de Champa*. Paris, 1928.

MAZZEO, D., and SILVI ANTONINI, C. *Civiltà Khmer*. Milan, 1972.

PARMENTIER, H. *L'Art Khmèr classique*. Paris, 1939.

——. "La Construction dans l'architecture Khmère classique," *B.E.F.E.O.*, XXXV, 1935, pp. 243–309.

STERN, P. *L'Art du Champa et son évolution*. Toulouse, 1942.

——. *Le Bayon d'Angkor Thom et l'évolution de l'art Khmèr*. Paris, 1927.

Burma and Siam (Thailand)

CLAEYS, J. Y. "L'Archéologie du Siam," *B.E.F.E.O.*, XXXI, 1931, pp. 361–448.

COEDÈS, G. "Birmania, centri e tradizioni," *E.U.A.*, II, Rome-Venice, 1959, cols. 604–13.

DUPONT, P. *L'Archéologie mône de Dvaravati*, 2 vols. Paris, 1959.

GRISWOLD, A. B. "Siamese, scuola," *E.U.A.*, XII, Rome-Venice, 1964, cols. 453–62.

———. "Thailandia," *E.U.A.*, XIII, Rome-Venice, 1965, cols. 528–43.

———, KIM, C., and POTT, P. H. *Birmania, Corea, Tibet*. Milan, 1963.

LE MAY, R. S. *A Concise History of Buddhist Art in Siam*, 2nd ed. Rutland-Tokyo, 1963.

Laos and Vietnam

BEZACIER, L. *L'Art vietnamien*. Paris, 1934.

———. *Relevé des monuments du Viet-nam*. Paris, 1959.

———. "Vietnamiti centri e scuole," *E.U.A.*, XIV, Rome-Venice, 1966, cols. 809–22.

COEDÈS, G. "Laos, scuola," *E.U.A.*, VIII, Rome-Venice, 1958, cols. 536–42.

MALLERET, L. *L'Archéologie du delta du Mekong*, 6 vols. Paris, 1959–63.

MERCIER, R., and PARMENTIER, H. "Eléments anciens d'architecture au Nord Vietnam," *B.E.F.E.O.*, XLV, 1952, pp. 285–348.

NGUEN VAN KHOAN. "Essai sur le dinh," *B.E.F.E.O.*, XXX, 1930, pp. 107–12.

PARMENTIER, H. *L'Art du Laos*, 2 vols. Paris, 1954.

———. *Inventaire descriptif des monuments cham de l'Annam*, 2 vols. Paris, 1909.

TRAN-HAM-TAN. "Etude sur le Van mieu (temple de la littérature) de Ha-noi," *B.E.F.E.O.*, XLV, 1951–52, pp. 89–117.

HIMALAYAN REGION

General Works

Archaeological Survey of India, Report XXVI (Excavations in Kapilavastu), Part I, 1901.

BENOIT, F. *L'Architecture: L'Orient médiéval et moderne*. Paris, 1912.

BROWN, F. *Indian Architecture*. Bombay, 1965.

FERGUSSON, J. *A History of Indian and Eastern Architecture*. London, 1876.

ROWLAND, B. *The Art and Architecture of India*, 3rd ed. Baltimore, 1967.

VOLWAHSEN, A. *Living Architecture: Indian*. New York, 1969.

Kashmir

COWIE, W. G. "Notes on Some of the Temples of Kashmir Especially Those Not Described by General Cunningham," *Journal of the Asiatic Society of Bengal*, XXXV, 1866.

GOETZ, H. *Studies in the History and Art of Kashmir and the Indian Himalayas*. Wiesbaden, 1969.

KAK, R. C. *Ancient Monuments of Kashmir*. London, 1933.

SAHNI, D. R. "Excavations at Avantipur," *Archaeological Survey of India, Annual Report*, 1913–14, p. 40.

———. "Pre-Muhammadan Monuments of Kashmir," *Archaeological Survey of India, Annual Report*, 1915–16, pp. 49–78.

Nepal

BROWN, P. "The Art of Nepal," *Journal of the Bihar Research Society*, XXXI, 1945.

KARAN, P., and JENKINS, W. M. *The Himalayan Kingdoms: Bhutan, Sikkim and Nepal*. Princeton, 1963.

LÜBKE, H. *Kunst aus dem Königreich von Himalaya*. Villa Hügel-Hessen, 1967.

SNELLGROVE, D. L. "Nepal," *Splendors of the East*, New York, 1965.

———. "Shrines and Temples of Nepal," *Arts Asiatiques*, 1961.

TUCCI, G. "Note e appunti di un viaggio nel Nepal," *Bollettino della Società Geografica Italiana*, LXVIII, 1937.

WALDSCHMIDT, E. and R. L. *Nepal (Art Treasures from the Himalayas)*. London, 1969.

Tibet

FRANCKE, A. M. *Antiquities of Indian Tibet*, 2 vols. Calcutta, 1914–26.

GORDON, A. K. *Tibetan Religious Arts*. New York, 1952.

HUMMEL, S. *Geschichte der Tibetischen Kunst*. Leipzig, 1953.

JISL, L. *Tibetan Art*. London, 1958.

RICHARDSON, H. E. "Early Burial Grounds in Tibet and Tibetan Decorative Art of the VIII and IX Century," *Central Asiatic Journal*, VIII, 1963.

ROUSSEAU, P. "L'Art du Tibet," *Revue des Arts Asiatiques*, IV, 1927.

TUCCI, G. *A Lhasa e oltre. Diario della spedizione nel Tibet*, 2nd ed. Rome, 1952.

———. *Indo-tibetica*, 4 vols. Rome, 1932–41.

———. "The Symbolism of the Temple of Bsam-yas," *East and West*, VI, 1955–56.

———. *Tibet: Paese delle nevi*. Novara, 1968.

———. *The Tombs of Tibetan Kings*. Rome, 1950.

———. *Tra giungle e pagode*. Rome, 1953.

CENTRAL ASIA

AL'BAUM, L. I. *Balalyk tepe*. Tashkent, 1960.

BELENICKIJ, A. M., *et al. Skultura i zivopis' drevnego Pjandzikenta*. Moscow, 1959.

BUSSAGLI, M. *Culture e civiltà dell'Asia Centrale*. Rome, 1970.

———. "Culture protostoriche e arte delle steppe," *Civiltà dell'Oriente*, Rome, 1961.

———. *Painting of Central Asia*. Geneva, 1963.

ESIN, E. *Antecedents and Development of Buddhist and Manichaean Turkish Art in Eastern Turkestan and Kansu*. Istanbul, 1967.

FRUMKIN, G. *Archaeology in Soviet Central Asia*. Leyden, 1970.

GRÜNWEDEL, A. *Alt-Kutscha*. Berlin, 1920.

HACKIN, J. "Recherches archéologiques en Asie Centrale (1931)," *Revue des Arts Asiatiques*, IX, 1936.

———, and CARL, J. "Nouvelles Recherches archéologiques à Bamiyan," *Mémoires de la Délégation Archéologique Française en Afghanistan*, III, 1933.

HAMBIS, L. "Asia Centrale," *E.U.A.*, II, Rome-Venice, 1958, cols. 1–25.

JAKBUOVSKIJ, A. J., *et al. Zipovis' drevnego Pjandzikenta*. Moscow, 1954.

LAVROV, V. A. *Gradostroitelnaja kul'tura Srednej Asii*. Moscow, 1950.

LE COQ, A. VON. *Bilderatlas zur Kunst und Kulturgeschichte Mittelasiens*. Berlin, 1925.

LITVINSKY, B. A., and ZEIMAL, T. J. *Adzina tepa*. Moscow, 1971.

MASSON, V. M. *Srednjaja Azija i Drevijj Vostok*. Moscow-Leningrad, 1964.

PUGACENKOVA, G. A., and REMPEL, L. I. *Istorija iskusstv Uzbekistan*. Moscow, 1965.

SARIANIDI, V. I. "Nekotorye voprosy drevnej architeltury eneoliticeskich poselenij geoksjurskogo oazisa," *Bulletin of Researches of the Institute of Material Culture*, 91, Moscow, 1962.

SISKIN, V. A. *Varachsa*. Moscow, 1953.

STEIN, A. *Ancient Khotan*, 2 vols. Oxford, 1907.

———. *Ruins of Desert Cathay, a Personal Narrative of Exploration in Central Asia*, 2 vols. London, 1912.

———. *Serindia*, 5 vols. Oxford, 1921.

TALBOT RICE, T. *Ancient Arts of Central Asia*. London, 1965.

TOLSTOV, S. P. *Drevnij Chorezm*. Moscow, 1948.

———. *Po sledam drevnichorezmijskoj civilizacii*. Moscow-Leningrad, 1948.

———, and BAINBERG, B. I. *Koj-krylgan-kala*. Moscow, 1967.

CHINA

General Works

BOERSCHMANN, E. *Baukunst und Landschaft in China*. Berlin, 1923.

———. *Die Baukunst und religiöse Kultur der Chinesen: Pagoden*. Berlin-Leipzig, 1911–31.

———. *Chinesische Architektur*. Berlin, 1925.

BOYD, A. *Chinese Architecture and Town Planning, 1500 B.C.–A.D. 1911*. Chicago, 1962.

CHANG, KWANG-CHIH. *The Archaeology of Ancient China*. London-New Haven, 1963.

CHAVANNES, E. *Mission archéologique dans la Chine septentrionale*, 5 vols. Paris, 1913–15.

CHENG, TE-K'UN. *Archaeology in China*, 4 vols. Cambridge, Eng., 1958–66.

CREE, H. G. *The Birth of China*. London, 1936; new ed., New York, 1954.

EBERHARD, W. "Temple-Building Activities in Medieval and Modern China, An Experimental Study," *Monumenta Serica*, XXIII, 1964, pp. 264–318.

FUGL-MEYER, H. *Chinese Bridges*. Shanghai, 1937.

GIN-DIJH SU. *Chinese Architecture—Past and Contemporary*. Hong Kong, 1964.

GLEN, T. T. "Chinese Cities, Origins and Functions," *Annals of the Association of American Geographers*, XLII, 1952.

GROUSSET, R. *La Chine et son art*. Paris, 1951.

HALLADE, M. *L'Asie du Sud-est*. Paris, 1954.

HENTZE, C. *Funde in Alt China*. Göttingen-Zurich, Berlin-Frankfurt, 1967.

INN, H., and LU, S. *Chinese Houses and Gardens*. Honolulu, 1940.

JENYNS, S., and ECKE, G. *Chinese Domestic Furniture*. Peking, 1944.

JIRO, M. *Manshu no Shiseki*. Tokyo, 1944.

KELLING, R. *Das Chinesische Wohnhaus*. Tokyo, 1925.

LIU HSIAO-P'ING. *Chung-kuo Chien-chu Lei-hsing Chi Chieh-kon*. Peking, 1957.

LIU TUN-CHEN. *Ching-kuo Chu-chai K'ai shuo*. Peking, 1957.

——. "Domestic Houses, Origins," *Chien-chi-hsueh pao*, No. 4, 1956.

MAKITA, I. *Jukka koseki to Chibetto Bijutsu*. Tokyo, 1943.

MIRAMS, D. G. *A Brief History of Chinese Architecture*. Shanghai, 1940.

MORTARI VERGARA CAFFARELLI, P. "Cina," *Dizionario di Architettura e urbanistica*, I, 1968, pp. 568–83.

MO TSUN-CH'ANG. "Architectural Decoration," *China Reconstructs*, IV, 9, 1955.

MÜNSTERBERG, H. *L'Arte dell'Estremo Oriente*. Milan, 1968.

PIROZZOLI, M., and SERSTEVSEN, T. *Living Architecture: China*. New York, 1971.

PRIP-MØLLER, J. *Chinese Buddhist Monasteries*. Copenhagen-London, 1937.

SICKMAN, L., and SOPER, A. *The Art and Architecture of China*, 2nd ed. Baltimore, 1960.

SIRÉN, O. "Les Capitales chinoises de l'ouest," *Japon et Extrême-Orient*, November–December 1924.

——. "Chinese Architecture," *Encyclopaedia Britannica*, 14th ed.

——. *Gardens in China*. New York, 1949.

——. *Histoire des arts anciens de la Chine*, Vol. IV (*L'Architecture*). Paris-Brussels, 1929–30.

SPEISER, W., GOEPPER, R., and FRIBOURG, J. *Arts de la Chine*, Vol. II. Freiburg, 1963.

SWANN, P. C. *L'Arte della Cina*. Florence, 1966.

TOKIWA, D., and SEKINO, T. *Shina Bukkyō Shiseki*, 5 vols. Tokyo, 1926–38.

WALEY, A. *The Temple*. London, 1923.

WANG-PI-WEN. *Chung-kuo Chien-chu*. Peking, 1943.

WILLETTS, W. *Chinese Art*, 2 vols. London, 1958.

WU, N. *Chinese and Indian Architecture*. New York, 1963.

YAO CH'ENG-TSU, CHANG CHIH-KANG, and LIU TUN-CHEN. *Ying-tsao Fa-yuan*. Peking, 1959.

YETTS, W. P. "Writings in Chinese Architecture," *Burlington Magazine*, March 1927.

Protohistory and the Shang Dynasty

CHENG, TE-K'UN. "The Origin and Development of Shang Culture," *Asia Major*, VI, 1957, pp. 80–90.

EBERHARD, W. "Bericht über die Ausgrabungen bei An-yang (Honan)," *Ostasiatische Zeitschrift*, New Series, VIII, 1–2, 1932.

HASKIN, F. J. "Pan-p'o, a Chinese Neolithic Village," *Artibus Asiae*, XX, 1957, pp. 151–58.

LOEHR, M. "The Stratigraphy of Hsiao-t'un (An-yang)," *Ars Orientalis*, II, 1957, pp. 439–57.

SHIH CHANG-JU. "Hsiao-t'un, I: The Site; II: Architectural Remains," *Archaeologia Sinica*, 1959.

Chou Dynasty

Ch'ang-sha fa-chueh pao-kao. Peking, 1957.

CHENG, TE-K'UN. *Archaeological Studies in Szechwan*. Cambridge, Eng., 1957.

CHIANG YUEN-YI. *Ch'ang-sha, The Ch'u Tribe and Its Arts*, 2 vols. Shanghai, 1949–50.

HAN-TAN. "Excavations at the Ruins of the Capital of Chao in the Contending States Period," *Archaeologia Orientalis*, Series B, VII.

HASKIN, F. J. "Recent Excavations in China," *Archives of the Chinese Art Society of America*, X, 1956.

KARLBECK, O. "Notes on a Hui-hsien Tomb," *Röhsska Konstslöjdmuseet*, Arstryck, 1952, pp. 40–47.

SEKINO, T. "Investigations of Lin-tzu of Ch'i," *Kokogaku Zasshi*, XXXII, 1942.

SOOTHIL, W. E. *The Hall of Light*. London, 1951.

WANG KUO-WEI. "Ming-t'ang miao ch'in t'ung k'ao" (German translation by J. Hefter), *Ostasiatische Zeitschrift*, New Series, VII, 1–2, 1931.

Ch'in and Han Dynasties

CHENG, TE-K'UN. *Archaeological Studies in Szechwan*. Cambridge, Eng., 1957.

FAIRBANKS, W. "The Offering Shrines of Wu Liang Tz'u," *Harvard Journal of Asiatic Studies*, 6, 1941, pp. 1–36.

FRANKE, W. "Die Han-zeitlichen Felsengräber bei Chia-ting, West Szechuan," *Studia Serica*, VII, 1951.

GEIL, W. E. *The Great Wall of China*. London, 1909.

LARTIGUE, J. "Au Tombeau de Houo K'iu-ping," *Artibus Asiae*, II, 1927, pp. 85–94.

——. "Résultats archéologiques," *Journal Asiatique*, May-June 1961, pp. 407.

LIU TUNG-TSENG. "Ta-chuang Shih Notes," *Chung-kuo Ying tsao Hsueh She Hui-k'an*, 1932, pp. 130–33.

MIYAZAKI, I. "Les Villes en Chine à l'époque des Han," *T'oung Pao*, XLVIII, 1960, 4–5, pp. 1–18.

MORI, O., and NAITO, H. "Ying-ch'eng-tzu," *Archaeologia Orientalis*, IV, 1934.

NEWTON HAYES, J. *The Great Wall of China*. Shanghai, 1929.

RUDOLPH, R. C., and WEN YU. *Han Tomb Art of West China*. Los Angeles-Berkeley, 1951.

SEGALEN, V., DE VOISINS, G., and LARTIGUE, J., *L'art funéraire à l'époque des Han*. Paris, 1936.

SEKINO, T. "Ancient Chinese Stone Shrines," *Kokka*, 225, February 1909.

——. "The Site of the Ling-Kuang Hall of Lum in the Former Han," *Kokogaku Zasshi*, XXXI, 1940.

——. "Stone Mortuary Shrines with Engraved Tablets of the Later Han Dynasty," *Kokka*, 225, February 1909.

WHITE, W. C. *The Tombs of Old Lo-yang*. Shanghai, 1934.

Six Dynasties

BUHOT, J. "Notes d'architecture bouddhique, I: Stupa et pagode, une hypothèse," *Revue des Arts Asiatiques*, XI, 4, 1937.

CHANG SHU-HUNG. "Tun-huang Memoirs," *China Reconstructs*, IX, 2, 1960.

CHU HSI-TSU, *et al.* "The Tombs of the Six Dynasties," *Monumenta Sinica*, I, Nanking, 1935.

GRAY, B., and VINCENT, J. B. *Buddhist Cave Paintings at Tun-huang*. London, 1959.

LO SHU-TZU. *Pei Ch'ao shih-k'u i-shu*. Shanghai, 1955.

MIZUNO, S., and NAGAHIRO, T. *A Study of the Buddhist Cave Temples at Lungmen, Honan*. Tokyo, 1941.

——, and ——. *Yun-kang, the Buddhist Cave Temples of the Fifth Century A.D. in North China*. Kyoto, 1952 ff.

PELLIOT, P. *Les Grottes de Touen-Houang*. Paris, 1920–24.

SUI KAO-JOUAN. "Tch'ong-k'an Lo-yang K'u lan ki, T'ai pei," *Academia Sinica*, 1960.

SULLIVAN, M. *The Cave Temples of Maichishan*. London, 1969.

WARE, J. "Wei shou on Buddhism," *T'oung Pao*, XXX, 1933.

Wen-wu ts'an-k'ao tz'u-hao, 3, 1956, pp. 62–64.

Sui and T'ang Dynasties

ADACHI, K. *Cho-an shiseki mo kenkyū*. Tokyo, 1933.

BULLING, A. "Buddhist Temples in the T'ang Period," *Oriental Art*, I, 2, 1955, pp. 79–86; 3, pp. 115–22.

CHENG, TE-K'UN. "The Royal Tomb of Wang Chien," *Harvard Journal of Asiatic Studies*, 8, 1944–45, pp. 235–40.

CHOBU, HIBINO. *Godaisan (Wu-t'ai-shan)*. Tokyo, 1942.

Chung-kuo chien-chu. Peking, 1957.

FEN HAN-YI. "Discovery and Excavation of the Yung Ling," *Archives of the Chinese Art Society of America*, 2, 1947, pp. 11–20.

FISCHER, W. *The Sacred Wu-t'ai-shan*. London, 1925.

LIANG, S. C. "The Great Stone Bridge of Chao Hsien (Hopeh)," *Chung-kuo Ting-tsao Hsueh She Hui-k'an*, 1, 1934, pp. 1–31.

SIRÉN, O. "Tch'ang-ngan au temps des Souei et des T'ang," *Revue des Arts Asiatiques*, 1–2, March 1927, pp. 40–46, 98–104.

SOPER, A. C. "A Vacation Glimpse of the T'ang Temples of Ch'ang-an, the Ssu-t'a chi by Tuan Ch'eng shih," *Artibus Asiae*, XXIII, 1960, pp. 15–40.

SULLIVAN, M. D. "The Excavations of a T'ang Imperial Tomb," *Illustrated London News*, April 20, 1946.

T'ang Ch'ang-an Ta-ming kung. Peking, 1959.

TWITCHETT, D. "Some Remarks on Irrigation Under the T'ang," *T'oung Pao*, XLVIII, 1–3, 1960, pp. 175–94.

WRIGHT, A. F. "Symbolism and Function: Reflections on Changan and Other Great Cities," *Journal of Asiatic Study*, XXIV, 4, 1965.

Liao Dynasty

LIANG, S. C. "Two Liao Structures of Tu-lo Ssu, Chi Hsien, Hopeh," *Bulletin of the Society for Research in Chinese Architecture*, III, 2, 1932, pp. 48–88.

NAKAMURA, R. *Manshu no Bijutsu*. Tokyo, 1941.

SEKINO, T., and TAKEJIMA, T. *Ryōkin Jidai no Kenchiku to sono Butsuzō*, 2 vols. Tokyo, 1925–44.

TAMURA, J., and KOBAYASHI, Y. *Tombs and Mural Paintings of Ch'ing-ling, Liao Imperial Mausoleums of the Eleventh Century A.D. in Eastern Mongolia*. Kyoto, 1953.

Sung Dynasty

DEMIÉVILLE, P. "Review of 1920 Edition of the Ying Tsao Fa Shih," *B.E.F.E.O.*, XXV, 1925.

ECKE, G., and DEMIÉVILLE, P. *The Twin Pagodas of Zayton*. Cambridge, Mass., 1935.

MOULE, A. C. *Quinsai, with Other Notes of Marco Polo*. Cambridge, 1957.

Ta-tsu shih-k'o. Peking, 1957.

YETTS, W. "Review of 1925 Edition of the Ying Tsao Fa Shih," *Bulletin of the School of Oriental and African Studies*, IV, 1926–28.

Yüan, Ming, and Ch'ing Dynasties

ARLINGTON, L. C., and LEWISON, W. *In Search of Old Peking*. Peking, 1935.

CHANG CHUNG-I, TS'AO CHIEN-PIN, and CH'UAN KAO-CHIEH. *Hui-chon Ming-fai Chu-chai*. Peking, 1957.

HOU JEN-CHIH. "Peking: Historical Sketch," *People's China*, October 1956.

JIRO, M. *Manshū no Shiseki*. Tokyo, 1944.

KOKU YAO LUN. *The Essential Criteria of Antiquities for Chinese Connoisseurship*. London, 1971.

LANCASTER, C. "The European-Style Palaces of the Yüan Ming Yüan," *Gazette des Beaux-Arts*, October 1948.

LING SSU-CH'ENG. *Ching Shih Ying-tsao Tse-li*. Peking, 1934.

MAKITA, I. *Jukka koseki to Chibetto Bijutsu*. Tokyo, 1943.

MALONE, C. B. *History of the Peking Summer Palaces Under the Ch'ing Dynasty*. New York, 1966.

NAI HSIA. "Opening an Imperial Tomb," *China Reconstructs*, VII, 3, 1959, pp. 16–21.

SIRÉN, O. *The Imperial Palaces of Peking*, 3 vols. Paris–Brussels, 1926.

———. *The Walls and Gates of Peking*. London, 1924.

SKINNER, R. T. F. "Peking, 1953," *The Architectural Review*, October 1953.

YOSHIKI, O. "Architecture of the Central Edifice in the Imperial Palace in Ancient China," *Paleologia*, XI, 1, 1962.

Modern Period

CHEN, C. "Modern Chinese Architecture," *The Architectural Review*, July 1947.

COLLOTTI PISCHEL, E. "Città e campagna nella Cina contemporanea," *Controspazio*, 1, January–February 1971.

GAVINELLI, C., and VERCELLONI, V., eds. "Cina: Architettura e urbanistica," *Controspazio*, 12, December 1971.

LIANG SSU-CH'ENG. "China's Architectural Heritage and the Tasks of Today," *People's China*, I, 21, November 1952.

PEN, C. "Chinese Vernacular Architecture," *The Journal of the Royal Institute of British Architects*, LXXII (1965), 10, pp. 502–7.

KOREA

General Works

Chōsen Kōseki Zufu (Korean Antiquities Illustrated), 15 vols. Seoul, 1915–35.

CLARK, C. A. *Religion of Old Korea*. New York, 1932.

DALLET, C. *Histoire de l'église de la Corée*, 2 vols. Paris, 1874.

DUPONT, M. *Décoration coréenne*. Paris, 1927.

ECKHARDT, A. *A History of Korean Art*. London, 1929.

FERNALD, H. E. "Rediscovered Glories of Korean Art," *Asia*, December 1931, pp. 788–95, 799–802.

FUJISHIMA, G. *Chōsen Kenchiku Shiron* (History of Korean Architecture). Tokyo, 1930.

GALE, J. S. *A History of the Korean People*. Seoul, 1927.

GOMPERTZ, G. ST. G. M. "Arte della Corea," *Civiltà dell'Oriente*, IV, Rome, 1962, pp. 1243–67.

———. "Corea, Coreani centri e tradizioni," *E.U.A.*, III, Rome–Venice, 1958, cols. 800–801.

GRIFFIS, W. E. *Corea, the Hermit Kingdom*. New York, 1911.

GRISWOLD, A. B., KIM, C., and POTT, P. H. *Birmania, Korea, Tibet*. Milan, 1963.

HAYASHI, T. *Chōsen tsū-shi* (History of Korea). Tokyo, 1944.

HULBERT, H. R. *The History of Korea*, 2 vols. Seoul, 1905.

———. *The Passing of Korea*. New York, 1906.

KEITH, E., and ROBERTSON SCOTT, E. K. *Old Korea*. London, 1946.

KIM, C., ed. *The Culture of Korea*. Los Angeles, 1946.

"The Korean National Commission for UNESCO,"

UNESCO Korean Survey, Seoul, 1960.

Kōseki Chōsa Hōkoku (Annual Reports on the Exploration of Ancient Ruins), 20 vols. Seoul, 1917–40.

Kōseki Chōsa Tokubetsu Hōkoku (Special Reports on the Exploration of Ancient Ruins), 6 vols. Seoul, 1919–30.

LAUTENSACH, H. *Korea: Land, Volk, Schicksal*. Stuttgart, 1950.

———. *Korea, eine Landeskunde auf Grund einige Reisen und der Literatur*. Leipzig, 1945.

LONGFORD, J. H. *The Story of Korea*. London, 1911.

McCUNE, E. *The Arts of Korea: An Illustrated History*. Rutland-Tokyo, 1962.

McKENZIE, F. A. *The Tragedy of Korea*. London, 1908.

MÜNSTERBERG, H. *L'Arte dell'Estremo Oriente*. Milan, 1968.

OSGOOD, C. *The Koreans and Their Culture*. New York, 1951.

ROSS, J. *Korea: Its History, Manners and Customs*. Paisley, 1880.

ROSSETTI, C. *Corea e Coreani*. Milan, 1906.

SEKINO, T. *Chōsen Bijutsu-shi* (History of Korean Art). Kyoto, 1932.

———. *Chōsen no Kenchiku to Geijutsu* (Art and Architecture in Korea: Collection of Essays). Tokyo, 1942.

———. *Kenkoku kenchiku chōsa Hōkoku* (Report of Research on Korean Architecture). Tokyo, 1904.

STARR, F. *Korean Buddhism: History, Condition, Art*. Boston, 1918.

UMEHARA, S. *Chōsen Kodai no Bosei* (Funeral Customs of Ancient Korea). Tokyo, 1947.

WON-YONG KIM, *et al. Korean Arts, III: Architecture*. Ministry of Public Information, Republic of Korea, 1963.

YANAGI, S. *Chōsen to Sono Geijutsu* (Korea and Its Art Treasures). Tokyo, 1922; reprinted 1954.

Prehistory

TORII, R. "Les Dolmens de la Corée," *Memoirs of the Research Department*, Toyo Bunko, I, 1926, pp. 93–100.

UMEHARA, S. *Chōsen Kodai no Bunko* (The Ancient Culture of Korea). Kyoto, 1946.

Lo-Lang Colony

HARADA, Y., and TAZAWA, K. *Lo-lang*. Tokyo, 1930.

IKEUCHI, H. "A Study on Lo-lang and Taifang, Ancient Chinese Prefectures in the Korean Peninsula," *Memoirs of the Research Department*, Toyo Bunko, Series B, 5, 1930, pp. 79–96.

KOIZUM, A. *The Tomb of Painted Baskets of Lo-lang*. Seoul, 1934.

OBA, T., and KAYAMOTO, K. *The Tomb of Wang Kuang of Lo-lang*. Seoul, 1935.

SEKINO, T., *et al.* "Rakuro-gun Jidai no Iseki" (Research on the Lo-lang District), *Koseki Chōsa Tokubetsu Hōkoku*, 1–3, 1925–27.

UMEHARA, S. "Two Remarkable Lo-lang Tombs of Wooden Construction Excavated in Pyongyang,

Korea," *Archives of the Chinese Art Society of America*, VIII, 1954, pp. 10–21.

Three Kingdoms Period

CHAPIN, H. B., and YO PU. "One of Korea's Ancient Capitals," *Transactions of the Korea Branch of the Royal Asiatic Society*, XXXII, 1951, pp. 51–61.

CHAVANNES, E. "Rapport sur les monuments de l'ancien royaume coréen de Kao-keou-li, *Comptes rendus des séances de l'Académie des Inscriptions et Belles-lettres*, 1906, p. 549.

Chōsen Kofun Hekiga-shu (Wall Paintings in Ancient Koguryo Tombs). Seoul, 1917.

COURANT, M. "Stèle chinoise due royaume de Ko Kou Rye," *Journal Asiatique*, IX, 1899, pp. 210–39.

IKEUCHI, H., and UMEHARA, S. *T'ung-kou*, 2 vols. Tokyo, 1938–40.

KIM, C. "Two Old Silla Tombs," *Artibus Asiae*, X, 1947.

———. *Two Old Silla Tombs*. Seoul, 1948.

SEKINO, T., *et al.* "Kōkuri Jidai no Iseki" (Research on Koguryo), *Koseki Chōsa Tokubetsu Hōkoku* (Special Reports of Research on Antiquity), 1–2, Tokyo, 1938–40.

UMEHARA, S. "The Newly Discovered Tombs with Wall Paintings of the Kao-kou-li Dynasty," *Archives of the Chinese Art Society of America*, VI, 1952, pp. 5–17.

Great Silla Kingdom

CHAPIN, H. B. "A Hitherto Unpublished Great Silla Pagoda," *Artibus Asiae*, XII, 1–2, 1949, pp. 84–138.

———. "Kyongju, Ancient Capital of Silla," *Asian Horizon*, I, 4, 1948, pp. 36–45.

Chōsen Hobotsu Koseki Zuroku (Illustrated Catalogue of Korean Treasures and Remains), Vol. I. Seoul, 1938–40.

COURANT, M. "Korea up to the Ninth Century," *T'oung P'ao*, Series I, IX, Paris, 1899.

HAMADA, K., and UMEHARA, S. "Keishu Kinkantsuka to Sono Iho" (The Golden Crown Tomb at Kyongju and Its Treasures), *Koseki Chōsa Tokubetsu Hōkoku*, 1–3, 1924–27.

KIM, C., and KIM, W. and P. *Excavations of Three Silla Tombs*. Seoul, 1955.

OGAWA, K., and BABA, K. "Rȳosan Fufu Tsuka to Sono Ibutsu" (The Tomb of the Couple at Yangsan and Its Remains), *Koseki Chōsa Tokubetsu Hōkoku*, 1–2, 1927.

YUSOP KO. *Chōsen T'ap-p'a ni Yongu* (History of Korean Pagodas). Seoul, 1948.

Koryo Kingdom

FUJISHIMA, G. *Chōsen no Kenchiku to Geijutsu* (Art and Architecture of Korea). Tokyo, 1942.

VIESSMAN, W. "Ondol Radiant Heat in Korea," *Transactions of the Korea Branch of the Royal Asiatic Society*, XXXI, 1948–49.

Li Dynasty

CHAPIN, H. B. "Palaces in Seoul," *Transactions of the Korea Branch of the Royal Asiatic Society*, XXXII, 1951, pp. 3–46.

GRAJDANZEV, A. J. *Modern Korea*. New York, 1933.

KUNO, Y. S. *Japanese Expansion on the Asiatic Continent*. Berkeley, 1937–40.

McCUNE, E. *Korea's Heritage: A Regional and Social Geography*. Tokyo, 1956.

———, and GREY, A. L. *Korea Today*. Cambridge, Mass., 1950.

PARK, L. G. *The History of Protestant Missions in Korea, 1910–1932*. Pyongyang, 1929.

JAPAN

General Works

ALEX, W. *Japanese Architecture*. New York, 1963.

AMANUMA, S. *Nihon Kenchiku Saibu Hensen Shozuroku* (Structural Transformations in Japanese Architecture). Tokyo, 1944.

———. *Nihon Kenchiku Zuroku* (Illustrated Treatise on Japanese Architecture), 6 vols. Tokyo, 1933–39.

BALTZEN, F. *Die Architektur der Kultbauten Japans*. Berlin, 1904–5.

DREXLER, A. *The Architecture of Japan*. New York, 1955.

GROPIUS, W. *Architettura in Giappone*. Milan, 1965.

ISHIWARA, K. *Nihon Nomin Kenchiku* (Japanese Rural Architecture), 12 vols. Tokyo, 1934–39.

ITO, C., INUI, K., and OKUMA, Y. *Meiji-zen Nihon Kenchiku Gijutsu-shi* (History of Japanese Architecture Before the Meiji Era). Tokyo, 1961.

ŌTA, H. *Japanese Architecture and Gardens*. Tokyo, 1966.

PAINE, R. T., and SOPER, A. C. *The Art and Architecture of Japan*, 2nd ed. Baltimore, 1960.

SADLER, A. L. *A Short History of Japanese Architecture*. Sydney-London, 1941.

SEKINO, T. *Nihon no Kenchiku to Geijutsu* (Japanese Arts and Architecture). Tokyo, 1940.

TAMBURELLO, A. *I grandi monumenti del Giappone*. Milan, 1971.

TAUT, B. *Houses and Peoples of Japan*. Tokyo, 1937.

YOSHIDA, T. *Japanische Architektur*. Tübingen, 1952.

Prehistory and Protohistory

KIDDER, J. E. *Japan Before Buddhism*. London, 1959.

TANGE, K., KAWAZOE, N., and WATANABE, Y. *Ise-Nihon Kenchiku no Genkei* (The Origins of Japanese Architecture). Tokyo, 1962.

Shinto and Buddhist Architecture

AKIYAMA, A. *Shinto and Its Architecture*. Tokyo, 1955.

BLASER, W. *Japanese Temples and Tea-Houses*. New York, 1957.

PONSONBY-FANE, R. A. B. *Studies in Shinto and Shrines*. Kyoto, 1942.

SOPER, A. C. *The Evolution of Buddhist Architecture in Japan*. Princeton, 1942.

Nara and Heian Periods

ASANO, K. *Horyuji Kenchiku Sokan* (Architectural Splendors of the Horyuji). Kyoto, 1953.

FUJIOKA. *Kyoto gosho* (The Imperial Palace of Kyoto). Kyoto, 1955.

SANSOM, G. "The Heian Capital and Its Palaces," *A History of Japan to 1334*, Stanford, 1958.

Kamakura and Muromachi Periods

KITAO, M. *Shoin Shosai Zufu* (Structural Elements of the Shoin-zukuri). Tokyo, 1955.

ŌTA, H. *Chusei no Kenchiku* (Medieval Architecture). Tokyo, 1957.

TOYAMA, E. *Muromachi-jidai Teien-shi* (History of the Garden in the Muromachi Period). Tokyo, 1934.

Momoyama and Yedo (Tokugawa) Periods

GROPIUS, W., and TANGE, K. *Katsura—Tradition and Creation in Japanese Architecture*. New Haven, 1960.

HALL, J.W. "The Castle Town and Japan's Modern Urbanization," *Far Eastern Quarterly*, XV, 1, 1955, pp. 37–56.

HORIGUCHI, S. *Katsura Rikyu* (The Katsura Detached Palace). Tokyo, 1952.

———. *Rikyu no Chashitsu* (The Teahouse of Rikyu). Tokyo, 1952.

KITAO, M. *Sukiya Shosai Zufu* (Structural Elements of the Sukiya Style). Tokyo, 1955.

MORI, O. *Katsura Rikyu* (The Katsura Detached Palace). Tokyo, 1955.

Gardens

NAOYA, S., and MOTOI, H. *A Pictorial Record of the Famous Palaces, Gardens and Tea Gardens*. Tokyo, 1935.

NEWSOM, S. *A Thousand Years of Japanese Gardens*. Tokyo, 1957.

TAMURA, T. *Art of the Landscape Garden in Japan*. Tokyo, 1935.

YOSHINAGA, Y. *Nihon no Teien* (The Japanese Garden). Tokyo, 1958.

———. *Nihon Teien no Kosei to Hyogen* (Character and Expression of the Japanese Garden). Tokyo, 1962.

Modern Period

ABE, K. "Meiji Architecture," *Japanese Arts and Crafts in the Meiji Era*, Tokyo, 1958.

BOYD, R. *Orientamenti nuovi nell'architettura giapponese*. Milan, 1969.

HORIKOSHI, S. *Meiji shoki no Yofu Kenchiku* (Western-Style Architecture in the First Period of the Meiji Era). Tokyo, 1929.

KOIKE, S. *Nihon no Gendai Kenchiku* (Modern Japanese Architecture). Tokyo, 1954.

TEMPEL, E. *Nuova Architettura giapponese*. Milan, 1969.

INDEX

LIST OF PLATES

432

LIST OF PHOTOGRAPHIC CREDITS

NOTE: *Photographs by Federico Borromeo. All those supplied by other sources are gratefully acknowledged below. The numbers listed refer to the plates.*

22.50

WITHDRAWN

A